SOME JUSTICE

SOME JUSTICE

A memoir of seeking truth and finding freedom

Cathy Byrne

Bathus

ISBN-paperback: 978-1-7647842-0-7
ISBN-epub: 978-1-7647842-1-4

Published by bathus, Tasmania.

Cover and interior design: Susan Young
Author photo on cover: Madeleine Waller.

The work of the bathus draws strength from the powerful country of Lutruwita. We acknowledge and pay respect to the traditional owners and their continuing custodianship of this place.

Events in this story took place on the lands of the Bundjalung nation of northern New South Wales. The author acknowledges the strength and patience of their elders, the sorrow of their stories and the majesty of those Aboriginal lands.

NATIONAL LIBRARY OF AUSTRALIA

A catalogue record for this work is available from the National Library of Australia

Millions of women avoid pursuing justice.
This true story sheds light on why.

Cultural change requires bravery but also patience.
Dear reader, allow your compassion to accompany these characters on their journeys, still unfolding.

About the author

Dr Cathy Byrne is an author, academic and social justice advocate. She has written for The Conversation and various academic journals. She has presented on radio and TV news shows and at the NSW Parliamentary Inquiry into Ethics in Primary Schools. Her first book, *Religion in Secular Education: what in heaven's name are we teaching our children?*, was published by Brill in 2013. She is known for her advocacy on children's rights and her support of women in surfing. This is her first work of memoir.

Contents

Author's note

This story is as true and real as I could make it. Conversations, recorded in extensive journal notes, emails, screen captures and text messages, document events across two years. At the time of my police reporting, it was important to keep records, not only as evidence for a court case; this note-taking helped me to keep track of essential information and to ground myself in a fracturing reality. Every word spoken was spoken. On legal advice, some details are changed. The general location has been broadened and the hometown name switched to a similar coastal town, but the details provided reflect actual event locations. To protect the people I love, identities have been disguised and mine is the only real name.

I wrote this to help patch my pieces back together and because society ought to know what happens when innocence is broken. The damage done to victims, and how to better support survivors, is not yet fully understood. We all need to find our way back to wholeness.

I hope this book provides some insight. For all victims and survivors of child sexual abuse and for those wondering if it's safe yet to speak, know this: a child cannot give consent.

IT IS NOT NOW AND NEVER WAS YOUR FAULT.

Cathy Byrne

An ending

He's waiting. I should go. Just thinking it, shrinks me into a fraidy little thing in someone else's skin. *What if he's angry?*

The mere thought floods prickly panic from guts into chest. Breath fights through a straw, then the back of my skull starts to rip. Heart thumping. Ears screaming. Sweat inside clothes. Tears and rain. Those are *my* hiking boots hitting the ground, running. Again.

No. Fear is not my ending. Now I'm stronger.

Let's begin slowly, at the upending.

The Upending 1

Truth shimmers

December 2020

Truth shimmers here like a shallow-trapped fish. A southerly squall chops the ocean with its blunt knife, swirling clouds into gusts, drowning everything in humidity.

It's morning. Take a moment. Breathe.

Fragility erodes the sun-side of the first dune, where I live, while heat seeps through Mum's tinder-dry house on the back dune, in the fire-risk scrub. I'm not sure which is more threatening, my sharks or her snakes.

On the beach pathway, we walk. She natters. The osprey circles as I float behind sunglasses, but light here is piercing; snags me back. A crow *quaarks,* angling downwind under a panicky seagull, entangling black with white.

'I'm nearly eighty,' Mum reminds me, pulling sleeves over arthritic hands. 'My sisters' hands are worse.' She boasts sibling rivalry, like cancer, through Irish skin.

'Mum, your sandal isn't ...' I squat and strap her old-lady shoes.

Today, she has a 'lunch date ... can't be late for my hairdresser'. Lianne, my eldest sister, will visit soon, the first time in months, now that Covid border restrictions have eased. 'I'll sweep the garage,' Mum says, 'and clean the walls, and oh, I can already feel that sun.'

Finally, she takes a breath.

'Mmm,' I murmur from harboured quiet, knowing Lianne will help. Mum's old house is crumbling and it's tough since Dad died. I do my share: skip surfs to make her tea, walk with her, drive her, make soup, type her community letters, report her health to *my* sisters. Mutually obligated, Mum babysits, shouts lunch, hems trousers, listens to my kids-at-school troubles.

We get a laugh. We're close.

Then the turquoise flash of a rainbow bee-eater makes me wonder if there's a wave today, and if it's bushfire I can smell.

We've stopped on the path where a sword of sunlight bullies through cloud. It feels like a portal. *Or a trapdoor.*

'I'm not sure I should tell you …' Mum shows rare restraint.

'Silence is golden,' I reply warily.

She cocks her head: intently watching me, her youngest daughter, now 53. Then she steps in, blocks my way. 'Cathy …'

I exhale, brace myself for whatever's coming.

'His name was in the paper.'

My *get-on-with-it* pose assumes she's referring to someone my well-liked father knew: a soldier; pilot; teacher? Mum enjoys making people guess.

'He's organising his mother's funeral.'

Looking for a clue in her grey eyes, I tilt confusion in my head. Two birds on a wire. Feathers ruffle.

'Who?'

Our eyes hold the wound closed. I suck in boiled air as sound evaporates. The osprey scans the shallows, readying to dive. A piece of me floats above water.

'He might be back in town.'

Cold inside hot. Not-breathing. Something flutters under my ribcage.

'Do you have a reaction to that?' she asks.

I notice looming thunderheads, my hand, covering mouth, but *I cannot name the feeling*. The wind-whipped osprey soars, without a catch.

'Good,' says Mum, 'you've moved on.' Her words sting, a slap of cold air.

Déjà vu clouds huddle as I remember the last time we spoke of it. Here, on this corner. I was 36 and pushing baby Kaleido's pram.

I crack my neck, taste weirdly sweet slime. Need to spit. *There's enough hurt already.*

'I could help you deal,' Mum said back then.

I'd wondered if she'd kept something. Maybe a letter I'd written? But I didn't accept her offer. I'd recently moved back to my beloved Tacking Point, a northern New South Wales beach town. After a decade of travel, work, marriage, a child, I'd mastered purposeful forgetting.

Now she peers, too close. 'Was it OK to say?'

'I'm fine,' I say, zipping raincoat over throat.

Taking my arm, she urges me up towards the old lighthouse. 'You know what "fine" means?' She chuckles.

I look ahead, wanting to speak, but avoiding her game.

'Fucking. Insane. Neurotic. Exhausted.' *Totally F.I.N.E.*

Her words melt behind rain curtains, blurring the view of Tacking Point's business district that Tacky locals call 'the island'.

Someone yells, far away. *Just a gull.*

'When are you working next?' asks Mum, pulling me into the gloaming hush.

'Don't know.' I feel nauseous.

Waking up

January 2021

A sticky night. My scratchy skin wanders through rooms and I squint at clocks. Barely midnight. Unable to sleep on the guest futon, I go back to our bedroom. Insomnia.

Lying still does not help.

Then a neighbour's alarm screams. Or there's a dentist drill inside my skull? This is new. *Painful.* I wriggle a finger into my right ear – the hearing one.

My left ear, deaf since birth, makes me so sound-sensitive that, like a Chihuahua, I hear extremely high-pitched noises. It's probably why I can wiggle my ears. Unlike dogs, my sound direction is poor. I remember Mr Kinner yelling across the playground:

'Cathy Byrne, are you half-deaf?'

'Yes!' I'd shouted, in the wrong direction. My honesty silenced him.

I try not to wake Mr Works-Too-Hard, but I can't get comfortable. I kick at tangled sheets. Vince moans, rolls, instantly snores. The ringing stops, but now my toes cramp. I launch forward, clutch my feet, puff-breathe, watch the shark-boat lights. *There.* Down near the Pebbly Beach streetlight, someone's lurking. *Just a shadow.*

Back in the guest room, I try dancing silently, soft-planting bare feet into floorboards, disco-pumping arms: 'Boogie Wonderland', 'Play That Funky Music', 'Hollywood Seven'. When the sun rises, I'll paddle across Shark Alley; surf into exhaustion. But now, in darkness, lungs feel waterlogged.

I tea-steam my dry eyeballs and give myself a proper talking to. *Be productive. Finish that Coastcare grant application. Do the 'Clean Up Australia Day' paperwork.*

Instead, I check the forecast. La Niña, the crying girl, will bring 'instability: turbulence; pressure troughs; swell blockages; and temperature regulation difficulties for all ocean life'.

I am a sea creature. Tanned, like my father. Emerald-eyed, like a deep-sea fish. I've surfed since I was 9. La Niña will disrupt my joy. But she's not here yet; fire warnings still crackle south of the river. Nothing makes sense in my once sparkling 'Tacky Isle'.

I rearrange letters: 'Tacky Lies'.

The place is a 1980s myth, a Pine Lime Splice pretend from my wild, free childhood: pretending to be a shipwreck survivor; belly-crawling along death-adder dune trails; swimming out through the rips; crying with a beached dolphin, too far from help. I imagined that Pebbly Beach held my heart in stasis while I travelled. Now I'm wondering why I returned.

You can't buy a Pine Lime at the Pebbly shop anymore, and the town's not really an island. Built on mangrove swamps, Tacky's canals were once sewage drains. The river, now often grey, makes my old town pride feel like a bleary hangover.

My 'LuvTacky' shark sticker makes more sense. The state government tried shark nets, which killed turtles, were ripped apart in huge seas and were removed in embarrassment. I tell myself I'm lucky to live on the beach where I grew up, but sharks make me nervous.

Tacking Point has always had predators.

Near sunrise, I head back to bed and enter a false sleep which holds me under; open-eyed, unable to move or scream. Breath skips across panic. I try kicking, but Brain is not Body. I lunge upwards, gasping.

Vince rolls me into a gentle hug. 'It's just a dream.' His calm radio-voice nestles me back, into my clean-shaven-handsome, loving husband of twenty years. *Just a dream.*

Once, on a nut farm, we made love under starlight. And so came Kaleidoscope: Vince's third child, my only. As a toddler, Kaleido enjoyed my storytelling, of the honey-coloured moon and why some children got magical blue eyes. Now 18 – studious and empathetic – Kal recently moved out, into university life. There is space here now, for me to deal with history, if I want to. *I don't want to.*

I remember being so chuffed, filling in Kaleido's birth registration. Next to 'occupation' I wrote 'Mother'. My only tasks: keep our child safe; play; aim for happy. The role is love.

My other 'occupations' hadn't worked so well. I always seemed to burn too furiously, give too much, needed to leave. *To run.*

I returned to raise Kal near the sea, in our leaky 1960s 'love-shack' made from beach boulders, old newspapers, and rusted-open windows. When the walls crumbled, we rebuilt small, the new house still crouching from sea-spray behind banksia hedges. I added blue walls and a tiny loft, so Kal could watch the moonrise. We still grow sweet potatoes and papayas … in compost, on a sand dune! I tell my Kal-school-mum-friend Gemma that 'I'll never leave my "belong place".' She knows I've moved ten times in the last ten years. This is the first haven I've not fled – yet, despite my current 'Plan D' occupation: teaching at my old high school.

He might be back.

In greying light, I see my world-travel mementos, my dusty juggling balls, my un-strummed guitar. I thought returning would tame my restlessness; that I could play-act happy here. *Lack of sleep makes me see more clearly.*

I scroll the news, wondering when I'll get a surf. Last week's low-pressure system raged down the Queensland coast and plonked a rain bomb, like a bloated toad, over 'Troubled Tacky residents'. Trapped in caravans and over-priced Airbnbs, holidaymakers lumbered about like zombies, hungry for streaming TV.

Lingering humidity weighs every surface with such slick stillness I'm relieved when sunlight finally burns the dark. I promised to help Mum in her garden. It might help my nausea. I leave Vince to sleep, grab his electric chainsaw and head to Bunnings.

In the parking lot, people take photos under a giant fibreglass oyster. They think it represents history. Another lie. It wasn't built until the late eighties and barely evaded demolition twenty years later. Confected outrage scored the mouldy shellfish a makeover. Now, a new tourism centre sells 'Tacky' oyster socks. Made-elsewhere kitsch.

Some creatures lie to survive.

Near Bunnings, Tacky's 'island' folds in on itself like a soiled wet wipe. Tidal creeks weave around workers' cottages and bling-boat pontooned mansions. The mangrove stench mixes with sulphur gas from the wastewater works, broiling my gut as I haul mulch into my Corolla. Heading for Mum's, I watch Richman Street pedestrians turn their noses up at rotting fish in king-tide drains. I drive slowly past the RSL Club, not-remembering. *Totally F.I.N.E.*

In her tiny courtyard, Mum trims grass with a push mower.

'We'll thin out the *Callistemon viminalis.*' She flaunts her Latin plant-name knowledge.

'The bottlebrush?' I ask, to peeve her.

'Above that broken branch.' She points, ignores, focuses on 'the visual', *her* perfect aesthetic. 'Trim it *exactly* how I want. Don't argue like your father used to.'

I nod, remembering Dad's patient acquiescence. The too-high branch requires me to stand on a ladder, pushing Vince's chainsaw beyond my reach. It's drip-sticky hot. My weak wrist points the saw skywards.

'Not there,' she fusses, '… higher. If you can't reach, I'll do it.'

She's taller, but I can't let her up a ladder. If Mother falls … well, I'm not good with blood. And my sisters might get angry. I balance on tiptoes.

'Did you watch the Australian of the Year Awards?' Mum asks in that dangerous moment, weaving her heron-neck through branches.

'No,' I mumble, shallow-breathing bark dust, the electrical cord wrapped around one leg. I'd seen Grace Tame, a child sexual abuse survivor and advocate, in the news, but hadn't read her story.

My sunnies are scum-flecked. Useless in blinding sun. I throw them down.

'She's very beautiful,' Mum continues, stepping back to assess my work.

'Brave,' I counter, not looking down.

'I was brave this week,' Mum counter-counters. 'I booked my first Covid vaccine. I'm nearly eighty, you know.' She's been reminding us for years.

Mid-saw, my grip falters. The branch twists the chain off, stalls the motor.

'Oh, you didn't quite reach,' Mum squint-points.

Rubbing my sprained wrist, I show the broken saw.

'Well, that's that then,' she decrees. 'Drag those branches to the bin,' she instructs. 'Can't leave it untidy. What would the neighbours say?'

I untangle as she easily manoeuvres mulch bags into her wheelbarrow.

Inside, I sip tea as Mum chats about her health issues. I don't mention mine because she'll list all the 'silly' choices I've made and ponder aloud how intelligent people astound her with their poor judgement. Then she says she wants to cut back on alcohol.

'I dropped from eight drinks a week to two,' I say, thinking my tracking method might help her.

'How do you know that?' she disbelieves.

'I keep a record.'

'No you don't.' She shakes her head, as if I've lied.

'I've been using a drink diary for years,' I insist.

She senses my annoyance. 'I couldn't imagine anyone doing such a thing.' Her attempt at an apology. I quietly rinse my cup.

'Oh, you're cross!' She snorts a belittling.

I'm too nauseated to take her on. If I get work next week, I'll need all my energy. Head pounds with the thought of it.

Driving home, the sight of the sea is no relief. Mud from Loggerville smears the coastline. I stow Vince's chainsaw and don't mention the damage. Money is tight.

Stay in the classroom

February, week 1

A 6:45 am work text coaxes me out of bed. An hour later, I drive ten minutes to the monstrosity in the centre of Tacking Point 'Island'. Rebuilt in 2019, the $8 million new high school is a state election 'innovation' from the Education Department's 'engineers of the future'. So said the brochures. Community consultations, held in the performance hall I'd rather forget, emphasised '21st-century' *open classrooms* and *sliding doors.* The brochure's ambitious idioms of 'student-focused outcomes' and 'evidence-based research' (as if there's some other kind) manifest here in noisy, walk-through rooms and a bring-your-own-device strategy of chaos and inequity.

The planners were so excited about architecture, they ignored demographic data. Student numbers outgrew capacity before the school opened; the 'green space' is now filled with demountable classrooms and disenchantment.

I breathe courage into being as I walk under the cantilevered bronze façade. Inside, steel beams pinch-hold floor-to-ceiling glass doors. The new performance hall has movable walls. *Dark spaces.* It connects to the local council's Sports Centre, suggesting that schools and communities have mutual responsibilities.

It was different back then. The school was our whole world.

My parents, here from the seventies to the nineties, were classically gender compliant: Dad taught industrial arts full-time, Mum, cooking and sewing as a casual. Now, casuals teach *all* subjects. *Fake it till we make it* ... to 3:30 pm. An endurance through four 70-minute lessons, playground duty, and a half-hour time-wasting session so the religious 2 per cent can pray.

Already sweltering on early duty, I find myself at Mum and Dad's old staffroom, the only red-brick building not demolished. All here in the heyday (Mum, Dad, my sisters Lianne and Maggie, me, and eventually little brother, Rocky) in a school of sports stars, academic achievers, and eisteddfod-winning musicians. *He might come here.*

Everything's different now. No longer blue, the uniforms are now oyster grey.

The bell sends me scuttling across bone-dry grass and dusty chip packets. To a one-word lesson plan: 'Shakespeare'. I ask thirty 14-year-olds to: 'Write a letter to Queen Elizabeth the First. Use these 16th-century English words to describe how tragic your comedies are.' None of them have seen a Shakespeare. At day's end all my pens are broken.

Hot westerly winds swirl beachward where the clover-coloured sea floats me into pink-orange sunset sparks and blissful forgetting.

Survival counts.

Week 2

I check the clock at 2 am, 3 am, 4 am, grabbing tiny sleeps on my stomach, like a turtle. It crinks my neck. Reports of fires doomscroll me until a work text drags me to the kitchen, where I won't eat because I feel sick. Vince is ready to leave. Covid border restrictions, and pressure from his boss, have raised mental-health concerns for his factory workers.

'Take care of your team,' I urge.

'They'll axe me next,' he warns.

'Don't let the bastards drag you down,' we boost each other.

If I glance sideways, I might see a real bastard.

I have not told Vince my story. *Am afraid to?*

South of the 'Isle' is a smoky haze. On Radio National: Perth copes with Covid cruise ships while a Federal MP promotes horse-worming pills for the global pandemic. Politicians avoid setting climate targets while Australia burns.

By 8 am, Tacky bakes at 30 degrees. Parked on oozing bitumen, I try to summon purpose.

I can make a difference.

Doubting my rear-view mirror face, whose career has devolved from international project manager and published academic, to last-minute-contract university lecturer, to perilously underemployed casual teacher, I laugh. 'Livin' the dream!'

As I climb the 21st-century staircase to the sign-in desk, a giant back-lit screen declares: *Innovation. Excellence. Diversity.* Nausea rides the updraft from an extraction fan, mixing canteen meat pie aroma with the stench of rubbish.

The engineers of the future make me sick.

The principal's motivational quotes cover the staffroom whiteboard: *Learn how to dance in the rain*, and *No phones in class*. Most casuals are required to show YouTube videos, which students ignore while sneaking their phones out. Last year, a senior boy refused to hand over his mobile, then ran from the school. I reported. Principal Palmer came to 'assist'. Her loud rebuke, directed at me: 'Stay in the classroom. Don't pick a fight.'

Reporting is pointless.

~

Bizarrely, rooms have heaters, not air conditioners. In class, two boys distract me while another turns heaters on. By ten thirty we're sizzling.

The day blurs with unexpected room changes (casuals aren't notified), quick runs to dirty student toilets (casuals don't get staff keys), an un-charged laptop missing software, and an increasingly fuzzy-hot headache.

At day's end, I bitch to Mum: 'I'm stuck as a casual.'

'*I* was a casual,' Mum reminds me. 'You need to come down to earth after all that international highfalutin. Spend time in the bog, with the little people.' She prides her station, wants it to be mine.

Slow boil

Seven in the morning, a ping: 'Cooking and science.' *Shit.* The radio warns of scorching conditions. Dry dust swirls as I ascend the nausea-uplifting stairs.

'Make do,' states the faculty head, busily organising catering for the Minister for Education. The government's shiny school bauble will be announced 'a success'.

Period 1 is a riot. Thirty Year 7 kids squeal-search for a room; we're sent elsewhere, and sardine-hunker into a space designed for ten.

A few shout 'Here, Miss!' into my directionless deafness, answering for absent others. I don't know their thousand names.

To quell their restlessness, I set up a game of Kahoot! The faculty head passes, yells at a boy using his phone. I'd given permission. He scowls at me. I mime-apologise.

~

Year 8 thought they'd be making chocolate brownies. They howl displeasure at me.

'Why can't we cook?' 'Aren't you a proper teacher, Miss?'

I ignore the protest-pen-throwing and shout-ask them to sit down. No-one takes a worksheet. Brandon struts in late, looks at me in disgust and pulls out a can of deodorant.

'Sprays are banned inside, Brandon.'

Defiant, he squirts his armpits. Revelling in their attention, he sprays over classmates' heads, smirks.

'Put it away. *Now!*' I try my big voice.

Brandon mocks my performance for his snickering table. Avoiding toxic air, I move towards the open door. Brandon raises his trophy.

'Brandon, this is your last warning,' I threaten.

So tired of not being listened to.

'It covers my masculine fragrance, Miss. Otherwise you won't be able to control yourself,' he taunts, stepping closer. Millimetres.

Enough. I reach out as Brandon twist-ducks under me. We both grab the can. My face wrestles a sting-chemical cloud of Lynx Africa.

'You can't take it, Miss. I know my rights!'

In absurd slow motion, a 53-year-old woman, the size of a 14-year-old boy, loses her footing. Embarrassed, I dash from the classroom, eyes streaming.

That moment, Principal Palmer sees Brandon stash the weapon, but she's bigger-fish-focused today.

Five of the thirty worksheets get completed, some scrawled with penises. I leave them on the teacher's desk. They'll be binned without a glance.

Should I put a report in the Behaviour Management System?

My last prohibited substance debacle ended with squashed strawberries in the carpet, my lunch break spent cleaning and typing, only to be told: 'Those reports don't get read.'

With too-few minutes between classes, the staffroom is a battle of kettles, microwaves, sandwich toasters, but only two power points.

The engineers of the future design mayhem.

I dry-swallow bits of protein ball on duty as my dehydrated head throbs under smoky sky. Cicada screams pierce every tonal space between handball shouts, pinging devices, and the thud of basketballs.

Stepping over squashed juice boxes, I challenge a boy who's discarded his half-eaten apple. He ignores me. I tell him to take pride in his school.

'Go on then, Miss,' he mocks. 'Be the change.'

He watches me pick up his slimy trash.

Avoid, don't confront. This armour I learned in the Ruin.

~

'Get to work, Year Ten,' and 'Put that away, Cade. No food in class,' I tell the ruffle-haired boy who peels a banana. Sniggers from his table draw expectant looks and the smell of pack dogs. My skin prickles.

I turn to a table of chatty girls and grab a sparkly phone, also prohibited. 'You can get it after class,' I tell the girl who's about to object, 'or … from the office at three-thirty.' She huffs as I pocket the phone.

'Mr Marsden wants your volcano research finished today.' I try to refocus them as raucous laughter turns me back to Cade, performing fruit fellatio.

'Bin it, Cade. Now!' My voice is lost in derision. Neck is a hot knot. I check the time and slow-breathe. *I'll be at the beach by 4 pm.*

Cade is distracting others, so I crouch beside him, my voice low. 'The principal is on walk-around, Cade. This will come down badly on you.'

'Hear that, boys?' he yells with a cocky smirk. 'She wants to come down bad on me.'

Harry laugh-spits his chips under the desk. Devlin, a weedy blond, drums his fingers next to my face, bringing my attention to the penis he's drawn on the table. My breath shudders and a drill screeches. *Inside my ears?* I look to the hallway, half-hoping to see Ms Palmer. No teachers in sight, despite all that glass. My ideal of collaborative learning is being trashed. My lesser goal, to be heard, withers under guffaws as Cade adds crude hand movements.

'Want banana yoghurt, Miss?' He licks.

My head flares red-hot lava. Gut lurches. I jump to vertical to beat the vomit. Hand over mouth, I stumble back to sit-hide behind a desk, drained by faking powerful.

I've been doing this forever. Coping.

I open my laptop to the news. Grace Tame, Australian of the Year, has 'EAT MY FEAR' tattooed on her hand. She's encouraging people to report sexual abusers.

'We need to hear from survivors …'

Cade walks too-close behind me.

'… because it's in their stories we find the truth.'

Another student raises a hand, moves their mouth, but I'm watching intently as a woman highlights the difficulties of speaking up. 'Miss?'

'Abuse is characterised by degradation, disempowerment and feeling like you have no voice.' Floatiness envelops me as the student tosses down an early leave note and storms out.

The bell goes. The sparkly phone goes. I stay, reading about Grace Tame: a schoolgirl in a culture of silence. *Brave Grace.*

Week 3

Tacky's dust-dry gutters smell of fish-rot. I sip coffee in my car, aircon at max, listening to radio news. 'A young woman reports being raped inside Australia's Parliament House …'

By 8 am, the sign-in desk is so smoky that breath skims oxygen from my throat. 'Oh please,' I beg of no particular god, 'can today be different?'

'At least we don't work in Parliament House!' responds another casual.

'Apparently she was *drunk*,' says a permanent, disparaging.

Vulnerable! I want to shout but – glance at my timetable – he's my supervisor today; my only shift this week. Stay in the classroom.

Scared of losing *her* job, Brittany Higgins dropped her complaint. The Minister called Brittany a 'lying cow'.

Brave Brittany.

Ants

The forecast wet struggles to make her presence felt. Instead, El Niño's dry heat hangs on, strangely heavy. Lines of thirsty carpenter ants form dark shapes at our front door.

Vince wants to spray. I suggest vinegar.

'Witchy rubbish!' He dismisses natural remedies.

I gather ants in tissues and toss them into the garden.

The ant man is overbooked because another rain bomb is forecast. Meanwhile, ants haul formic acid into my walls, slowly moving my foundations west, over the dune, towards Mother. But I don't visit. No work this week; I don't want to be reminded I'm over-educated.

Too clever.

I resort to my cure-all: surfing for two hours, three days in a row. Ocean therapy. I joy-ride the nose of my dinged-up mini mal all the way into shore, cackling as I flop onto sand. Wind, sunburn and sightings of a large sea turtle steady me into gratitude.

At night, the moon glows through our flimsy curtains like a nuclear lollipop. Recalling Grace Tame's words, 'Share your truth, it is your power', I lie awake, buzzing with radioactive ideas. *He might be back.*

Saturday morning, Vince agrees to walk. We chat about our soon-to-be first grandchild, guess possible worst names. 'Esmerelda,' he jokes. 'Morticia,' I counter. 'Barnaby.' We laugh.

Out on the river breakwater, the swell thunders.

'You should have a surf,' Vince encourages.

I convince myself that the river's testosterone-zone is too crowded, that the water isn't clean enough. But the truth is, I'm worried about schoolboys hustling onto my waves.

While Vince watches booming tube rides, I stretch in my daggy shorts, try to suck in air. Despite the sparkling sunshine, something feels ominous. Breath shallows. I squat, hands out in front, and stand too quickly. The blood-rush drains. Head pounds. *Have I eaten?* I look down. *Are those my feet, way down there?* I spiral sideways in slow motion, down and around, like a salt-drunk shark, watching cement rush up to my face. A hand breaks my fall. *Mine?*

When I open my eyes, my outstretched left leg is twitching. Mouth is frozen, like in my paralysis dream. I can't yell. Can't move. But I'm awake. *It's just like …*

I want Vince to turn. Leg still jerking, won't bend. Mustering all I've got, I clench, kick and explode into gasping breath.

Vince acts normal. 'Come on,' he says, offering his hand.

Did he see me flapping like a landed fish?

He pulls me to his chest, where I hang on longer than usual. I don't want to worry him.

~

Later, I google 'low blood sugar fainting' but nothing makes sense. Was it vestibular? Abnormalities in the inner ear can cause floating sensations. *Yeah, nah.* Cervical spondylosis? Parkinson's? Or … psychiatric disorder? *No.* Anxiety can cause dizziness. *I'm not anxious.* Depressed? No. I rarely feel 'low' … There was that time in college when a monstrous cloak of sadness knocked me to the floor … and I did drink into oblivion through my twenties. *Well …*

Maybe I'm dehydrated, or worried about not getting work? I'm hungry, but nauseous again. I look up causes; see that 'gut disorders are associated with trauma'.

That's not me. Don't click.

I write 'nausea' in my diary, next to 'no work this week'.

I burrow down more internet rabbit holes and find myself staring at research that connects depression and sexual assault. Breath hits a sandbar. *Click.*

Chanel Contos, a former high school student, sexually assaulted at 13, didn't realise it was rape. Now 22, Chanel is calling for 'consent education'.

Consent? The concept sloshes into my numb bucket.

~

My sister Maggie, a nurse, warns against internet advice. 'Standing up too quickly can drop your blood pressure. It's orthostatic hypotension. See a proper doctor.'

~

Medical tests show my blood pressure is down, sugar levels dangerously low. But it doesn't explain the nausea, or the red-hot seltzer-fizz behind my ant-nest skull. I force myself to eat, which makes me want to puke. Breath doesn't have enough space. I need to empty sour monoxide. Something is wrong. Something Vulcan is stirring, shaking. Rupture feels imminent.

I walk the cliffs. It doesn't help. Ocean squalls rain me into disillusionment. In desperation, I read *Breath: The New Science of a Lost Art* by James Nestor. I do the exercises. Breathe in for four and hold for two. Eight steps … breathing out, and hold. Slowing. Four steps in. Hold. Eight steps. Slower. Out. And deeper now.

Already I've forgotten the ants. Breathing helps.

~

Weeks of intense heat vaporise every drop. I get no work calls. It's for the best. I'll step down from my bottom rung into Mother's breathless bog. I'm *F.I.N.E.* with that … and with staring across the supermarket carpark for … how long?

I drive the groceries home, tune out of head static into radio news: Chanel Contos has prompted thousands to share their stories. Education ministers hold crisis meetings with principals. Commentators blame alcohol, porn and parties. Chanel's survey reveals 'a toxic Australian rape culture of male entitlement and slut-shaming … leading to attitudes where assault and harassment are normal'.

I sit in the garage, listening, scratching ants.

Brave Chanel.

'Every single person contributes to this rape culture, unless they actively don't.'

Her words upend my numb bucket over my head. Leaving groceries in the car I find myself at my laptop. In an article titled 'Do they even know they did this to us?', Contos urges: 'Understand what was wrong with the past.'

Muddy tides haul my past into present: *Every single person contributes to this rape culture, unless they act* … Time dulls the ripples. Now, they intersect, circles growing wider, breaking through buried awfuls.

He might be back in town.

Incident reports

Week 4

I dizzy-trudge up the stairs, kneel at the computer trolley and review my class list. Mr Jones sees me mutter a quiet 'fuck', steps out from the staffroom, asks which students I have.

'Tacky's finest.' I show the list.

'I'm marking. Hopefully you won't need me,' he fake-smiles.

Only February, but everyone is already stretched thinner than old rubber bands. I'm straw-sipping smoke haze, balancing six half-charged iPads, thirty worksheets and my laptop. I grab a handful of pens, for students who will try it on: 'Can't, Miss. No pen, Miss.' In my allotted glass cavern, one side opens to a railing over a twenty-foot drop. *Engineer-designed danger.* Every sound is amplified.

I connect laptop to smart screen as the bell rings and the away-teacher's instructions arrive in my email. I write them up. No sound on the video! I ask a boy to find help. He argues. I plead. Students sit as far away as they can, making faces through glass walls, pretending I don't exist. Latecomers shout inane questions.

'D'you surf today, Miss?'

'Where's Gardo, Miss?'

Their distractions will bury me. 'OK, I need six groups, one iPad per—'

'You should answer me, Miss,' interrupts Devlin, hovering like a summer midge.

I pretend not to see his phone. When I'd reported his penis drawings, his file read: *learning difficulties and frequent porn-viewing.*

'Find a group please, Devlin.' I turn away.

'But Miss ... my breakfast.'

'Take your pie outside, Devlin.' He stomp-chomps towards the door, dripping gristle. I repeat my instructions, magically find another volume control.

A girl yells: 'What's the code, Miss?'

'On the board,' I shout-point.

A chorus in reply: 'Doesn't work, Miss.'

The code links to a blank page. Mercifully, another student has correct links. I write new instructions as one boy leaves. 'What's his name?' I ask. No-one will say.

Few students watch the video or attempt the worksheet. All my pens are gone.

Devlin bounces beside me. 'We've already watched this, Miss.'

'Show me,' I challenge.

'Can't, Miss. Already submitted.'

Others join in: 'We did this already!'

Cacophony erupts. Several boys head to the danger-rail. I watch in horror as Ewan starts climbing, glare-dares me to react.

'Gardo won't be happy you're wasting our time, Miss,' he taunts.

'Hop down, Ewan!' I shout. *He wants me to panic.*

Too close behind me, Devlin yells: 'Jump, ya cunt!'

Mr Jones escorts Ewan to the staffroom. Devlin dashes around a table of girls, offers 'chicken chips for a blowie', crinkles the packet in my face. Nausea slops up my throat. I want to shove the skinny prick, but he lacks parental attention.

Stay in the classroom, don't pick a fight.

Suddenly, a piercing alarm slices my right ear. Not inside my head this time. Powerless, I plug my ear in crouched confusion. *I am their target.*

Mr Jones steps back in, wishes he hadn't. He booms: 'Quiet, boys!'

The hidden phone siren stops.

'Some respect for Miss Byrne.' He waits for simmering quiet, then exits.

The boy that left is back, kicking the wall behind me. *Thud, thud, thud …*

I ask him to stop. He doesn't. Then, another student throws a lidless, half-drunk bottle of milk up the wall.

'OK!' yells my deepest voice. 'No-one leaves until that's cleaned up.'

When the bell goes, no power can stop them. I stand against the one solid wall and close my eyes for a millisecond.

Like a goblin, Devlin is there, his grey eyes flicking over me. Every cell of me recoils. 'I know you reported me, Miss,' he sneers. 'They showed my parents.'

I taste acid bile. 'Step back,' commands my shuddery voice.

He doesn't move. I raise my hands to push and he jumps back.

'She molested me!' he yells maniacally. 'I'll report *you*, Miss,' he threaten-skips around the room.

It's only 9:50. Mr Jones brings Ewan back and sternly repeats that no-one is leaving until the milk is cleaned up. He stares them down until two boys go for cleaning supplies. I spend the last fifteen minutes shrinking into my sandals.

After the bell, Mr Jones advises: 'Don't let students leave the room. You're responsible for their welfare.'

I ask what a casual can possibly do.

'Write an incident report,' he suggests.

'Are they even read?'

'Well …' He lets it slide.

I practise letting-it-slide for the rest of the day. I ignore the nail polish, deodorant, phones, food and verbal abuse. My earlier Lynx-boy report backfires; I'm told to 'find the good in the kid'.

Lessons: *This is an income, not a profession; reporting is not worth the trouble; bog-dwellers cannot change the world.*

At 3:30, I trudge through burnt air and the shrill of victory-dancing cicadas, hoping the ocean will wash off defeat. But today, even sea-salt can't scour me. Smoke hangs, a grey curtain, slinking the sun down.

Back home, the outdoor shower is so hot it stings. Vince is inside, pouring shiraz, cooking pork. The stench enters me.

'That smell makes me nauseous,' I tell him, for the umpteenth time.

'It doesn't smell.' Vince denies my reality.

I open all the windows, close the bedroom door and don't come out.

The breakout room

Week 5

'Year Ten, we're doing sections one to four.' I hand out maths workbooks and mark the roll. 'Has anyone seen Devlin?'

'In the breakout room, Miss,' comes his disembodied reply.

Devlin stares through darkened glass. I'd like to ignore him, but I need this job.

'Devlin …'

'Miss Sherwood lets me,' Devlin shouts.

'Not today, Devlin,' I say calmly. 'Principal's instructions.'

'I've got permission!' he protests.

Half-tempted to leave him, I imagine Principal Palmer's harangue.

I don't want to be anyone's target.

'If you finish the work,' I use my determined, not-raised voice, 'you can come back.'

A reckless promise. I take his bag to a table.

'Don't touch my stuff, Miss,' he whines, but follows.

I remind students to complete sections one to four. Every other minute, Devlin steps into my space: 'Can I go to the breakout room, Miss?'

'You haven't finished section one.' I move on. He's bouncing, trying to start conversations. An outsider, he annoys other students. I feel sorry for him.

I sit with a table of girls who are working. They ask to use the breakout room.

'Finish section four,' I repeat, turning to find Devlin in my face again.

'Miss, I've done more than everyone. *Come* ... and see.'

I sigh, step towards the table of noisy boys. Devlin opens his workbook to a drawing of a penis, resplendent with pubes. 'See, Miss ... Not that!' He slowly turns the page. '*Here's* my work, Miss. Can I go now?' He's done two sums.

'Devlin, you have to *finish* section one.' I point to his torn workbook, 'and section two, and three, and four. *Then* you can come and see me.'

'I can *come* on you after that, Miss?' – I ignore the sexual reference – 'You lied, Miss,' he shouts, grabs his bag, heads for the breakout room.

Principal Palmer exits the library. I muster my big voice, step into the breakout room doorway: 'Devlin, stay in class and finish your work.'

Devlin steps defiantly into the doorway, facing me. We both watch Palmer walk by, purposely looking away. Then Devlin growls: 'Hard cocks are good for lesbians!' His spit burns my skin. 'You want it, Miss.'

'I want ...' *you to fuck off,* I think, but blurt: '... to drink whiskey.'

'Me too, Miss. Let's go,' he guffaws.

~

Outside on duty, Armageddon-orange sky presses heat into my eyes. There's a fire south of the river. The hotter the day, the louder the male cicadas bang their tymbals. Today they punk-rock with primal pleasure. My char-scratched throat wishes I'd brought my water bottle. I remember a Covid mask in my pocket; try breathing through my mouth so I won't smell dead things; try not-breathing.

~

I'm outside my body, somewhere Dali-esque. A basketball thuds as they surround me: banana-boy, his circus crowd, two senior boys I put on detention, and Devlin, somehow taller, glaring, bouncing the ball, slow and hard. Time telescopes outwards. I'm still not breathing. The posse circles in the haze, as Devlin's grey eyes bore into me. I say nothing. Don't. Move.

Between each slow-motion bounce, Devlin rubs his genitals. My head thuds. Legs want to run. But they're inside cement. The thud of the ball slows in my chest. I hear a sharp alarm. Not the school bell. It's inside my head. Say something. Do something!

Phoooff, my held breath launches me from nightmare, sweat-soaked. Stained.

Vince makes tea and leaves to catch a plane. Away for a week.

I hunker. Survive on miso and crackers. Revel in the power of the TV remote.

A news report alleges that Australia's Attorney-General once raped a 16-year-old girl at a school debating tournament. The Prime Minister backs his legal man, who accepts hidden donations to rescue his 'ruined' reputation. She suicided.

I call Vince. He doesn't answer. My sister Lianne calls. I don't answer.

Every single person contributes to rape culture, unless they actively don't.

Clinging to Vince

I miss Vince's cups of tea, want to hide beside him. He's under pressure to bring in the big deals, but I wish he was here, helping me deal. *Will I tell him?* I refuse several days' work. We need the income, but I can't face it. The hot prickling in my gut slides under my skin. Stronger than reluctance. Ghost-cold. Powerful.

This shadow-surge I cannot name. It feels like fear.

Morning radio says Australia's Chief of Defence gave female cadets a '4A's strategy': 'Avoid sexual predators' by not being 'Attractive, Alcohol-affected, [or] out Alone after midnight', as if victims are responsible for sexual assault.

I think about Chanel Contos's survey on consent. *Did I . . . ?*

~

I accept work. Try to be grateful – for staffroom jokes, occasional teaching moments, an income – as I tight-rope walk up those stairs. *Is he watching me?* I navigate increasing food allergies and cold feet. Body is tetchy. Twitchy. An afternoon swim under smoky sky washes off the mild insanities. Dinner is toast.

I stupor-cope. Walk to work. Force-feed another hideous school day down my bilious throat. Now, I'm waiting for Vince to pick me up, across from the nearby greasy takeaway, desperate to see Vince's truck. A gang of Year 10 boys are watching.

'WhereYaGoinMiss?' one shouts and plays the phone siren, but I have my earplug in.

He can't hurt me.

Another yells: 'I know where you live, Miss.' Ugliness hisses into my skull. I squelch down, barnacle-hollow my once-confident self. By the time Vince pulls up, I'm inside-crying. But I won't drag him through my awfuls. *He'll think less of me.*

March forth

March 4th is my annual gratitude day. Sometimes I clean house. Often I've moved house; futile attempts to gut and leave the bits behind. This year is a countdown: 04/03/21. I resolve to skip alcohol for a month.

'You could give up pork,' I suggest to Vince, who's not a member of my cult.

'Don't start,' he growls.

I focus my energy on Coastcare's annual Clean Up Australia Day. We've recruited volunteers, posted notices, set up a Facebook page – something I swore I'd never do. 'Facebook is powerful and evil,' I tell Kaleido, 'but I need some tips.'

Kal laughs at my hypocrisy.

The positive vibe of 'making the world a better place' reels in another day's work and a rare free period. I read news about women organising a March4Justice. They want the government to respond: to the reported rape of a Ministerial staffer; to the accusations of rape by the Attorney-General; to online disclosures of schoolgirls' sexual assaults; to an Australian Human Rights Commission report. *Click.*

The report shows that sexual harassment in Australian workplaces is pervasive; that prevention relies on addressing unchallenged behaviours. There's a surge in the zeitgeist of the braves. 'Speak Up,' they say, 'Seek Justice and Truth!'

I wish for change to be possible. But a speck in the bog survives by staying quiet. What value lies in justice? Or truth? Slippery shimmers in a stormy sea.

Smoke chokes me through the day. I fulfil my hot-hazed canteen duty and rejoice in a Year 10 class of only five students. I scroll job ads I won't apply for because I can't face another knock-back. Each time I update my CV, I remove more qualifications and experience because 'they don't want a too-confident, too-clever smarty pants.' My mother's description of me watermarks my life. I'm not clever enough to see what traps me here. *It's what I deserve.*

At 4 pm, I run to the sea, dive deep into green and dissolve.

March 7

Clean Up Australia Day is sunny. Our Coastcare volunteers collect a tarp-full of turtle-killing detritus. The local paper re-posts my Facebook photos. Uplift restores my faith in this town; in the possibility of goodness; in my capacity to handle rubbish. I accept another day's work.

March 9

Too smoky to walk. I drive nausea and black coffee to school. On radio news, the Fire Rescue Service warns of 'extremely unpredictable winds and high temperatures'. I resolve to keep cool. 'I *will* make it through today *without raising my voice*,' I declare over radio babble. Then comes the talk show's focus question: 'What role should teachers play in educating young people about sex and consent?'

I park my oath and yell: '*Lock the pedos up!*'

~

Period 1: In a too-damn-hot-to-play ping pong lesson, a student twice my size shout-stalks his opponent to the gym and grabs a 10-kilo dumbbell. Insanely, I step between them.

'You *made* him win, Miss.' Jake turns on me.

I step backwards, ignore panic, ego-stroke the big-guy down. *I know how.*

~

Before break, I chat with senior girls about jobs, tell them they can do anything. Two of them 'want to work at a brothel, to get out of this town!' They're just trying to shock me.

'Don't *you* want to get out, Miss?'

'I did,' I say, 'and I came back to contribute to this community.'

They eye-roll me back into my overqualified, no-hoper corner.

I check the outside temperature: 35 degrees. The new air conditioner squeals as I drag failed job applications into laptop trash.

Stay in the classroom.

~

Period 3: I bin my half-eaten protein ball and walk past dehydrated gardens to the demountables. As I step out from the main building, a tennis ball slams down an inch ahead of me. I flinch, look up, but can't locate the laughter. *Keep going.*

Thirsty, ready to ignite; *I will not raise my voice.*

In class, neither fans nor air conditioner work. Open windows suck in the smoke-dust. Everyone sits on gritty edges as I play the video, dry-gulp a Panadol.

I send Harry outside to finish his lunch. As I check the roll, another boy upends Harry's bag and a large, black object rolls to my feet. Boys giggle and mutter. Girls go quiet. Eyes widen. *I will not raise my voice.*

The foot-long black object is penis-shaped. *A giant dildo?*

Harry re-enters, cheeks stuffed, to see his embarrassing trophy on the floor. He swallows, sits down, as if the thing is not there.

'Put it away, Harry,' I say, calmly. He slowly wipes grime from his mouth, dusts off his hands, crunches his pie bag into a ball.

'What, Miss?'

I point.

'Not mine, Miss,' he says, punching the boy's arm. The two erupt in a tussle.

I will not raise my voice.

Harry squirts hand sanitiser onto the giant penis. 'It's just a bottle opener, Miss,' he says, throwing it across the room. Another boy shakes the ugly prize near a squealing girl's face as a support teacher enters, appalled.

I will not raise my—

Then it's waved in my face. Heat prickles the base of my skull, setting ears ablaze. Enough. I muscle up my boss voice. 'Year Ten!' I roar. 'Sit down. Shut up. Do. Not. Move.'

Oath crushed.

I kick the thing into a rubbish bin and tell the support teacher I need to step out. She blanches.

'You'll be fine.'

As I exit, Devlin steps full-frontal into me, grinning over a tennis ball.

'You're late,' I hiss.

Then his throaty growl: 'No breakout room, cunt!'

Nausea explodes up my chest. I suppress the retch, step around him, rush to the main building and boil up the 'be the change' steps. Enough. *E-fekkin-nuff.*

I storm into the deputy principal's office. 'I'm sick to death of your boys!'

'My boys?' he objects.

'All the boys,' I shout. 'Entitled. Harassing. Sex-obsessed. Porn-fed. Menacing boys!' I yell. 'And men. Rape. Domestic Violence. Harassment, *didn't-mean-anything-by-it* bullshit blokes,' I shout. *Inside myself?*

'I'm sick of the power-gaming filth of it,' I rant … or think? *Sick that so few people understand the damage.* I slow down to speak up. *Sick that I've silenced myself for so long. Sick to my soul that I'm numb and dumb.*

'Finished?' he asks.

'No!' I take a long, shaky breath. 'Why doesn't anyone *do* anything?'

My throat spasms violently. *Why don't I do something?*

He stares as I protest my own clear judgement. *I'm the bottom rung,* I defend. *No excuse,* I counter. Hands shaking. Close to tears. *No more.*

The deputy goes to rescue the support teacher. It's not even 2 pm.

Out the window, my car tyres distort in the scorching street. I can't think of one reason to stay. I stuff my jokey-coper face into my bag, shove the laptop through the tech window and heart-thump nausea down the *Innovation* stairs.

Do not look back.

Those are *my* sensible sandals slapping the ground, running from the bronze monster, into searing light. I hear a sharp *tick-tick-tick* as my mouth fills with metallic slime, vomits into the gutter. I taste bubbling bitumen, smell flinty dynamite, the diesel of the detonator.

Inside my Corolla-chariot, the air crackles.

Then comes the *whoomph* of the bomb, the scalding white sky. I pick up my phone and dial the police.

Be brave now.

2 Little Brave, Asking

Say his name

March 9, 2 pm

'Thank you for calling the New South Wales Police, River Region. If this is an emergency, hang up and dial triple zero. To report a breach of Covid-19 restrictions, select one. For road closures, select two. For bushfire information, select …'

'FerrFekkSake!' I toss my phone and drive towards the sea. Choices singe me.

If not now … Never! *What's to lose?* Everything. *Why rock the boat?* He's still out there. *He should have the chance to atone.* Why? *Forgiveness is …* Bullshit! *But I'm afraid.* Of …? *Unravelling.* Of Him. The Teacher. Bastard. Ruiner. Rapist. *Pedophile.*

I stop at the lighthouse, sipping smoky air.

If I don't report my own childhood abuse, how can I expect more than moral blindness in this world? If *I* don't speak up, I'm no better than those who failed me.

I am the adult now. Justice matters.

I pick up my phone. 'Thank you for calling … Covid, road closures, bushfires … If you'd like to speak to an officer, select four.'

Oh. Press 4.

'Tacking Point Police Station. Officer Michael Kay here.'

'Um … hello. Do you have any female officers on duty?'

'What is it regarding?'

Pause. 'I'd like to report an historic sexual assault.'

'Just a moment …' Officer Kay is cordial. 'Yes, there's a female detective on duty.'

'I'll be there in ten minutes.'

Driving back towards town, tension plumes in a prickle-rash across my scalp. Somehow, in slow motion, I ascend the station ramp. *Why are my feet here?* Brain, not involved in this decision, stalls at the door, wants to run. Body breathes heat. Slow drag in. Long out.

Just go home. *No!* Push the door.

Inside on the walls, Missing Persons posters. *Where am I?*

'Can I help you?' asks a smiling uniform. *Oh, I'm not invisible.*

He's barely 30. Moon-faced. Clean-shaven.

'I rang earlier, requesting a female officer,' a little voice manages.

He squints at his computer. 'What's it in relation to?'

Could I dive under this blue carpet?

'Um …' Mouth opens. 'It's about … child sexual abuse …' Throat spasms. 'I was told a female … detective was on duty.'

'I'm sorry, she's not available.'

Gut roils. *Don't do this. Run now, back to irrelevance.*

'We take these matters seriously,' he adds. 'You could talk to me. Without the details. Just get something on file. It won't take long.'

I try to turn, but I'm anchored. Chest implodes into a black hole of shame, swallowing children from every culture, time and place.

I must do my bit.

'Um … OK.' Body steps into a grey interview room, to officially become the victim of a forty-year-old crime. The aircon is blasting.

Two bodies in a freezer. I'm shaking and holding myself tight, fighting the urge to run.

'I know you're busy … This was a very long time ago …' I try to not-begin.

'We take these matters seriously,' he repeats the training script, eyes sincere.

We wait for the old computer. I fold my arms, squeeze-shut my eyes, mouth, thighs.

'Do you know the name of the perpetrator?' he asks. *Blech.* I nod.

'Can you tell me?'

Tongue runs along slime-coated teeth. I've not spoken that poison in forty years.

Head moves side-to-side. *No.*

'You'll have to name the perpetrator,' he says firmly.

Head moves slowly, up-down. Yes. But a frozen thing shakes inside. Perp expects silence. *He'll come for me.*

I try to clear my throat. 'His name …' *Can a headless body report a crime?* I ask for pen and paper, write it down.

An initial report is lodged. Good. *Difficult.*

Smiley cop says a detective will be in touch. *I can still back out.*

Leaving the station, BodyBrain surges with energy; wants to track down Perp's address, graffiti his driveway: P-E-D-O; hire a skywriter; print a T-shirt: 'I survived Mr X.' *Vengeful?* No, I don't want to hurt anyone, not even him. I just want people to know. Maybe we could perform an 'It's not OK!' cabaret on that RSL Club stage. This time *he'd* be the naughty one, tut-tutted by the audience. *Ridiculous.* I should just send him a letter; reveal the anguish he's inflicted. On all of us. Gut clenches.

No. He's had forty years to say sorry. Let's list him on Pedos-Insta! Let's tell this whole bloody town what he did.

At home, I google 'delayed reporting for child sexual abuse' and read about the legal complexities of my forty-year time lag. Key witnesses might have died; the word 'witness' frightens potential supporters, implying they 'saw something'. Older communities don't understand that 'evidence' can be a cumulative story, not just fingerprints and hard facts. Floating apart from myself, I read that delayed reporting is common when the perpetrator was a trusted authority. I read about how abused children fear consequences for their families; how they often protect their abuser; how perps take advantage of fear, maintaining compliance through secrecy and loyalty, making the child feel … Responsible. Me.

Brain rejoins Body. *Oh.* I notice the familiar pouring back into myself, without knowing I've been gone.

~

Detective Serena Herd phones the following afternoon, suggests I seek counselling before giving the statement, rattles off a phone number that Brain manages to write down. She reminds me I'll have to 'say his name'.

Brain wants to remove larynx.

'Will your family support you through this?' Herd asks.

'Of course,' I assume. 'Should I bring someone?'

'Well … they can't be in the interview room,' says the detective, 'and you can't speak about the details with your family.'

Wait … *What!? Because we might collude?*

For decades I've glossed over, medicated, buried 'the details'. Now, finally braved up, I might need help dredging them from the deep. But I cannot speak to the only people who might remember? I cannot help them to recall? My impossible choice plummets into gut. The splash tastes of bile. Head pounds against the brick-walled system. I dizzy-crouch onto the guest room futon, dial the number Herd gave – a rape crisis service – am surprised to hear a human.

'Um, I've just made an initial report about … historic sex abuse, and …' A torrent of uncertainty snakes up my gullet. 'What happens now?'

'Jewel can help you with that,' says an encouraging voice.

Jewel speaks friendly words, but ants bury information under my skin. She says I can get a payment. Sounds like hush money. My head is a hot worry.

Did she say I'm supposed to do something? Go somewhere? Fill in a form?

Brain is unplugged. Body feverish.

Jewel's voice is serene; seems to think I can do this.

'Do historic cases get justice?' I blurt-ask.

'It's highly *unlikely* you'll get the justice you're after.' Jewel demolishes my expectations. 'The stats aren't good.'

Scratching at ants, I realise I've not eaten today.

Jewel asks me to take slow, deep breaths. 'It's important that you speak your truth. Try not to think about the outcome. Take it one step at a time,' she reassures Brain and Body, and some other watchful presence. Then Jewel asks what 'justice' might mean for me.

I've never thought that far forward.

Jewel encourages patience. 'Criminal justice takes a long time.'

Through my half-drawn curtain, I see a baby magpie, hanging upside down in a tree, swinging awkwardly by one claw, squawking. Mother bird feeds it.

I'm still hanging upside down, when Jewel says: 'You can't know how things will pan out or what evidence will be uncovered …'

My chest flutters.

'Will your family support you?'

'Y-yes.' I swallow, holding a hand over fibrillation, believing in Mum and Lianne and Maggie and Rocky. Vince too, but we met long after this was buried. *Can a man respect an awful-ised woman?* I can't tell him 'the details'. Not yet.

Even the feminist hides behind the skirts of a damaged girl-child. Shame is sticky.

Jewel suggests I write a timeline of the first, worst, and last interactions with the perpetrator. I try to take notes, but frosty hands tremor. 'Get some photos. Try to eat and sleep.'

Her words fall to the floor, with my snotty tissues and the snakeskin of fear curling around my ankles. *How long before Perp finds out?*

~

Vince's plane is delayed. Heating soup, listening to Nina Simone's 'Sinnerman', I ask myself too, *Where can I run to*? Her 'Power' chorus dances me, until determination blooms in my chest. Until I scroll-read that the 'epidemic' of child sexual abuse is an 'under-reported crime … difficult to prosecute', historic offences 'a poor fit for adversarial criminal justice'.

What was I thinking?

I read how judges and jurors lack the knowledge to evaluate evidence; how guilty pleas are less common than for any other offence. I stir soup and open a bottle of soda fizz to settle my nausea. It sprays across the floor.

Reporting won't change anything.

I find the stats for my state. Each year, thousands report sexual assault, though less than a third of victims go to the police. Of incidents reported, only 3 per cent result in conviction. Even my leaky maths-brain understands those numbers: most perps walk free. Then this line from a New South Wales parliamentary standing committee: 'Children are to be protected from all sexual conduct, even if they are willing participants.' I was not willing. *I got on his motorbike.* I did not scream or run. *He locked the doors.* I was not frightened – why would I be? I had no idea what was about to happen. What *did* happen? Pieces missing. At 53, I realise I do not understand consent.

Why didn't I tell someone? The question sickens me. I'm afraid of what the answer might unleash. Disbelief carves my guts. *Perp was never held to account.*

Shit. The soup is everywhere. I rescue what I can, put some aside for Mum. Vince will be home soon. He's under pressure. I can't fall apart on him. Delirious from tiny turtle-sleeps, I leave my mess and walk to the sea.

Gentle jade swells massage my spine. Bubbles percolate through shell grit and I breathe in the purpling sky.

Walking home in glorious stillness, I'm finally calm enough to acknowledge: *I'm a mess.*

From the outdoor shower, I see Vince pull into the driveway. He drags exhaustion from his truck, wipes red dust off his face and slumps into a deckchair.

'We just won a multi-million-dollar contract, and the boss bought me a thirty-five-dollar shirt!' he declares, faking celebratory finger-spins.

'I made soup.' I offer what's left, eat toast, afraid to add to his stress, afraid that Vince, my safe, broad shoulders, will see me differently if he learns 'the details'.

You are afraid that your scent, of submission, will embolden him. That he'll want what others got: free rein. But Vince never hurts me. Not all men ... *How would you know? Your love-abuse gauge is broken.* It's not Vince I don't trust. It's *me.*

I hate secrecy, but this old family shame must be addressed with old family.

Asking Maggie

I visit my closest sister. Two years older, Maggie is the family style-and-social queen; the only sibling to inherit Dad's skinny legs and community service commitment. She's a generous, caring nurse – a profession Mum is proud of. A fiercely loving mother to her own children, Maggie is the 'fun, naughty auntie' who treated Kal to their first burger and fries.

When I was 6 and hungry for attention, I ran away from home with a plastic bag full of green beans and hid in a gully on Pebbly Beach, ready to tough out the world. Maggie found me, took me home. Later, travelling to college, I'd arrive at Maggie's Sydney apartment as she slept off night duty. She always let me stay, drove us to the beach, fed me chicken pies.

Maggie has a nostalgic, Disney-esque view of the world; she doesn't understand why everybody can't *just get along*. Her wishful thinking *does* conjure real magic, but as a dream-scaper, she had trouble coping when our coming-of-age 'coming out' realities weren't fairytales. To me, she's a lighthouse in rough seas.

Maggie makes tea and we sit in her re-styled loungeroom with 'oyster grey' cushions and 'carnival orange' proteas.

I sip and stall, remembering Maggie's school friend, Lucy, Perp's target before me. I don't know what (if anything) happened to Lucy and can't remember who else knew. I guess no complaint was ever made. 'There's a thing,' I say. 'A big thing.'

'OK …?' Maggie sips.

I breathe in slow, out long.

'Just say it,' she says, a touch impatient.

'I went to the police … about what happened in high school.'

'The teacher?'

I nod.

'About bloody time!' She places her hand on mine. 'I'm proud of you.'

Her support opens a bubbler. 'I just … didn't deal for so long. I thought I forgave him years ago … but he's never taken responsibility.'

'No,' she says, putting her cup down.

'He hurt all of us.'

'Yes,' she admits. 'He *stole* your childhood.'

'Oh, he took more than that.' I tremble teacup to table.

We sit and sip the darkening. *Breathe.* Ask: 'Do you think you could write down what you remember? For the police?'

'I won't lie for you,' she says, too quickly.

Chin dives for neck as Body shrinks into gut.

I don't want her to lie! I want her to remember. Should I mention he's back in town?

Something slides across Maggie's face. My erroneous history?

Fear. Blame.

'Cathy … I didn't *see* anything. Did he threaten you?' She exits to the kitchen.

'It wasn't like that,' I reply, feeling cold-numb on this warm afternoon.

His manipulations were hidden.

She sees I'm crying, comes to hug me. Cries too.

'I will try …,' Maggie says, 'to get the balance right.'

Nausea swirls into confusion. *What needs balancing? Is she divvying up blame?* I want to be angry, but I'm sick-dizzy with disappointment. I'd hoped Maggie would shine.

Then, in dwindling light, I recall a moment, just months ago, when Maggie disapproved of my old, stretched swimming bra; told me I needed a new one. I'd smiled in admission; the elastic was fully gone. I hate shopping. I'd told her about paddling out another day, holding my board through the waves, when one boob escaped. 'I had to shove it back in!' I'd laughed. 'So yes, these boobs need a new top.'

Big sister had bossed me: 'You don't want some guy seeing your tits and going home to rape his wife.'

Wait … *What!?* Surely I'd misheard? But child-self had learned to stitch lips tight. My sister's reprimand had stunned me into silence. I'd walked home, replaying her judgement: *Cathy, the risk-taker, the female at fault.*

Maggie sits away from me now, silhouetted. My throat constricts.

'Maggie … before he came after me, the pedo targeted one of your friends …'

'Lucy. Yes. She was worried about you, always on his motorbike.'

'Can you ask Lucy if she'd make a statement?'

Maggie looks into her empty teacup. *For guidance?* The pause stretches, and my pseudo-feminist rubs humble pie all over my pathetic face.

'I can ask,' Maggie says. Heavy air hangs above cold teacups and stiff, oyster-tinged cushions.

She hugs me out the door. My legs, semi-attached, wobble me up her driveway, scuffing my shoes on ideas of 'sisterhood'. Body drives into town for groceries, but I sit in my car staring at nothing for … *how long?* I forget three things on my five-item list.

Back home, Vince and I binge-watch children's TV. I can't watch anything violent.

I'll have to tell him soon.

Asking Lianne and Mum

'I totally get it,' says Lianne – my three-years-older sister – on the phone. 'I want to be there when you tell Mum.' We agree on Saturday. Her support relaxes me enough to step outside and do some weeding, but I keep alert, checking for cars.

Perp knows this street.

Lianne has strong bike-rider legs and freckled Irish skin. She's tougher on the outside than the rest of us, like Mum, and can militantly pack a tarp and tent, like Dad. When we were younger, Lianne thought I got more than my share. She had to watch over me. I've felt her resentment sometimes.

When I was 5, she twisted my missing-a-bone wrist in a shocking arm burn so I wouldn't dob on her for nicking Minties. I got blamed.

In our twenties, when Mum implied I'd 'forced Lianne out of the closet', we helped each other through Mum's Catholic-Wrath-cum-Darwinian 'it's not natural' monologues and Maggie's naively hetero judgements. Lianne stored my stuff so I could keep travelling, keep not coming home. She didn't, but sort-of did, begrudge me. Her mixed signals make her difficult to know, but we get along as opposites: she's anti-social, sun-shy, fears boat-rocking.

A germophobe and scientist, Lianne keeps her distance from the mess of children. When I announced my pregnancy, she was 'so sorry'. Some people struggle to celebrate another's joy if they can't picture themselves happy in it. I admire her clarity for what she doesn't want.

It's a Mum trait. Efficient, but lacking imaginative empathy. 'Why would anyone want that …?' their shared refrain. Despite it, Lianne literally had my back at Kaleido's birth. She loves Kal, is fiercely loyal to Mum, and to the memory of Dad.

Saturday, March 13

It's sweltering, but meteorologists and cicadas disagree on whether the next catastrophe will be flood or fire. I appreciate Lianne's long drive to get here, to the big old house Dad helped build. Blocked from sea breeze, in the scrubby dunes, it sinks deeper each year in fine grey ant-sand.

A migraine shovels insomnic exhaustion behind my eyes. Lianne makes tea, talks about her work. Mum, proud of Lianne's stable, single-employer career, tries to listen but dithers from pantry, to fridge, to the window.

'Think you own the place, do you?' Mum suddenly hollers.

Bewildered, we watch Mum dash out and hose a slither of tail near the compost.

'Careful!' yells Lianne.

'It's just a python,' Mum retorts, returning inside. 'I think.'

~

For my police statement, I need to look through the family photos; to plot a timeline. My notes are a single sheet of place names and question marks. I need help but can't mention 'details'. *Impossible.* Justice cuts me off already. I'm afraid to hurt them, again. The last time we aired my awfuls, I was 22. Dad was here. Mum yelled blame at me, and I destroyed all photos of the 'family friend'. I hacked him up with Mum's sewing scissors.

I sip soda to dampen nausea. Body swings between crazy-hot in the head and too cold in my toes. Anxiety ants crawl under prickling skin.

Oblivious, Mum offers, 'Spinach roll? Malt biscuit? Hummus?'

My dry eyes plead with Lianne, who says, 'Mum, just sit down.'

The fuss-bothering continues until Mum finally sits. A sip. A bite of biscuit.

Speak now.

'Mum, I went to the police.' I don't look up as guts wrench. 'I'm reporting what happened in high school.'

Mum pales. Her mouth stops chewing, opens. Closes. Her cup clatters, tea on fresh tablecloth. She fusses. Lianne gets a towel.

'Mum, it's not your fault.' I rest my hand on hers. 'I don't blame you.'

Voice is timid as I change shape, shrink. The electrified outline of a headless child, sitting in my chair, drips in fear-blame. Cannot move. Eyes will not lift. Ears flame.

'I know I lied.' The forgotten voice feels guilty in my mouth. Part of me detests being this pathetic. *Disgusting.* 'I covered up for him.'

I am no longer 53 but this is not the 'Rebellious Thirteen' I'm told I was. *Naughty.*

Mother stands now, partly horrified, partly … *what else?*

'I'm sorry for dragging you back here,' I plead. Words slough hurt from our edges, old fuel ready to ignite. Body flakes in smoky cinders. All the shame I've caused and carry.

Mum pats my outstretched hand, a kind-of hug. 'It's about time,' she says.

I let out a stale puff, hand over mouth, realising I've forgotten to breathe. 'I need to look at photos,' I manage, '… to get dates.'

Unfolding notes from my pocket, afraid to look Mum in the eye.

'You destroyed our photos,' Mum jabs, as Lianne grabs my notes, breaking the rules of justice. *I need help.*

Mum leaves the mess at the table, pulls out several albums from the cupboard, plonks two in front of me. 'These are from the nineties,' she says, 'and I have a timeline of family milestones on the computer. I've recorded those since …'

She leaves the room to navigate her own discomfort.

'Since 2014,' I finish her thought. *Dad's crash.*

I go to the cupboard, select albums from the eighties.

Mum yells out confused questions from her computer. 'That's not right.' *It is.* 'You were older.' I wasn't. 'I'm sure he went on the swimming club trip.' *He didn't.* Her panicked avoidance of unwanted memory swirls into maelstrom. She re-appears, her face a mask of disbelief: 'How did you do so well at school?'

Ignoring her question, I stumble on the only remaining photograph, flinch from the shock. Him, still menacing, here in Mum's living room. It's a picture from the camping trip. Not wanting to be Fifteen again, I jump up from the table, fingers covering mouth. I'm standing near the TV. *Breathe.*

'Who invited him?' Lianne asks.

'Cathy would have,' Mum accuses.

Stop, I try to say, but swallow myself quiet. Neck spasms. Dentist drill screeches under my skull. 'Stop,' I beg. 'Please listen.' Mum dashes back to her computer. 'I did *not* invite him,' I insist, but they're not listening.

I taste the bile of unforgetting: I quashed vomit back then too, in this same spot, where I pretended I wasn't horrified. *Why didn't I object to that invitation?*

Body is a heatmap of guilt-memory. Ants dot the grey sand, burrowing.

Mum is a silhouette against the kitchen window, a dark gathering of forces.

'How did you do so well?' she repeats, as if rape rules out academic talent. Then her voice is a turgid whisper: 'You were *too* confident, *too* clever.'

Little Brave is choking.

'I'm glad your father isn't here,' Mum spits, in a bizarre reversal of seven years' grieving. 'He'd be *mortified*.'

'I wish he *was* here,' I defend. 'He might've helped me.'

Focus. Keep going.

I flick through fading pictures, half-listening to Mum's fable of 'Cathy the Capable.' An abuse victim does not fit inside her idea of clever. She's frightened. Bitter.

'This isn't new, Mum,' I say, tired and struggling with her panic.

'How did you get to his house?' Her voice is loaded.

'I can't talk about "details",' I hiss, hating the rules of justice. 'I've told you before about his motorbike.'

'I never saw you on his bike,' she declares, punching air from my truth.

Lianne, at the table, conflicted in red-faced silence, remembers the ugly telling of the Ruin, years ago, and the family folklore of 'Cathy the Black Sheep'. I seek refuge in her eyes. But she's snagged on an old version of me that she doesn't like.

Something flaps in my chest. Hand flies to mouth. What if they *all* still see me as a willing participant?

'How did you get to his house?' Mum demands.

'I can't discuss details!' but I offer my notes.

'I don't want to see that,' she shouts, recoiling.

Someone's head pounds, enroute to the bathroom, searches the mirror's face. *Who was that terrified child?* I press a wet washer to my neck. Rinse. Repeat.

Back at the table, Lianne tries to remedy. 'I don't remember much,' she admits, 'but I do remember walking to his skanky apartment and chucking his keys through the door. I didn't want you going there.' *She remembers!* 'Do you need someone at the station?'

Grateful for the offer, I know Lianne has to get back to Brisbane.

Mum pipes up. 'No. This is Cathy's thing; she must do it by herself.'

She still sees my false projection; my inexhaustible adventurer.

No Mother, child abuse is not my thing. I close my eyes and picture the sea. My thing.

When I was 3, I insisted on joining Dad's swimming lessons for older kids. I spent more time under the water than above it, which freaked Mum out when we swam at Black Lake. Eventually she stopped worrying; I could hold my breath for fifty metres before I turned 10. Dad taught me to love waves. He was one of the first to argue against misogyny in surf lifesaving and trained women for the bronze medallion. When Lianne and Maggie got boogie boards, I got a surfboard.

I rode my first tube at Pebbly Beach when I was 12. Salty marmalade ribbons reflected overhead, sparkle-wrapping me, zooming the nose of my six-foot-seven orange and yellow pintail. So much light and colour; the joyful stuff of then-me.

Surfing is still *my thing.* Waves infuse my being with a smiling glow that lasts for days. No matter time or place, I can transport myself back to myriad breaks. As a kid, I'd imagine surfing alongside the car; 'cut-backs' through forest shadows, 'reo's' off clouds. Once, on a real wave at Rainbow Bay, Dad on his surf ski, a dolphin leapt between us. I re-live that memory whenever I need to. Like at Dad's huge community funeral, when I eulogised how he was 'a good man', who 'always did the right thing'.

'Cathy?' Mum wrenches me from reverie.

I lift my head off the table, unsure where I've been.

'Well, this explains your controlling behaviours.'

She chooses *this* moment to critique my over-protective parenting style! I glare.

She shrugs. 'It's where my head went.' Her usual defence.

Breathe. Don't get derailed. *Look at them.*

Little Brave asks: 'Will you make a statement?'

Support evaporates as two pale faces register what police reporting means. 'I didn't see anything,' says Lianne. 'He was a dickhead, but …'

Mum pushes her chair back, her face a sheen of steel. 'I don't have any *evidence*. I don't need to go there,' she says, lips thinning. 'Your father's crushed plane sat for weeks at the back of that police station.'

Compassion squeezes out of me for Mum's trauma after Dad's death, and its association with Tacky Point police station. But I'm confused by their complete withdrawal.

'I'm old,' she sighs. 'I don't need to go back over all that.'

'I'll be getting counselling, Mum, you could access help.' I reach for her but she pulls away, snorts disgust.

I must not hurt my mother.

Desperate now, one hand supporting my feverish head, I try to coax.

'It's just telling the police what you remember, Mum,' I say gently, 'about how Perp was always around, for *years*. You must remember that?'

'I don't remember anything,' comes her armoured reply. 'That's my statement!'

The shrill *pee-wit* of a mudlark pierces the air as I step off Mum's patio, shoulders hunched, neck cricked. Those are *my* legs, heavy with old sand, dragging the heat home.

Big little brother

Sunday, March 14

The surf is blown out, so I walk the cliffs. The southerly forces oxygen into my lungs as I stand too close to the edge, arms out, leaning.

Rocky phones. 'Hey Cath, I hear you reported that prick. He groomed you and our whole family,' he says. 'It's disgusting what he got away with. You should've been protected. I totally support what you're doing and will help if I can.'

Crystal clear. Relief pours into me, drips down my face.

Five years younger, Rocky still remembers the camping trip; me and the man-boy in the waterhole. Ten-year-old Rocky felt something was wrong, was uncomfortable sharing the men's tent with the 'bossy boofhead'.

Rocky tells me that, some years ago, a podcast stirred difficult memories about my abuse, so he called a New South Wales Police taskforce. 'I wanted to make sure he wasn't still teaching,' he explains. 'They'll have my report on file.'

~

One of the family folk stories is that, as a child, I was jealous of Rocky's attention; that I trod on him as a baby. I don't remember that, but I do recall once wanting to smash his spoiled-Mama's-boy skull, for some forgotten reason. Luckily, I put that brick down, back when I could still hear my inner voice. I was mean and cruel, as siblings can be, but I watched out for him in the surf, made sure he came up through big waves.

Mum revelled in the glory of Rocky's dark curls and the fact he was a boy. But Rocky wasn't fooled; his mild paranoia often claimed that if a pumpkin fell from the sky, he'd be the one knocked down.

As teens, Rocky and I shared a rebellious spirit. We saw Midnight Oil and The Pogues and paddled through sharky waters. Later, we both bore the brunt of Mum's disapproval of our media professions and relationship choices. We broke the box of what she meant us to become.

Grown-up Rocky is a warrior father to his three children – a gentle homebody who's worked hard to master the dad skills. But little brother hasn't been close to any of us for a while. Maybe since Dad died. Maybe before. We grew up, then apart.

Our unpatched issues seem to get the scabs knocked off at family gatherings. At first, Rocky 'could only stay a while'. Eventually he stopped coming. I thought he was avoiding us. More likely he was protecting what little of himself had escaped this careless town. Rocky got out, but not without scars. Like all of us, he'd sometimes fallen out with Mum's famous insistence on having the last word. Only now do I recognise his self-erasure.

'Mum has a duty to speak,' Rocky says, without condemnation.

'I don't have the energy to convince her,' I say.

'You shouldn't have to.'

~

Back at Pebbly Beach, grey clouds stab lightning into the horizon. A sky-flash alerts my arm hair. Gut twinges. Thunder booms. I taste ozone.

How many children drown under the weight of silence?

I feel the first fat raindrops and phone-check the forecast: storms. Tomorrow requires truth-telling. I'm not ready.

I argue with myself: *Why plant trees for the future if the child of your past cannot breathe?* Society is sick. *One in four girls and one in six boys are sexually abused before they turn 16: more than half of those before age 10.* The pedo-teacher saga is not my whole story. *Rescuing others can drown yourself.*

I carry deluge home on my distraught face.

'What's happened?' Vince asks as I howl-collapse into him.

'I'm going to the police tomorrow,' I splutter, 'about something awful from high school.' I don't say more. Afraid of losing the one strong hand I can reach.

'I'm here for you,' he says gently, 'whenever you're ready.'

Supremely patient, supportive without needing details, Mr Lovely runs me a bath.

Big Brave, Telling 3

The details

March 15, Day One, a.m.

Vince kisses me into the downpour as Maggie pulls into our driveway. Trying to be helpful, she passes me a photo from her 21st birthday: the pedo at our childhood house.

'Who invited him?' Her question burns through my numb.

It wasn't my birthday! I climb into my car.

My driving-mind drifts seawards, over bruise-grey swells. What *did* happen at her 21st?

I was 19 by then, had escaped. I'd left Maggie's party to avoid him; went to the beach with her Sydney nurse-friends, poured whiskey into throat and dived into darkness.

Radio news tugs me back: 'Thousands have joined the March4Justice, calling for action on sexual violence.' The Prime Minister boasts that in other countries, such marches are met with bullets.

Men sometimes misinterpret women's voices.

La Niña smears my scrawled notes as tingly feet trudge up the police station ramp. I'm armed with a few photos, my emerald water bottle, and no idea what justice might mean.

Stay brave.

I remember Detective Serena Herd from Dad's plane crash investigation. Greying hair in a sensible bun. Dark silk shirt, practical shoes and holstered gun. We walk into the same interview room. Grey desk. Old computer. Cheap tissue box. A used teabag clings to the rim of a small bin and cold air tightens me into shivers.

Through the blinds, the glass wall amplifies gloom. Rain smashes a cement path, a high grey fence. No view to the river. No garden.

Detective Herd remembers me, too. Not just because Dad died horribly, taking property photos for a friend, while flying an ultralight, near trees, on a windy day – *risk-taking* – but because of secrets I was supposed to keep. Feeling guilty, the 'friend' bullied me into hiding Dad's camera, lying to the police. Mum also wanted to protect Dad's reputation.

'Strong Cathy' can cope.

'They should know!' I'd yelled at Mum in the hospital, in front of my siblings, over Dad's tubed-up body.

'Know what?' Rocky asked as Lianne reddened in alarm.

'*You …!*' Mum lasered her strong one into silence.

I'm finished with secrets.

'Cathy?' prompts Detective Herd, hooking me back. 'The more detail, the better.'

I cramp in the sub-zero as ants swarm under my collar.

'It's strange being here today.' I stall, scratch my neck.

'Why?' asks Herd, intrigued.

'The March4Justice,' I say. 'Calling on people to report sexual abuse.'

'I don't know about that.' Her comment shreds my enthusiasm. Suddenly I'm not part of something bigger; not ridding the world of depravity. Just alone in my awfuls.

'I don't know if justice works for women,' I think aloud, think of leaving.

'We'll do our best,' says Herd.

Already muscles are seizing. Scalp tingles as Herd opens a document, types: STATEMENT OF A WITNESS.

Witness? I didn't see what happened. I live it.

Herd waits, fingers poised over the keys.

Unfolding my notes, I deep-exhale, then words rush out:

'I startedAtTackingHigh in1980soo ... IwasThirteen-WhenImet ...' *Swallow.*

'... him.'

'His name?' Detective Herd peers over her glasses, into me.

Can't I just point to a photo? Breathe.

'Rob...ert John Cunning.' *Cough.* I tongue-scrape a foul taste. 'He was ... TwelveYearsolderNearlyTwicemyage', I rush-gulp my notes.

'HeGroomedRapedAbusedmefromAgeThirteen ...', speed-garbling. 'InMyuniform.BeforeandAfterSchool, Rehearsals, Soccer. OnbeachesAt hisParents', InApartmentsIn our garageOn afamilyholiday ...'

Potholes of blame clench my knuckles. *I want this to be over.*

'Let's go slowly,' suggests Herd. There's warmth in her brown eyes. Body is freeze-boiling as I float behind a hot head.

She asks if I remember his birthdate. Weirdly, I do.

'Can I just call him "Perp"?' I ask, bouncing cramp-cold feet, tightly crossed legs.

Detective Herd nods, keeps typing. 'You met him ...?'

'I was checking the surf at Pebbly Beach, wearing new summer white shorts and a baby pink boat-neck top.' *I see the details.* Those shorts had shiny white embroidery that made my legs look extra tanned. The open-weave top only partly covered my teen bra.

I would have looked so strawberry ice-cream fresh.

'I said hello to a man with a moustache, sitting on a dark Honda motorbike. He was wearing very tight, very short shorts.'

'Eww,' says Herd. We both grimace.

'He introduced himself as "Rob". Dad had a Honda too, so we probably talked about motorbikes.' *He was handsome.* Ugly! 'He was like an overweight Tom Selleck from *Magnum, P.I.* He told me he lived in Loggerville, with his parents, that he was a music teacher at Tacking Point High. I said my parents taught there too. He wanted to meet them, asked where I lived.' I realise, only now, he already knew my parents; would've been in staff meetings with them. 'Innocently, I invited him up the road. Mum and Dad offered him tea, a biscuit, a chat.'

I invited a stranger home. But my parents trusted him, a teacher.

'Sometime soon after – *or was it before?* – at the school swimming carnival.' I slow down, remembering: 'Perp, a big guy, wearing only Speedos and T-shirt, leaned over me and … He let spit droop from his mouth, then sucked it back. It made my skin prickle.' *Still does.*

Detective Herd shakes her head, keeps typing.

I describe how Perp grabbed opportunities to build trust. 'He played babysitter, transport-helper for Mum, while Dad was …' *Where? Surf lifesaving? Training basketball? Army camp?*

Herd watches me wade through a fog of questions.

'Pretty soon, the "family friend" would visit with his guitar. Maggie and I both played. We'd sit around singing.' I ramble on, keeping gut from launching. 'Perp and Maggie had beautiful voices …'

I check my notes.

'On a Saturday in May 1981, Perp drove me, just me, to Loggerville to watch him play soccer.' *He was slow, played the back line.* 'After the game, we drove back to Tacky in his green Ford Falcon with a front bench seat. He pulled into Byrne's Lane, about halfway home. It was a cold evening, the windows fogged up. He leaned over and kissed me on the lips.'

First kiss. A man kiss. Surprising. *Exciting?*

'He held my hand, told me: "No-one else will understand our love. Let's not spoil it by letting anyone else know. This is our special secret."'

'At home, I marked an "X" on my wall calendar, wrote "Byrne's Lane". When Mum asked, I said it was the first time I'd seen our name on a road sign.' *First lie.* 'Perp rewarded my secrecy with fancy chocolates he kept in his car. He told me I was a "good kisser", that I "must've been practising".'

He decorated his abuse with my child's idea of romance.

'What were you like before you met him?' Detective Herd looks over her glasses.

I sense something under the desk.

'I was the only girl in the surf-rider's club,' I detour. 'I won trophies, against boys.' Herd doesn't see the blame bucket. She peers into me.

'I'd kissed a few boys.' Guilt squirms.

'In primary school, girls weren't allowed to play soccer, but high school got me kicking balls! I was a fast mid-fielder for Tacky Point Women's. We won the grand-final and ...'

'So, you were a virgin?' Herd asks directly. I sit back.

I *had* kissed boys. *Only* kissed. Only *boys*. 'Yes.'

'Sport was "my thing",' I insist. *That was before.*

Herd types as I rub frosty, fist-balled fingers, to stop them pointing at myself. 'After his kiss, the "thing" was letting him touch me, on the arm or leg; backstage at rehearsals, in classrooms, under the desk.'

Under the radar.

Grooming is an insidious takeover, an intangible crawl of oversight, from carer to predator. It smears guilt over innocence. My parents must've felt twinges of nothing-to-worry-about. Mum would ask where I'd been, in her accusatory tone. Maggie's friends wondered what was going on. 'Just mates', I'd say, trying to be mature, while the hunter crept towards possession. Always touching.

'Gifts and favours were carefully spaced. A child pick-up for Mum. A beer with Dad. Chocolates for me.' One-on-one time became unfettered access. Thirteen and worldly-wise, I thought it was love. 'He gave me a gold Libra necklace to match his Scorpion.'

He whittled my boundaries, not yet built.

Detective Herd types, brow furrowed.

'He took up *trying*-to-surf, to keep other guys away. He got me into the school band, though I couldn't read music. He became my soccer coach, though he wasn't a good player.' *He inserted himself into every aspect of my life.*

'We'd make plans outside the music staffroom. I'd call him from the

Pebbly Beach shop phone. We held hands and kissed in his car. He'd drive me halfway up our street, getting my story straight. Neighbours and surf buddies saw us together every day.'

Herd nods, types.

'Sometimes, Dad or my sisters would come to the beach with us. Perp always swam too close to me. Every time I got out of the water, he'd look at my nipples and whisper "Are you cold or pleased to see me?"' *Didn't they see how much I hated that?*

'Perp, in his mid-twenties, hung with the kids. At school, he was the fun guy.' The man-boy splash in a small-town puddle.

He hid among the privileges of adolescence.

'When I was still thirteen, Perp moved just over the hill from my parents' house. Already divorced at twenty-five, he lived alone in a dark, one-bedroom apartment. Looking back, it reeks of creep.' The detective eye-rolls agreement.

'I rode there on my bicycle. He'd give me five bucks to do his ironing, or clean his motocross leathers, or vacuum. I was saving for a new surfboard. He always had lollies.'

I'm freezing in this little interview room, watching the battering rain, clutching my smudged notes.

'In June 1981, my parents let me travel six hours north with him to Kingaroy, to watch motocross. Lianne came as chaperone. We left before dawn and returned after midnight. We kissed under the grandstand. I watched him race and saw that he was hopeless. His grooming overrode my gut instinct; I never liked the guy. Lianne fumed that I'd left her alone all day.' *Will Lianne give a statement?*

'That year, Maggie and I were in the school musical. Perp was the director. Dad built the sets. Mum made costumes. I was in the chorus. Maggie was a dancer. So was her friend, Lucy.'

Will they give statements?

'Perp would brush by me backstage. Dangerous kisses behind curtains.' *Exciting.* 'Maggie and I had different rehearsals, so Perp would drive me home. A smoochy touch, a chocolate. "This is our secret," he kept saying.'

On closing night, under spotlights and camera flashes, the principal declared the show an 'overwhelming success'. *Everyone applauded the Hero-Perp.*

I'm shaking, trying to hold myself together. 'It's freezing,' I tell Herd, zipping up my vest. She brings me tea in a Styrofoam cup.

'Shall we keep going?'

'Momentum is everything,' says Big Brave.

The Ruin

'On a weekend in August 1981, Mum, Dad and Rocky went to visit Nan on the Gold Coast. I stayed home with Lianne and Maggie, who had weekend jobs. Perp took me for a motorbike ride. I wore yellow summer jeans over my crimson bikini.'

I show Detective Herd photos of me in these clothes, the only Byrne girl with teen boobs.

Is that why it happened to me?

I dry-retch, sensing the blame bucket. *I didn't tell anyone where I was going.* My gut contorts and I become small. My throat constricts and something slides up into my chest cavity. Truth wants to choke me. *Or fear?*

'OK, Cathy?' asks Detective Herd.

'He led me into the dunes on a remote beach. He wanted to sunbake!' *I'm a surfer.*

'I probably said "Sunbaking is stupid."'

Detective Herd looks at me strangely, listening to this child-voice.

'He stripped to his Speedos, told me to take my jeans off. I didn't want to. His voicegotGrowly.I keptmyjeanson.He stormedbacktothe-bike.I hadtofollow. IwasA longwayfromhome.He—'

'Breathe, Cathy,' says Herd.

'—rodeoffsofast I …' *Why was he so mad?*

'Ihad toHangOn. Tight.' I realise, only now, on the in-breath, that I *was* frightened.

In the police freezer, my muscles clamp. An ick-sweet taste stirs a panicked flutter, high in my chest. Then the breath escapes in a sharp *whoomph!* like a fireman-squeeze. Something trapped wants to stay hidden. Fingers tap over mouth. Every nerve clings sinew to bone. I'm not just cold. I'm *terrified.*

I want to run, but ice-feet are encased in concrete. Head afloat, torso swaying. I exhale frost as the glass wall weeps a river of rain.

'Take your time,' says Detective Herd: a woman, a mother. She nudges the tissues. Patient, listening, believing.

Hand still tapping over mouth, I'm afraid that words will come.

All that blame. Who will it stain?

I close my eyes and deep-breathe into belly. Musty air squeezes up through arched chest, *whoomphhh!* The expulsion pushes words into mouth:

'We stopped to get fuel. "Stay here," he commanded and went to pay.' Inside the memory, legs want to run. *Why didn't I?* 'I remember sensing danger, stomach churning, but then the trusted teacher was putting on his helmet.

'"Maybe you didn't sunbake because there were people on the beach," he said. He knew a "more private place".' *What people? How will I get home?* 'We rode for half an hour to Loggerville, to a yellowish bungalow near the soccer fields. No-one was there.'

In the icy interview room, I close my eyes and step into his parents' house: wooden panels, lace curtains, knick-knacks. I hear the bolt slide as he locks the door. *I didn't click then.* But I flinch now, in sound-memory. My skin prickles.

'Wait here,' his dark whisper, another *slide-click* at the back door. Even now, a door locking sets me on edge. Thirteen didn't know the danger she was in.

'He seemed very calm,' I tell Herd, aware of the *shoosh-shoosh* in my ears, the thumping in my chest. *Underwater now. Shark and his target.*

'Perp took me into a room with a big, white-lace-covered bed,' I tell Detective Herd.

'His parents' bedroom?'

No longer in the police station; I'm there with Thirteen, a chest of drawers, framed photos and crochet doilies.

'We'll sunbake here.' He lays two towels on the bed.

I'm cautious, curious, clueless. *Not afraid? Shoosh Shoosh.*

'Let's try bikinis,' he says.

Avoiding angry, I take my jeans off and the man-boyfriend lies beside me. Deep in my *shoosh* hollow, Thirteen shuts off the ugly scene unfolding. *I am not afraid*, she pretends, burying her coloured lights.

A large man climbs onto a small girl and pokes his tongue into her teeth.

'Relax,' he says, his hairy hand on her boob.

'Did you kiss back?' Herd prods.

'Probably?' I respond to her intrusion. 'I'd seen it on TV.'

My bikini bottoms are off. I try to stay in the glacial room with Herd, but I've gone back to terror, where his sweaty body is ragging me about, shoving hurt. Everything is sharp-throbbing but I hang on. Tight.

Is this sex? Painful. Traitorous.

'Stop,' I said. He didn't.

'Bend your knees,' he said. I couldn't.

'Stop, please stop, it's hurting.' Three times, I asked.

He wrenched my knee up, kept crunching.

'A bit longer,' he grunted his hungry-slurping into my hearing ear. 'Almost there.'

My pain does not matter. My voice does not count. I am deep under ice.

'Cathy?' Detective Herd tries to find flat-frozen me.

Now I'm mopping my face with tissues, trying to feel my toes as rain pounds out of me. The crying girl has finally arrived. She weeps and weeps and thaws, and just beyond the police station, La Niña dredges the murk of Loggerville through Tacky's River.

'He pulled his thing out,' I start.

'His penis?' clarifies Herd.

I nod. 'Spurted smelly white slime across my stomach.'

'Stay still. Don't move,' he commanded. Got toilet paper. Wiped his grime off me.

'I was sore, confused, embarrassed.' Tears blur the heartache of the gagged hostage. *Permanently stained. Thirteen.*

She knows the adult secret now: that sex is horror, tarted up in gifts, taboo, and intrigue. That romance, sold as happy-ever-after, is a sham.

'I was shocked by the blood,' says Thirteen. *Slick-shiny. Red red.*

'Menstrual blood?' asks Herd.

'No.'

In the interview room, I puff out cold-smoke, wipe snot off my face. The back of my head pulses hot-itchy. I try to steady through the sway. Nausea rages up my throat. The big thing, the rape, the awful details, finally spoken.

Brave Cathy.

'You're doing really well,' encourages Herd. 'Do you need a break?'

I breathe myself into half-ebbing calm but can't shake the sight of blood. 'He said he "popped my cherry",' I tell Herd.

All I knew was that I was corrupted, beyond naughty. *Evil.* The carnal sin those shouty priests and nervous nuns had warned me about, sex-before-marriage, was *in* me now, forever ugly. Now there is me and *not-me.*

'Cathy?' asks Herd, waiting for *us.*

'I have no memory of exiting that house. I suppose we rode home. I don't know the route we took, if we stopped, or how I hung on.'

I was absent. Even years later, I could not locate that memory; not at college, not with a psychologist, not while crying in bathtubs around the globe. The blankness astonishes me. The missing is still guarded by electric wires and scream-alarms. *Danger!* The siren pierces me now. I plug my right ear with my pinkie finger and support my flaming head with my left hand.

'We should take a break,' Herd urges across the grey desk.

'I'm OK,' I say, determined. *Typical Cathy.* I stand and shake legs out. Glance at the potential vomit bin. Try to breathe but shudder. Freezing and boiling. Something is flapping in my chest. *What lurks, still unspoken?*

'I thought about telling Maggie, but I knew I'd be in big trouble. I was exhausted, and still asleep at midday on Sunday when my parents came home.'

Daytime sleeping is not my normal.

'Why are you sooo tired?' Mum asked. *Could she see my sinner's face?*

I don't remember what lie I told *her*, but I rehearsed my lines for when I next saw him: 'I don't want to do that *ever again*. I don't want to see you anymore.'

Detective Herd is typing furiously.

'Monday morning, he met me in the Pebbly Beach car park. I must have said something,' I tell the detective, 'because he used his growly voice: "People will call you a slut," he said. "We were special. I thought you were The One." He tsk-tsked. "Your parents will be soo disappointed."'

Disappointing slut-child.

Detective Herd does not know I've slipped into the back-then; into ant-riddled skin with cement-for-guts. *A slut cannot reveal herself.*

He holds my hand. 'Let's talk like grown-ups, because you *are* now.'

I want to say *No*, but I'm a hollow-boned bird in the screeching wind.

'No-one else knows how special you are,' he says. 'Your parents won't understand.'

He made me distrust my protectors.

'Sex the first time is difficult, but it gets better,' he says.

I believed him.

'It's what *you* wanted,' he says. *I suppose I must have.* 'I love you,' he says. 'I had such hopes for us; travelling the world, playing music together.' He kisses my hand. 'We can get married.' He promises to remedy the sin.

I don't want to do that ever again.

Fear coils around my windpipes. The practised lines are swallowed. Then the monstrous silence slides right up my throat, chokes off the air, engulfs my tongue.

Stay still. Don't move. My future selves take a sharp breath.

'My mouth didn't work,' the ice-buried child yells at a glass wall.

Thirteen unravels, rises with seagulls. I'm going too. Away ... reaching for a silver thread.

'I'm above myself on the beach,' I shout at Herd. 'A silver ribbon is twirling out through my head!' I'm desperately grabbing for that lifeline. *Is this dying?* 'I can't ...' I fling cold hands across the desk, yelling. 'I can't reach her!'

The detective stops typing. There is a long, guttural howl; the 53-year-old's realisation: 'That's where I trapped myself!'

I upend the blame bucket over my head. *I stayed silent.*

Then, in that frosted grey room, Fifty-Three hears the horrendous *craaack.*

A blaze of pain explodes from my coccyx, up my spine. Hands grip blistering head as shards of skull fling. 'Oooh, noo. No!' I yelp in the ripping, severing sensation. Lava meets ice, hissing into thick, black, boiling bubbles. Body swaying. Brain frantic.

The detective leans closer, frowning, not taking notes. *Did she hear my brain erupt? Can she see it spitting rocks?*

I rise from the magma, a throbbing migraine. A high-pitch squeal punctures my right ear. Head *thunks* onto desk in agony. Detective Herd watches the apocalypse unfolding. This is no historic case. This is *now.*

'I should call the hospital,' she says, about to dial.

'No,' I slow-raise my eruption off the desk, wiping tears and snot. 'That memory, floating outside myself ... I just re-experienced it.'

Detective Herd nods, but her face holds deep disturbance.

Does she think Cathy lies?

'You're obviously distressed,' she says. 'We'll think about what to include in your statement. Right now, you need to take care of yourself.'

I'm too disoriented to drive. Maggie brings her painkiller-stash, drives me to her house. Says it was probably an adrenaline spike.

'The fight-flight response floods the body with hormones,' she explains, being nursey. She rubs my neck, being sisterly. 'Does Vince know?'

'Only that I'm reporting something old.'

I don't say *I'm worried he'll see me differently.*

When did I learn that women can be blamed for men's behaviour?

We drink tea. Three cups. Then Maggie drops me back to the station; to my attempted rescue of Thirteen, forty years too late. The murky river reflects ominous clouds. I numb myself with painkillers and step back into freezing. Ear still ringing, breath shallow.

Revisiting the Ruin is raw, painful and bizarre. *I have no idea what comes next.*

Criminal Justice 4

I am not evidence

March 15, Day One, p.m.

'Will my earlier breakdown be reported?'

'No,' says Detective Herd. 'The Statement is just for facts. You can write about how you felt later.' *Fact: that fracture was not an emotion. It was a chemical explosion.*

I'm shocked. Wish I'd been recorded. Scan the room but see no cameras.

The detective looks bothered. Thirteen raises her guard.

'Cathy, I don't want to upset you,' Herd placates 'but we should clarify what happened on the beach. It's probably *not* good to include the out-of-body experience. It could be' – she steps around words – 'damaging in court.'

Breathing stops. *I'm being silenced.*

'It happened,' I insist. 'I've *never* forgotten *that*.'

Watching myself, from above myself, desperately reaching for the top of my own head.

'Yes.' Nodding patiently. 'But it might be used to substantiate mental health problems.'

I scoop in air. Straw-breathe out. A psychosomatic response to rape is evidence of rape. Trauma resulting from rape is evidence of rape. I am a body of evidence. But I am not a fact.

Breathe.

A jury expects rape victims to cry. Some can't. But my howl will not be heard. Only hard facts. No sodden tissues. No eye-witnessed eruption.

They won't believe me.

I never revealed the broken one. *Why didn't I?* How did I go on each day, each year, pretending it was love?

No. I did not pretend. The confused child *believed.* She bore the quick sex, drowned the terror. Ran, far and fast, so danger could never catch up. *I chain-locked those horrors in a dungeon and swallowed the key.*

'I've never done this before,' I defer to Herd. 'I … suppose I should be guided by you. If this gets to court, I want my statement to be useful.'

'Trust me,' she huffs, 'you don't want this ending up in court.'

But that's why I'm here! I want him to face his criminal damage. Too exhausted to speak, I nod in confusion. The painful re-telling, *re-living* is reduced to: 'I felt disconnected: unable to say what I needed to.'

The UNDERSTATEMENT OF A WITNESS is inadequate. *A lie?*

Detective Herd gently asks why I kept the abuse secret.

'I was already ruined,' I whisper-shrug. *You can't soil filth.*

Part of me believed our secret was special. At 53, his 'love' is fully realised as abuse. The comprehension, still rumbling through me, feels as traumatic as the rape. Thirteen blamed herself; got good at faking great, pretended she was *F.I.N.E.* Subjected herself to later punishments with other men.

I survived all that. Must keep going now.

More details emerge from the muck. I tell Herd how Perp introduced himself as a 'family friend' to my Uncle Bill, who refused to shake his hand: 'Bill knew something was off.'

Herd looks up. 'Would Bill give a statement?'

'He's dead,' I say bluntly, thinking of others who'd whispered 'She's too young', who'd muttered. Tut-tutted.

'I rode to Perp's place on the hill after school. Maggie often saw me turn in, to do his "domestics". She'd wondered why he had such power over me. Then she repeated my lies: "Just similar interests; soccer, music, surfing."' *Just friends.*

I buttressed the façade; did extremely well at school and sports. Panic-paddled for so long under the surface that I learned to breathe in a drowned world. *I looked happy. Was?*

'School buses passed our bikes up that hill,' I tell Detective Herd. 'Carol, a brassy girl in my year, would yell from the Northshore Bus: "You're with Cunning, you're with Cunning!" Other kids laughed.' Parents and teachers saw me ride down his driveway, into the open secret.

I show Herd a photo of me inside his bachelor pad. *Those brown walls.*

'I remember being there, in my school uniform, lying stiff, just like the first time. Like every other time. It only lasted a few minutes …' I float off again. 'He gave me lollies,' I say from the faraway, 'and money to fold his shirts. They had to be *perfect.*' A shop-fold for his T-shirts: front down, arms in, neck-hole centred, bottom third up, top third down, flip, stack.

'What happened if you didn't do it right?' Herd asks, watching my knuckles whiten.

A *whhoomphhh* of metallic air bursts from my lungs. 'He'd get angry,' whispers the chest-flutter. *Get what he wanted.*

'Clothes-fussing is the mark of a serial pedophile,' I tell Herd, who guffaws.

She brings me another foam cup of tea. We go on.

'Perp was jealous. Always wanted to know when I surfed, and who with. He told me what to wear, was always at our house, at my soccer, in my waves. He was claustrophobo-clingy. This was "love".' Thick-sticky and choking.

What could the shackled child-slut say? To whom?

'When I was fourteen, Perp dressed me in lacy lingerie and took photos … so he could "hold me close at night".'

Detective Herd shakes her head, types. *Does she think about her own children?*

'It was scratchy, nylon, with white boob-triangles, a flouncy belly-veil and frilly knicks,' Shame describes the bridal fantasy costume. 'He hid the photos in his wardrobe. When he moved house, he kept them in his briefcase.'

'Perp took me and my best friend to the Loggerville Show,' I tell Herd.

'Can you contact her?' pounces Herd.

'Maybe?' Hannah's in England. *How will I find her?*

'I demanded every fluffy-toy prize and show bag,' knowing he couldn't afford it. My only power: treats and throwaways.

'One morning, Perp and I hid at Miners Beach. He wanted sex, but I spied Dad jogging up the beach he *never* jogged on. Mum probably sent him to find us,' I tell Herd. 'We watched Dad turn back. I hated hiding.' *Lying.*

It must have been stressful for Thirteen, Fourteen, Fifteen, Sixteen …

My lies diverted suspicion. *Busy adults avoided looking too carefully.*

'Cathy?' Detective Herd encourages me to recall 'specific interactions, places, times'.

'There were so many.' *Every day before or after school.*

'Why didn't you say no?' asks the detective carefully.

'I'd already tried,' Thirteen grumps. 'I got on with the job of it. Besides,' I shift into his fantasy, 'we're *in love*. He buys me ice-cream,' Thirteen defends him.

Looking backwards, she wanted the sex to be over. In, out. In, out. Flat-frozen. Smell of semen. *He never asked if I was OK.* Numb was normal.

Now I'm tired. Detective Herd urges me to find exact addresses. 'Drive around, try to get unit numbers,' she suggests, as if I'm capable. I've avoided those streets for decades.

I hiccup. 'Can't you just ask him where he lived?'

'It doesn't work like that,' she says. 'He's under no obligation to talk to us.'

'So *I* have to do all the work?' I ask, exhausted. Hiccup.

'Yes,' she says. 'You've a long way to go yet.'

The anvil of injustice concaves my chest. I've spent six hours in the grey room and we've only covered the first year.

Detective Herd walks me out, into rain; reminds me not to speak with family.

Still shaking when I get home. Vince bear-hugs my hiccup-shudder-howls. My comments about teacher-rapists, while watching Grace Tame on TV, have clued him in to what's happening. He doesn't ask for details. He's focused on his own stress. We're supposed to be heading south tomorrow, to the rainforest. It's his first day off in a year, but a huge low-pressure system inundates the region. Vince doesn't want to get flood-trapped. He cancels our cosy cabin. I cry in the bath.

Dorrigo crossover

March 16

Awake before dawn, listening to pounding rain, I take my laptop to the guest room. I google 'out-of-body stress' and find that 'dissociative amnesia' is a 'common response to child sexual abuse, often accompanied by memory loss'. I do not understand the words, but I learn that during severe perceived threat, the brain's speech centre gets switched off.

My mouth didn't work. It's chemical, not rational.

Reading through tears, I learn that child abuse survivors can experience intense distress when recalling traumatic events. Confused by the enormity of the betrayal, my young, terrified brain shut me down. Silently weeping, I return to bed, holding my little self.

Then I'm underwater, peering through dark bubbles. Can't breathe. Body paralysed. I see the surface but can't propel myself up. My arms are stuck to my sides; my legs wrapped in writhing layers. My chest cavity shrink-spasms into a tight knot. I'm squeezing my last seconds through muddied lungs until … *whooomphhh.*

Body heaves through the quagmire with a rasping, desperate breath.

Vince flips over. 'What happened?' he asks, as I puff-panic. 'You're OK. Just a nightmare.' He hugs me back into now. 'You can talk to me,' he encourages, wiping my tears. He makes no demands. Lets me draw strength from his unquestioning loyalty. I snuggle into his warmth and watch the shark boat, in greying light. 'Rainforests are rain-lovely,' I coax Vince, using my cheery adventure voice. 'Let's get out of here.'

He's not keen. 'You can stop for crispy bacon,' I tempt him.

We grab jackets and boots and drive through dangerous squalls. Finally, on the ridge, we read and rest under a motel blanket. Later, as with twenty-year-happily-marrieds … things progress.

Then something slides through my guts and suddenly, I'm unsure whose arms are around me. *Cannot see his face.* Skin electrifies. Hands tremor. Mind prepares to flee … *from under the monster.* The hairy arm … *is.* Shallow-scream. *Voice doesn't work!* Leg muscles freeze-burn, already running but … too frozen. Chest gallops.

Wait … *What? No!* Adult Brain tries to help. Body opens eyes, grabs hold of who I'm with. No, you cannot have this. *Get out.*

I hang on through it as time chokes me. Trepidation spreads fresh nausea across old ruin. *Nothing will ever be safe again.*

I cry in the motel shower and wonder: Will *we* survive?

~

The emerald forest is calming, grounding. Green. Revitalised, we find Saint Pat's Day Irish tea and shower the leeches off. Vince is too tired. *Hallelujah.* Sleep is mercy.

Giant squalls piss on the River Region, threatening to cut roads. Vince has to get back. We head home early. I spend time trimming the banksia, spreading mulch. Dirt under fingernails feels good, but I breathe through watchfulness, wary of my own heartbeat.

Perp knows this street.

Unsafe survivor work

Detective Herd is away for training. I say 'no' to work and spend several days at Tacky's library, scouring dusty newspapers and school yearbooks. I need help but feel alone.

The survivor does the digging.

Coffee-brave in the teeming rain, I drive to his old addresses, walk right up to doors. I hear his name and look over my shoulder, skin-ant alive. Gut spasming.

He's not here, says Brain. *Breathe.*

Perp's privacy is protected, his innocence assumed. I'm not protected, then or now.

To check dates, I venture to a Facebook school reunion page but recoil when I see Pedo listed as a classmate's 'friend'. Ants feast.

What if he finds out? He could run, or … My gut drops. *Or attack.* I hate Facebook!

Days become fraught-filled. I jump at loud noises, lumber about in a haze of fret, staring at nothing. Sometimes walls fall to the floor, and I step unsteadily.

Vince tries not to show annoyance. He's stressed that I'm avoiding paid work. *I should tell him more.* Digestion is a struggle. I can't eat, then I'm starving. Then sweet-metal-mouth, then gut pains. My organs twitch and I wonder if it's *my* body at all, *schluck*ing down this plughole of sleepless paranoia.

I take some work. Stay in the classroom. Survive.

Details fall out of my head, like forgotten shopping. Once a clever media manager, now I lose cups of tea. I'm beside myself; literally outside myself.

Keep swimming. And I do.

When the sea is sparkle-green, I float, letting earth's magnet spin-close my eyes; listening to heartbeaty-thump waves. Ocean never fails me. I glide in cooling shallows and shower with water dragons. Then, connected to my salty self, I hum on long walks and speak in '*zee-zer*'s – nonsense syllables which relax my jaw.

Lianne phones. 'Things were different then, Cathy … even now, reporting sexual assault is difficult.' She worries what justice might do to me – and Mum.

'He raped me,' I protest. 'I thought it was love.'

'Imagine that conversation in a courtroom.' Her words slice bleeding pieces off me. Bits fall into the sink. Maybe she's right. I'm overwhelmed at the effort of just speaking.

'What are you hoping for?' Lianne asks, with a nebulous sigh.

'I don't know,' I admit. So tired I can barely lift eyelids. 'I guess I want an apology?'

'Think about *Mum*, Cathy. Imagine her in court!' Mum would droop into her sandals.

Part of me knows Lianne cares for me, but the guilt-trip works. I see my mother, ululating in shame, claiming frailty: 'I'm nearly eighty … I don't remember!'

'After all she's done for us,' Lianne adds.

I think of Mum's blood pressure, her asthma, that her father died of a brain aneurysm. *Imagine the blame … if Mum had a stroke on the stand!*

'I'm trying to trust the process,' I say, while feeling something horribly bad is about to happen. 'I don't *want* this to go to court.'

'Then why do it?' she challenges.

'I want *justice*,' I splutter.

She laughs: 'There *is* no justice, Cathy … watch Saxon Mullins on *Q&A*.' She hangs up and I search for the TV show.

I find Saxon's own assessment: 'My search for justice ended after two trials, two appeals, an acquittal, and no resolution … a four-year ordeal with no closure … the mistaken belief that consent was given. I was labelled an unreliable witness to my own story.'

Brave Saxon.

A mercurial barrister will twist my story too, into one of a sexually curious girl, luring an upstanding teacher. I click and read 'The Myths of Consent': that flirtatious girls initiate sex; that victims fight or flee; that assault involves visible injuries; that the victim will appear distressed; that rape is provoked by females – what they wear, how drunk and pretty they are.

I hopped on his bike. Went to his apartments. Did not run screaming.

'I tried to keep my jeans on, your Honour,' says a faltering Thirteen in my imaginary courtroom. Then Fifty-Three spits: 'Curiosity is *not* consent. He has lived unchallenged, without a thought for what he did.' Holding my dressing gown like a black legal frock, I strong-voice around my kitchen: 'Forgiveness, without atonement, is false. Remorse requires *transformation*' – I embolden my performance – 'a change of heart, and actions to prove it. I don't need his punishment. I want something *bigger*,' I declare. 'Social change is a *sine qua non*' – dramatic pause and turn to the jury of pot plants – 'a *requirement*, and' – I raise a finger – 'a *possibility*.' I swirl-flop back to my laptop.

Saxon Mullins highlights that justice depends on the legal support victims can afford. 'A good barrister will degrade you, cut you to shreds … make you look like a liar.' Vince and I have limited funds. Besides, I've already paid for Perp's crime, and other, later but consequent sexual violence in my life.

I google 'justice in NSW': More than 90 per cent of reported sexual assaults receive no formal justice.

Fear blooms. I hug untethered daze.

~

'I didn't think I was frightened,' I blather to Maggie as we beach-walk. 'Why would I have been? I had no idea what was coming.' She listens. 'I *still* don't. Or who I can contact, or who he's still friends with …' I panic-prattle, gulping salt air, careful not to reveal details, because: 'I'm not even supposed to talk to *you*!' I yell at Maggie.

'Why?' She looks bewildered.

'In case I'm just a liar? Bullying witnesses?' I gulp the wind, realising

I'm still frightened: of him, of being blamed, of dragging Mum into accusations of … *wilful neglect?*

I need Mum's support.

The situation, for her and me, then and now, is dangerous. My gut spasms, frantic, as I head home. Car brakes squeal and I squat-flinch, clutching my right ear. I don't know what's happening to me. My super-alert switch is 'ON'.

Back home, I find myself on the New South Wales Victim Services website. It offers 'free counselling & financial support' to 'help victims recover from the psychological and emotional impacts of a crime'. But my tech-savvy skills have deserted me. Not-Clever can't even complete the 'Registration' form. Popping my trauma bubble has pilfered my super-achiever gas. Deflated, I leave it.

I drive to the local Rape Crisis Centre for my one-hour appointment with Jewel, who somehow believes in me and might help prepare me for whatever follows a police statement.

Jewel's shelves are full of hand-sized tactile objects, small toys and crystals. I chatter about the spiky Ninja Turtle. She asks if I've registered for Victim Services, tells me the process is 'fairly easy'.

'I tried, but … wasn't feeling up to it,' I admit.

Jewel completes and submits my form. *Helpful.*

I get sidetracked into my more recent, more frightening abuse. Not by the Teacher, but another violent man. 'He called himself "The Beast".' I feel ill. I'm wandering off into patterns that got me stuck. Patterns taught by Cunning …

Jewel patiently listens, sees I'm overwhelmed, suggests focusing on the Teacher.

I revisit the telling: *grooming, rape, missing memories.*

'Memories can go missing because the brain stores trauma differently.' I hear Jewel from a distance. 'Fear … the amygdala … slivers of vision and sound get locked away. That's why you remember some things with extreme clarity.'

Jewel describes how the ancient reptilian brain protects: 'To focus on immediate safety, the body overrules the brain.' *Brain listens, Body nods.* 'The freeze response, or "going away", is like an animal playing dead, blocking sensory input; so we don't "feel" the violation.' As she speaks, she puts *her* hand to the back of *her* neck.

I immediately feel cold in *my* body, heat at the back of *my* neck. I'm floating above the beach. Reaching. Shaking, I panic-suck a sharp breath. Unpleasantly tingle … *Oh no!*

In an instant, I'm howling in excruciating pain. A high-pitched drill pierces my ear and prickly heat throbs my again-shattered skull. '*No. No.* Not again,' I whisper in disbelief, hunch-helpless, as shudders rumble through me.

When the drill subsides, I unplug finger from ear and press palms against the agony-swirl behind my eyes. I focus on the rain outside, wipe snot and tears.

Seriously? Is this a thing now?

Jewel makes me tea and scrounges a Panadol from another counsellor. She tells me that out-of-body responses are common for chronic child sex-abuse survivors.

Is that what I am now?

Jewel suggests holding something firm and rough, to help me stay present, in Body. 'Push the spikes into your hands.' She offers the turtle. 'Your young brain was shocked into emotional detachment,' she reassures me. 'This can manifest as numbness, confusion, out-of-body experiences, digestive issues, muscle spasms …'

As I emerge from another splintering, Jewel offers more tissues, asks if I've experienced flashbacks. I try not to think about Dorrigo, but tears river my face and she knows already. I am afraid my awful will drown Vince. I can't allow the spoil.

'It's probably not a good idea to push yourself at the moment,' she says.

She means sex with Vince, an intimacy I've been navigating for twenty years. Sure, I avoid, but we manage. He doesn't really know I'm broken. Suddenly, our once-happy, irregular sex life slams me into sorrow. She lets me cry, offers the bin for my sodden tissues.

Jewel does not check her watch. She tells me that 'dissociation during childhood trauma is a predictor of serious later-life stress disorders.'

I should look up that word. Dissociation. Is it freezing or floating? The significance does not compute. *Both.*

'I think your police statement has triggered you pretty badly,' she explains.

'It's forty years later!' I'm astonished.

Again, more carefully, Jewel speaks about the shutdown. 'If we're trapped when the brain floods with stress hormones, we can be paralysed. The "freeze" can create psychological problems. Some people have no recollection until memories emerge, sometimes decades after.'

Jewel spends more than her allotted hour, makes me feel I'm doing the right thing. She tells me that child sexual abuse can affect the development of the central nervous system, the map of *who we think we are*. 'Being repeatedly raped by someone who you and your caregivers trusted made you feel there was no-one in the world to protect you.'

When a child is afraid, they hide.

'You've been hiding stress in your body for a long time. Suppressing your intuition for decades,' she says. Jewel encourages me to listen to Body, not push sensations away. 'Now that the cork is removed, your nervous system might give unexpected responses as you adjust, as you relearn how to trust. You'll need professional support.'

Kindness from this stranger, her simply listening, makes me cry even more.

On the rainy drive home, I stop at Chicken Mania, which I never do. I eat one too-yellow chip, dipped in oily gravy, then toss the box in the bin. Nausea does not know how to feed me.

I am awake at 1 am, 2 am, 3 am. Detective Herd will be back from training soon. I get up at 5 am, do dishes, hang laundry, shirts sideways, pegs shoved in the centre. I listen to k.d. lang's 'Crying' and suddenly I'm on the floor, grieving my lost child-self.

I forget Jewel's advice to make a doctor's appointment.

Blue balls, pearls and a real boy

March 25, Day Two, a.m.

I have painkillers, scarf, vest, water bottle, and a blue spiky ball to push into my hands.

'We'll be here all day,' Detective Herd reminds me. 'Ready?'

I nod, determined. Roll blue spikes along already twitching thighs.

'Perp tried to teach me saxophone so I could go on school band trips.'

Other students knew I had privileges.

'We need specific incidents of assault,' Herd gently redirects.

'When I was fourteen, he fingered me in the garage, in my purple Fred Flintstone nightie. My family was finishing dinner. He eye-signalled me to go downstairs for his special goodbye.'

'Just that one time?'

'Dozens.'

'Could you have stopped going downstairs?'

Herd's courtroom manoeuvre turns my mouth upside down.

'I tried once …' Thirteen falters.

'And?' asks Barrister Herd.

'At our next band practice … he embarrassed me in front of everyone because I couldn't read the music.'

The predator's game.

Herd sits back from the computer, frowns.

Wasn't it normal, to keep allowing? Wasn't it love? *A creature, trapped, digs deeper.*

'Perp was a megastar,' Thirteen continues. 'He broadcast radio shows from the school roof.' Herd is not taking notes. *Who would have been believed?*

As an adult I know where shame *should* have landed. I press blue spikes into hands.

Detective Herd senses that I'm lost. 'Do you remember other specific assaults?'

'Perp invited me to "check the sound equipment" for a school concert in Kempsey. We stopped at Devils Lookout, for "a sunset surprise". I remember pink shine on every gum leaf. It was stunning. And then it was stupid. He was dripping sweat and checking his watch. We didn't even take our shoes off. He stuck it in-out-in-out-in-out and then spurted goop on the sand and wiped his hands with those leaves. Then *I* got in trouble for being late.' Herd types.

'Another time he collected me early. My parents thought he was taking me to a surfing contest. He took me to his apartment, for sex, *Cheech and Chong* and lollies. He told me the "surfing boys" weren't gentlemen, because they said "fuck".'

Herd and I eye-roll the irony. Perp imagined himself a gentleman.

'He took me to Back Beach on his motorbike and I watched a field mouse while he did it on me under the pandanus trees. I got in such trouble for being late home that I asked a neighbour to lie for me. Mum warned she'd be checking my story. I was so anxious.'

Herd types.

'Variety concerts brought money into the school. In 1982, the RSL Club auditorium was packed with parents and teachers.' I show Herd the *Tacking Point News* clipping; me in my poetry-reader costume.

'Perp told me he was "ready to tell the world about our love". For two nights, he played a song called "Cathy" on his red guitar; performing our secret. I can still hear the sickly lyrics. I watched from behind the curtain with another student who explained that "Cathy" was his ex-wife's name. *Weird – I never asked him. I* knew who the song was for. *I* worried about the audience reception.'

I look at Herd, bewildered. 'Why didn't anyone do anything?'

She frowns, shakes her head, types.

No-one was listening.

'Cathy?'

'I … I, um …' The grey walls topple, and I wonder who owns these 53-year-old hands.

'Tell me more about soccer,' Herd prompts.

'Perp played for Loggerville, but he helped our Tacky Point coach carry me off when I hurt my knee. He kept sending his "hungry-eyes" up my shorts.' Detective Herd is typing. 'Then, Perp became our "co-coach", supposedly a surprise for me. I didn't want his second-rate tips; just another way for him to access sex.' I look to Herd. 'Is that *specific* enough?'

'Keep going.' She glances at her notes.

'I had lots of physio during the '82 season. Perp often took me to appointments. When the physio asked if Perp was my father, I said he was my *boyfriend* and she was horrified.' Detective Herd tries to find the physio online, asks if I ever told any adults.

Should have told the PE mistress. Didn't.

'Perp was a big-shot director.' I show Herd the yearbook rave about the 'artistic and financial success' of his musicals. In 1982, two hundred students auditioned for *Thank Zeus It's Friday*. 'He cast me as Goldie, "the virgin sacrifice".' His little joke. 'He'd whisper that he knew I wasn't. Other students joined in the joke; 'Cunning and Byrne' were *a thing*. Dad made a wooden Parthenon. Mum made my thigh-revealing white satin toga. On opening night, Goldie-the-Virgin entered the stage to a chorus of wolf whistles. Perp didn't like everyone *knowing* I was a slut.

'We had night rehearsals at school and the RSL. We'd stop at his apartment for sex – before, after. Sometimes both.' I look at Herd, who's patiently awaiting *details*. 'It happened so often … it's difficult to separate incidents.' She nods.

'Perp moved to another place in Tacky.' I show Herd last week's nausea-blurred photos. 'Another brown-carpeted hovel he lived in, alone, curtains drawn. My bicycle was often visible at the top of that driveway.' *No-one reported a thing.*

'Perp took more sexy-pose photos here, and …' I straw-breathe, hand over mouth. Butchered innocence blurs into drudgery. *Why couldn't I stop it?*

'I thought this was love,' I flounder, as Herd turns back to the computer.

At home, my parents expressed frustration, but I was a regular, selfish teen.

I was a cocky smart arse.

'I didn't do housework, except his. I was exhausted, always in trouble. He suggested I "do more to protect our love" ... "empty the dishwasher, set the table, sweep the stairs".'

Mum's reluctant to support me now. 'Will you ask Mum for a statement?' I ask Herd.

'We'll get to that,' she assures me. 'Do you remember anything else?'

I trawl my notes.

'Sometime in '82, he showed me a condom. It was gross'.

'"I'm only doing this for you," he growled. "It's like wearing a raincoat in the shower."'

Detective Herd is back at the keyboard.

This was the first time I had to touch his animal. I'd never had my face so close to its bulging veins. I couldn't get the floppy round thing onto the hard wrong thing. 'Eventually, he did it himself.' Herd waits. 'That time, he didn't hose stink-jelly on my stomach.'

'He made me practise.' On and on and on. Condom lessons. Sex. I got quicker. 'He told me I knew how to "turn a man on" and, after showing me, asked how I knew the moves.'

He made me think sex was my idea.

~

I tell Detective Herd about Christmas 1982, the road trip to Mildura.

'Your dad just invited me!' Perp said, rushing inside. My innards churned but I faked excitement, cemented near the TV. 'It was supposed to be a *family* surfing safari. I wanted time away from Perp's cloying control. Instead, my fifteenth Christmas was spent with Dad, Rocky, Lianne, a trailer, two tents, and a pedo I couldn't escape.'

'We stopped south of Sydney at Wattamolla waterhole.'

I show Herd the only photo I have of the prick; the two of us jumping off that cliff. Years later, mother yell-blamed me: 'He should never have been invited.' *No*, I'd silently agreed.

Herd says I need exact locations. But I can't talk to family. Lianne says justice isn't real. Maggie didn't come on that trip. Mum is a 'fluster-cuck'.

On a break I text Rocky, who recalls every place we visited.

Back in the station, nausea burns throat while feet sting-tingle into frozen. It's about to get ugly. Ice-preserved memories do not fade. *They pierce.* I see Fifteen in the thawing mess.

'We spent a rainy Christmas Day in Ulladulla, eating tepid lasagne and pudding.' Herd is surprised at my clarity. 'Then we travelled south, to Eden.' I lurch and puff out metal-air. Herd is poised, sees my shiver-storm brewing. I wrap my scarf tight, push-roll spikes into thighs.

'It was a full moon, late December. Perp whispered into the "ladies' tent" to "come and see the moon",' I tell Herd, who types as I continue. 'Lianne told me to "be careful". Dad and Rocky didn't stir. Near the palm-treed beach, Perp spoke about how risky sex would be.'

'Lianne's still awake,' I stressed. 'I don't want to.'

'Haven't you heard of blue balls?' he hissed.

'No.'

'When a man gets a stiffy, but doesn't come, it can make him so sick, he can *die*.' He built the pressure. 'I can show you something else,' he said. 'Kneel down.'

Stay still. Don't move. Don't tell.

In the police station, a detective types, blue spikes press into shaky hands. Itchiness infiltrates somewhere near my wrists. Bubbles crystallise behind my eyes. Nauseous, I cry.

'You're doing really well,' assures Herd, opening another box of cheap tissues.

I sip water, draw hands over mouth: 'I've *never* told anyone this.'

'OK,' she says. Her fingertips keyboard-hover.

My legs clamp to the chair. Torso freezes. Ears shoosh-burn. I hear the high-pitch-ring, stuff fingers into both ears. *Inside or outside my head?* I puff-breathe, then stand and shake out legs and arms.

'OK?' asks Herd.

Still puffing, sitting, nodding now swaying.

'I knelt behind a palm tree and Perp told me to "give his dick a little kiss". I pecked it and pulled away. "Come on," he coaxed, "open your mouth, lick it." I must have leaned in.' Fifteen grips the police station plastic chair, neck retracted, fingers ice-cold. Body rocks.

I try to allow it, his thing, but I pull back each time he shoves the grizzle-snake forward. Suddenly his dick punches deep into throat. 'He grabs my head, one hand holding my chin, the other over my right ear. My warning ear.' I hear only gagging-on-slime. *Can't breathe!* Want him to slow down but hurry up. 'I'm trying to look up, can't pull my head away.'

Choking is felt in your guts. Not like ocean breath-holding. In the sea, you loosen, and the wave lets you go. This fear, on a beach, in a police station, has *intent*. It's voracious, violently shaking me, thrusting me deep under mud.

I gag-retch and desperately extract from cruelty, eyes stinging with tears. 'He shirks off behind a tree.' Herd waits. *It didn't feel like love.*

'I remember having a horribly sore throat, faking my period, not speaking for days,' Fifteen admits. 'Until the safari turned inland, to spend time with my cousins. I was happily distracted until Perp made me do his laundry. He got angry when my tissues stuck to his clothes. Lianne said "He should do his own bloody laundry."'

I'm not sure which words make it to the police statement.

Day Two, p.m.

I leave the station for lunch but can't eat. I look up 'epididymal hypertension', sometimes called 'blue balls'. It's *not* life-threatening. Damage *is* inflicted, however, by men who shove their dicks in children's mouths, causing palatal haemorrhaging. My gag reflex is now so strong I have to warn dentists. Mouth x-rays are impossible. That scar never healed.

'Did he ever give you alcohol?' Herd asks when I return.

'He poured ick-cheap Riccadonna Asti at secret "oyster picnics" in his apartment. Him sweating in his white shirt and bow tie.' *Did*

I know it was illegal to supply alcohol to a minor? Did it make a difference to the sex? For years after, I was still and straight as a board.

Numb-normal.

'What did your family think of him?' asks Herd.

'Dad and Maggie enjoyed his guitar-playing. Lianne and Rocky didn't like him. Mum once jibed, "He's old enough to be your father. It isn't right."'

'It' got me in trouble, made me anxious. We were seen in his various cars, at beaches, on his motorbikes. In town, at school, at performances, in music rooms. I was 'accused' through snide comments from Mum, raised eyebrows from other teachers, derisive chortles from other kids. I hid in their ambivalence. They suspected but refused to question. No-one ever asked how 'it' started.

I want to vomit.

'I practised reading music and eventually played a sax solo. Perp joked in rehearsals about teaching me the song "String of Pearls". I didn't get the joke.'

Neither does Detective Herd. In a freezing police station, two females in their fifties google-learn that a 'string of pearls' is to ejaculate on someone's neck.

'Who did you first tell about the rape?'

'Garry,' I say. 'Captain of the Starship!'

Herd frowns over the rim of her glasses, puzzled. *Sigh.*

'In 1983, Maggie and I were in a Star-Trekky musical. I played a flightdeck robot who had to soprano-solo the opening bars. I didn't have a high voice,' I blather. 'Perp humiliated me. I asked to swap parts with Maggie, who was cast as an alto, a drunken pirate, but Perp wanted me at every rehearsal.'

'Garry?' prompts Herd.

Sigh.

'Garry was a sweet boy my own age, the male lead – Starship Captain.' Herd starts typing. He had curly hair and puppy-dog eyes and he could sing! We listened to Billy Joel. 'We were fond of each other.

He wanted to "go steady", I had to tell him I was "damaged goods". Garry insisted on knowing who my "relationship" was with.'

'Do you sleep with him?' Garry asked.

'We don't *sleep*,' I tried to minimise the awful but didn't tell him about the rape until years later.

Garry and his best friend, Scott, tried to convince me to end it. Confused and trapped, I had no idea how to navigate back to 'first love', to innocence. *I was already ruined.*

'Perp used Garry's interest in me to lessen suspicion.' The more time I spent with Garry, the more Perp pulled my strings. 'Now I can tell everyone how much of a slut you are,' he'd mock, and, sulkily: 'I thought we'd get married.'

I was disappointed when Garry left school for the Army, but too numb to ask for help. My childish mind thought my only option was to marry the abuser. I had no-one else.

I take a sharp, shallow breath. 'Will you contact Garry?'

'I'll talk with your family first,' Herd says.

'Be gentle with Mum,' I urge.

'Yes.' Herd understands. 'Let's talk next week.'

I can still back out.

Later, I walk the perilous cliffs, sucking in salt air, when I notice someone walking too close behind me. I flush-panic and crouch as if tying my laces. I'm embarrassed then, at the paranoia trickling into my shoes.

He could find me, follow me. Push.

Tea with Mum

Late March

There's a break in the rain, so I attempt normal, accept a few days' work at the school, walk barefoot to check how Mum's coping. We're different.

I'm an iconoclastic feminist sociologist. She's a gender-conventional rule-obeyer who's afraid of lesbians and 'doesn't like social workers'. I desperately need her help, but she avoids my awfuls.

Today, I will also. *I'm too tired.*

As I step onto her patio, I see ominous stacks of notepaper on the dining table. Before I can swallow angst, Mum opens the screen door and peers into me.

'I thought about it. … All night,' she declares.

Where's her head headed? I stand awkwardly in the doorway.

'You make tea,' she commands.

I feel a conciliatory breeze as I put the kettle on.

'I've written a statement for you,' she says. *Oh.* 'I'd like you to read it.' *Breathe.*

'I'm not up for that today, Mum,' I say, worried about Brain-Body erupting. I don't have my spiky ball, or painkillers.

'It won't take long,' she insists. 'It's just a little thing, to help explain …'

Explain, not help.

I bring her tea and sit near the door. She sits too close, offers me a stale gingernut biscuit.

'No, Mum, I have to be ready to talk about this stuff, I might—'

'Well.' She cuts me off then robots at me, 'You. Asked. For. A. Statement.' It's what *she* needs. 'I'll sit with you while you read it,' she prods, unaware that my body is already coiling.

I exhale panic-puffs. *Slow in, long out.* I spot a butcher bird in the gum tree. Hear the distant thump of waves. *Slow in, long out.*

Mum's 'statement' is handwritten shakily on old notepaper. It starts with a dramatic, double underlined 'It's all our fault.'

'Mine, and your father's,' she clarifies, finger-stabbing the underlines.

I remind her she's not responsible for Perp's actions.

'We didn't know it was sexual,' she pleads.

Her truth silences me. So I read on, about how 'busy' she was, 'with four children; all their sports and music'. She notes that 'Cathy was infatuated.'

I feel the prickling heat.

Her statement concludes: 'We are all suffering, from the guilt and shame.' She pokes the words. 'That's true, isn't it?'

'I suppose?' *Where might her army of marching reasons spiral me?*

'Then why did you email your sisters? Asking them to consider their language?' *What email?* 'We all have a right to say what we need, don't we?' she continues.

Oh, that email – asking not to be blamed for 'inviting' him, on a family holiday, or to Maggie's 21st.

'Yes?' I say, confused.

Mum refuses to blame the criminal who walked freely into her house. She grapples with memories of Cathy the feisty teenager who always got what she wanted. *I never told her otherwise.* She does not know me. *I should drop this whole thing.*

Sipping cold tea, Mum suggests I was 'praised too much', that my childish expectations were 'too grand'. Nausea surges in a chemical flush. She takes flight on this toxic thermal, riding higher through justificating clouds, her pure logic speaking *at* me.

'You were wild and free. Too big for your own boots. Too clever and confident.'

An adventure-seeker. My risk-taking made me a liar. My lies kept us all safe from the hurt of knowing. *She's justifying why no-one bothered to rescue? Because I wanted too much from life? That I *deserved* this?*

Brain is in fluster mode, flicking bits of Mother's assessment off my chest, searching for some reason why *any* mother would say such a thing.

'We *all* have different recollections,' Mum continues.

She doesn't want to hear my truth. Wants to speak hers.

Her words open fault lines. Shockwaves ripple around us.

'If *we* see things differently, *we* have to say what *we* think happened,' she adds.

I realise … she's recollecting the evil girl-child, manipulator of a good man. Brain feels the bubbling volcano.

'You can't control what other people say,' says Mum, as I *phoopth* out metal-heavy air, 'especially in court. You can't manipulate their version of—'

'Oh noo …' My slow moan interrupts her. Searing magma under my scalp. Mum stands with her scrap of statement, still spitting words. I hear the oncoming siren, feel the prickling ants. I hold my head as excruciation rumbles through me; leaving me hollow. Drenched.

Seeing me reduced to this, she moves in.

'It's good to see you cry.' Her tone motherly but also callous. *Baited.*

'I need … Panadol,' I manage, 'and … something sharp … to hold.'

'I only have out-of-date drugs.' She dawdles off to her medicine cabinet, returns with two pills. 'They probably won't kill you.' She chuckles.

I dry-swallow the pills, worried that my escape legs have crumpled. She hands me a piece of Dad's rough-cut opalised stone. I scrape my hands waiting for relief, slow-breathe myself back into Body, look around; dumbfounded.

'Mum, you can say whatever you need, to the police,' I whisper.

'Oh, I don't need to go *there*,' she announces. 'I don't need *that* stress.'

The piece of scrap she's wielding is not her police statement; it's a command for me to not challenge others. She'll probably put it in the compost.

The ants have knitted numbness through me. Legs walk me off her patio, past home, straight into the sea. I dissolve disappointment in green oblivion.

A statement. Now what?

March 29, Day Three, a.m.

Detective Herd is on call. 'I might have to leave,' she warns.

I want to leave, myself. I'm waiting for news of our first grandchild, worried about Vince's eldest daughter, Lee, giving birth during a Covid lockdown.

Herd asks if I remember anything else. I haul back into awfuls, show some more photos, wonder if *he* ever had to lie. I recount the school band trip to the Sydney Opera House. Perp was bus driver, but I sat with friends until the last pitstop when Perp ordered: 'Sit up front.' I swapped seats with Miss Brownlow. Perp pulled a blanket over our laps, kept checking the rear-view mirror. He whisper-wanted me to 'keep him awake'. I put my hand into his already unzipped pants.

'You're really good at this,' he kept saying. 'You like this.' I was terrified of being caught. *Why did I not refuse?*

Herd types. Another memory floats to the surface.

'Near my sixteenth birthday, Perp went on a date with a Canadian exchange teacher. After everything I'd been through for his promise of marriage, I was confused. *Angry?* I let myself into his apartment, threw the lingerie, photos, poems and cards across the floor. When the prick came home, he seemed scared I might tell. He told me he wanted to visit Canada. But then kissed me. Then angry. Then the usual.'

'What about senior school?' asked Herd.

'Perp didn't have enough students for his "beginners" music elective. He convinced me to enrol, but I changed to engineering. "Cathy thinks she's too smart," he told the class.

'I didn't do what Mr Angry wanted.' Herd smiles at my proud voice.

'But I could still be slut-shamed, and burned in sex-before-marriage hell.'

I had not outgrown those shackling beliefs.

'I worked at Woolies, studied hard, was still in band, musical, vocal group. I had actual feelings for a real boy, and a desperate need to escape. I didn't handle any of it well.'

Eighteen could get married. Didn't want to. *Thought I had to.* 'I was so stressed at my school farewell at the RSL (wanting him to dance, wanting to escape him); one of my eyes stayed dilated for hours,' I sob. *Was that a stroke?* Herd pushes the tissues over.

My phone buzzes and I smile through nicer tears. 'I'm a grandmother!'

Herd smiles. 'Congratulations!' My granddaughter's world needs to change.

~

'So, you finished school?' Herd prompts.

'I went to college in Bathurst. Far enough away that I didn't have to tell Perp who I was with, what I was wearing. At the end of first year, he came to visit; assumed he'd get sex.'

This time, my 'Go Away' lines were practised. On long walks. Quietly in the library. This time, I lectured the mirror: 'It's over.'

'I arranged for friends to check on me while he was in my room; I stayed standing, kept the door open. He tried to cajole, but I finally voiced the words I'd long strangled: "I don't want to see you anymore."'

'Mr Angry stormed off and I got drunk that night.'

Despite my perfect grades, that last few weeks of college dropped me into deep depression. I remember a heavy black cloak knocked me to the floor. I'd crawl to my room, sometimes not make the bed, and not get up for hours; 'I thought it was all my fault.' My head plonks the station desk.

'That's the last time you saw him?' asks Herd, brow arched.

I raise and shake my leaden head. 'That Christmas, I bumped into Perp on Richman Street. He wanted to show me his music studio.' Zombie-like, I walked with him. But my body revolted. 'I refused to step through that door.'

I sit back into the plastic chair, take a deep breath.

'The last time I saw him was at my sister's 21st in January '87.' I show her Maggie's photo. 'And I … did *not* … invite him.'

I close my eyes, float away from the image, from all of it.

'Well done, Cathy.' Herd's tone remains sombre. 'You've managed the first, worst, and last. I'll need a list of everyone you've ever disclosed to.'

'Well … there's Garry, and a psych …' I mumble.

Herd is typing, nods me on, into sludge.

~

'In Sydney, '89, straight out of college, I escaped from my first boss – a violent Beast who ...' *Shoosh-shoosh*, I fight-breathe to stay in the room. 'He ... But I ...'

Those are my 21-year-old's sensible work shoes, slapping along Military Road, past The Oaks Bar and Grill, quickly. Quickly! He's waiting.

'I escaped ...' I sit in my shame-filled confessional, puffing panic-clouds. Herd sits back, confused by the detour.

'Let's focus on the teacher,' she says, not understanding the connection.

The lessons taught, of choked obedience, ignoring my gut ... led me inexorably into life-threatening, sexual, emotional, physical and financial abuse.

What a fine education that Cunning teacher gave me.

'When I escaped the Sydney Beast, Uncle John arranged for me to see a psychologist, Frank Somebody,' I tell Herd. 'It all poured out: the teacher, the motorbike ride, the locked doors, the missing bits, the Ruin. It wasn't until I escaped the second abuser that I understood how it all started.'

Herd's computer keys clatter.

'Frank Somebody was the first person to say "It's not your fault",' I bawl, still grateful for those diamond words. 'But ...' I grab tissues, blow my nose, and speak into the flat grey desk. 'I contacted Frank last week. He didn't keep a record of my visit. He never suggested going to the police.'

Herd sighs. 'It wasn't mandatory back then.'

Scrolling through her notes, Herd mutters, 'And that's when you told ...'

'Garry,' I finish. 'After Frank diluted my guilt, I phoned Garry, told him Cunning had raped me. That's when I destroyed my family's photos; cut Perp out with Mum's scissors. I *tried* to tell Mum, but ... Rocky was still at school.'

'When did you tell your sisters?' Herd asks.

'*Urghhh!*' Gut spasms as I press blue spikes into thighs.

'Breathe, Cathy,' soothes the detective. 'Take your time.'

'I numbed myself on whiskey and weed for New Year's '93 at the RSL Club and danced with some guy until I blacked out. I woke up with scrapes all over my back.'

Re-re-damaged goods. Maggie lectured me for 'getting myself into that position'.

Walking the cliff edge doesn't give someone the right to shove. She was talking about New Year's, the Beast, the Teacher. I know getting senseless was stupid, but I was tired of blame.

'Maggie and I exchanged heavy letters about responsibility. I described the rape and apologised for my lies. Maggie showed Mum, Dad and Lianne my letter, but Mum was being very Catholic about my emerging homosexuality (I found safety with women in my twenties but I'm not keen on labels. Sexuality, like gender, can be fluid). I told Mum she was focused on the wrong "crime". We fought a lot.'

'Did you keep that letter?' Herd's fingers hover.

'Probably in Mum's compost ...' I sigh.

Herd glances up. 'What happened next?'

'I ran away. Overseas.'

'No wonder,' she empathises and prints my statement. 'Double-check it, sleep on it.'

But I'm done. In my car, I speed read, take nothing in, sign anyway.

Everything else will be easy.

'What happens now?' I toss and catch my blue ball.

'I'll talk with your sisters,' Herd says, adding warily: 'And your mum.'

I gulp, nodding slowly.

'Of course,' the detective whispers carefully, 'there's the most obvious thing.'

Thirteen's electric fence snaps on. 'Oh?'

'We get you on the phone with him.'

I fall through a dark chasm. 'With Perp?' peeps Thirteen. Heart rate doubles. *How will I react to his voice? What if he comes after me?* 'Don't you have enough to arrest him?' I plead.

'Think about it,' she says.

Somehow, I drive home.

Pickling in raw fear, I google 'child sex offender psychology': Often narcissistic, they minimise the consequences of their actions, blame external circumstances, frequently live alone and enjoy their immaturity, which affords them contact with children. Offending usually starts in their early twenties.

My whole abdomen spasms. *Did he hurt his first wife? Or Lucy? Are there others?* Something crushes my chest to the floor. Pain squeezes my heart. So tired of the enabling silence, I wonder how I'll ever speak shame to where it belongs, doubt I'm brave enough.

I simply cry and cry.

Outside, it rains.

5 Family Justice

High school 'bestie'

I find a contact for my school friend, Hannah, email 'long-time-no-chat' niceties and …

> *Did I ever tell you? I probably only showed my happy-achiever self. But later, I might have been honest about a certain teacher?* [I don't name him]. *Do you remember? If so, could you contact Tacking Point police?*

Hit send.

I spend forty-eight hours knitting torso to knees. Hannah replies. Breathe in, open her email … Don't exhale.

> *Of course I'll help. I hope you have support. You didn't tell me then, but I learned about it after. In hindsight, it's inconceivable I didn't recognise grooming behaviour. I was a child, as you were …*

Phhooophhh. I flush with relief.

Hannah will write down what she recalls of the 'relationship' *(Sorry,* she writes, *I can't think of another word)* with Perp [she names him].

There were plenty of adults and other kids who knew. I'll send a statement to the investigating officer.

Yes! Someone who knows. Cares. Does not blame me.

Hannah named him. I print our emails and walk to the police station, slow-squeezing blue ball into hands, mantra into breath, Brain into Body. The bearded duty-officer fobs me off but a voice forces my larynx: 'Detective Herd requested information.'

'The file says you'll be contacted,' says Officer Disinterested.

I text-ask Lianne for her detective's name.

Ping.

'Can I see Detective Balding?' I ask, loudly.

The officer, bothered by my persistence, calls upstairs. When burly Detective Balding appears, I apologise for interrupting, show him the emails. He looks at me strangely – *assessing witness credibility?* – and asks if I'll do The Phone Call.

'Maayyb-be …' Panic arises.

'We'll help you prepare.' *Oh? Relief.* 'Let's wait for Detective Herd,' he says, slipping the emails into a dusty pigeon-hole.

My life is only this; a desperate wait for justice, avoidance of what must come, and endless bloody rain.

Not good Friday

Delightful Kaleidoscope is home. We share dragon stories, sci-fi movies and ice-cream. But I'm glad Kal is out when I argue with Vince, who's cooking bacon.

'It's just a *smell*,' he says, not understanding. *Let it slide.*

I take nausea outside, wait for dead-pig to waft away. From our deck, I notice giant tree trunks, pushing the mud-sea north.

Lianne phones from the police station. She's driven three hours, through squalls, to see Detective Balding. She'll go to Mum's after.

Stomach broils, waiting.

Lianne's statement – which I won't see for months yet – confirms Perp *ingratiated himself into the family*, that he *moved from Loggerville to a nearby apartment*, that *Cathy was often on his motorbike*, and that during the Kingaroy motocross, *Cathy went missing*. Lianne remembers the camping road trip: the cold Christmas lunch and warning me to 'be careful'; that Cathy *left tissues in his washing* and Perp *made a big, angry scene* … She recalls *once, when they were lying together, watching TV, they jumped apart when I entered the room.*

Lianne was tired, being questioned for hours about events from lifetimes ago. Her memory of tossing Perp's keys into his apartment doesn't make her statement.

Will she help Mum remember?

In the sorry April rain, I watch broken dragon-logs.

Come to Mum's, Lianne texts.

~

For a minute, we avoid each other's eyes. And then …

'I don't know what you think you'll get from this police thing, Cathy,' discourages Mum, arranging her rain-bashed lettuce. 'Your sisters don't have time to make statements, and I certainly won't be going near that station.' She turns my need for support into a 'selfish Cathy' act from the family folklore. Mouth tastes sky-metal.

I eyebrow-ask Lianne why she hasn't told Mum she's already been. In the kettle's reflection, Mum flits from kitchen, to dining table, to fridge. I hold compassion, roleplay the contrite daughter. Brain drifts out the window.

There are times when Kal challenged me. Times I got mothering completely wrong; when my way was neither wanted, nor appropriate. Times I had to listen, learn and change; when love was more important than my opinion. *I hope I'm a good mother.*

'Cut some tomatoes,' says Mum, slamming me back into skin. 'Not *that* knife,' she commands, 'use a *sharp* one.' Through the thrum of rain,

I listen to her fuss-bother; a show for Lianne, whose last Covid border escape was also ruined by my history. Mum swirls the flamboyant skirt she 'got out for the occasion'.

'Boiled eggs. Sourdough, drizzled with macadamia oil,' Mum announces.

Oh. Not concentrating. Thinking about The Phone Call. A slug of blood oozes into sink.

'You've made a mess of those,' Mum reproves, shaking her head at uneven tomato chunks, not noticing the blood.

I re-boil the kettle, suck my thumb, think about how Mum always provided: healthy food, clean clothes, art classes, long drives to scholarship interviews. Practical, education-focused, Irish care. My otherwise achievement-filled life must be a frightening contradiction to her concept of abuse-survivor. She bristles at me.

It's just her way. Mum manoeuvres to confirm the 'true' version of reality – *hers*. Strategically undermining anything that challenges her rules: 'women with babies should stay home', 'homosexuality is unnatural', 'obesity is a poor choice', 'other religions are worse than Christianity', 'Anxiety? … life is a struggle; deal with it'. These views are common in her generation, and she has 'every right to express those opinions'.

Maybe she's defending her 'housewife' life: a rural upbringing, a teaching diploma, raising four kids. *Maybe she's jealous of my world-wandering?*

When I returned from adventures, got married, then pregnant, she aimed to 'bring me down a peg': 'You think you can do anything,' she'd bittered.

Why can't I whisper truth against her wall? Her false belief that I controlled my world?

Because I am perpetually exhausted in her arena. Because she gave everything to build her acceptable version of me. Because she denies all knowledge, performs an impish frailty. Because she will forever circle back, closing the noose of her guilt around my throat.

For Mother, my story confirms the myth: *the flirtatious teen revelled in the upstanding man's attention. The blameful girl must be protected from her mistakes, because 'men do what men do.'*

Lianne finally admits her police visit. 'I spent three hours there this morning, Mum.'

'Why would you do that!?' Mum's wide-eyed response punches my lungs. 'You don't have any evidence.' Her understanding feeds on TV forensics: *Silent Witness* and *Vera*. Not unreliable unspokens.

'I'm supporting Cathy,' Lianne affirms, avoiding eye contact.

Doesn't Mum realise ... her own statement is a requirement, not a choice?

'*You* could make notes, Mum,' I prompt. 'Just what you remember.'

'I don't need to,' Mum scoffs. 'I don't know anything about it.'

The three of us sit in humid history. Ghosts circle. Toxins surge.

'Oh, Cathy,' Lianne severs the silence. 'Your lies didn't help.'

'Of course not,' admits my shame-numbed self.

I watch them fill, then empty, their plates. Cannot bring myself to eat. I try to imagine more palatable words in their mouths: *I'm sorry I didn't protect you then, a child. I'll help you now, however you need.* But empathy is ant-dust under this house.

They don't understand. How could they? I can't comprehend it myself. It took years to use the word 'rape'. They tried recalibrating. But some memories are deep-scratched records. *Cathy, the naughty one.*

Months later, when I get to read my sisters' statements, I'll see how Lianne's adult judgement pinned Thirteen to the courtroom wall: *Cathy was politically savvy and a good actress. She knew how to work the room.*

Back home, I google why abused children lie. Shame is a deterrent to disclosure. The child turns liar, under threats, for enticements. 'Your parents will be disappointed ... People will call you a slut ... I'll marry you ... Have a chocolate.' Perpetrators reinforce self-blame. 'It's what you wanted ... You really like sex.' He dressed me, then told me I was seductive.

Mum *still* thinks I was in control. Anything else will destroy her. Adults find the child's apparently normal state incongruous. People think *they* would not cope. It's a horrible irony: my ability to fake OK made it impossible for them to believe me when I finally spoke. I was so 'in love' that I hid how sick he made me feel.

All that oyster-grey puke inside my shiny green self.

Easter eggshells

On Easter Saturday, Lianne drives Mum to the graves of long-dead relatives. I tag along in the miserable wet, hoping Mum will feel my freshly excavated hurt. She doesn't. I get a moment with Lianne on the southern breakwater, watching agri-poisons pour into bog-grey sea.

'Move on, Cathy,' Lianne instructs.

Only sharks keep moving, because if they stop, they drown. Lianne wants me back in false-happy. But I won't abandon myself again. I must dig now, deep down to where I left Thirteen in the frozen faraway. It's time for all this bloody mindless 'moving on' to STOP!

And still, I avoid anger; the sharp flint of my sisters' mothers' husbands' raised voices makes me feel small. If I told Vince how Mum's been responding, he would explode in fury. *It would burn me … and I still need her help.* So I walk them all about on Easter eggshells.

Back at our house, Mum delights in rare male attention. Her sons-in-law serve tea and hot cross buns with 'proper butter', on 'fancy plates'. Outside, under the rain-hammered deck, three sisters whisper in a dark-sky huddle. Maggie has also spoken to the police.

'I told them what you said once, driving to Loggerville, that you were raped.' *Good.* 'I was a bit mixed up,' she adds. *Oh.* 'We never had the chance to clarify … It happened on that hill? In the purple house? With a funny roof?'

Her face grows whiter, mirroring mine. Blood drains into my ankles. *No!* Incorrect. *Over the hill,* I'd said while she drove, down near the soccer fields, in that awful yellow house.

'I got it wrong?' Maggie panics. 'Should I change my statement?'

I'm deep under black ice.

'No!' booms Lianne in her eldest-sister voice, blocking my attempt to resurface.

I straw-breathe into cold limbs and smile as I respond: 'If justice can't cope with fuzzy memory … we're *all* in trouble.'

My sisters flick fear and bun crumbs off their chins.

Months later, I read Maggie's statement; she too confirmed Perp's laundry obsession: *Cathy wouldn't hang out her own washing, but she was always doing his.* I'm relieved she mentioned Lucy, Perp's prior target, and that a PE teacher was *suspicious.* I wish I'd told the PE mistress. A mother of two girls. She didn't let Perp coach girls' soccer. She would have helped. But she's dead. It's up to adult-me now, to show some grown-up courage.

It will take more than I can imagine. Possibly more than I've got.

~

Mum's Easter Sunday guest-fuss replenishes her. As dark clouds gather over the dunes, I take my chance: 'Mum, have you thought about a police statement?'

'You were *infatuated*,' she hacks me down, slicing the lamb, her grey eyes absolving herself behind mint sauce. 'We didn't know it was sexual.'

'Lots of people knew something was … off,' I protest.

'Well, *I* didn't,' Maggie jolts loose a memory that slips away before I can catch it.

'You lied!' Mum ramps the volume, 'I tried to keep you apart.' *Why?*

Unaware of her almost-admission, Mum's moral obligation crouches on the table. Nobody else notices. Their glares scorch my face. *I want to vomit.*

'Mum did her best.' Lianne holds serving-fork swords across potato salad, defending. 'She doesn't have to relive it. She can say "No."'

We try to be civil at the table, elbows millimetres apart. Sharp knives scrape the silence, pierce my ear. Brain is too tired for another meltdown; Body too nauseous to eat.

Looking uncomfortably sticky, Lianne scrapes cold gravy off cutlery. She is champagne-careless now. 'I remember being sent to find *her* once …' Red-faced, she doesn't look at me; or take a breath. 'I had to ride out along Miners Beach. By the time I got back she was already home, spouting crap about doing his cleaning.'

The venom-soaked air simmers as Lianne warns Maggie: 'Cathy wants her day in court. Can you imagine Mum being cross-examined? … In front of a jury of locals?'

I step outside and diffuse into grey, gum leaves in rain.

'I remember *her* jumping on his bike.' Lianne makes sure I hear. 'It will all come out … her *participation*.'

The word slices my innards, releasing a horde of ants.

Maggie joins me outside, sipping wine. 'I honestly don't remember much.' She sighs her hand to my shoulder as Lianne appears, flustered. 'He never threatened you,' Maggie continues. I swallow uneaten gristle. *She doesn't get it.* 'I don't remember you ever being upset or afraid, Cathy. I thought you were *happy* with him.'

I begin to cry as the ironclad sky rumbles.

Maggie pleads for solidarity: 'Rocky wants us on the same page if this goes to court.'

Lianne scoffs: 'Rocky hasn't been anywhere near this family's page lately. Poor Mum. Perp was *always* here!' she struggles to whisper.

Maggie looks for a seat on the 'please everyone' fence. 'I want to help Cathy *and* protect Mum.' *Impossible.*

'I will protect Mum,' warns Lianne.

A mudlark shits a white smear on the Lianne-freshly-painted garden seat as Mum joins the honesty soiree with a jollying tray of dates and lemon cake. 'Such an operatic dress …' Mum nods to the bird, which shriek-pierces my ear. I wander off into the gloomy afternoon.

'Pity about the singing voice,' she chortles.

Did she notice I was gone?

'Free' therapy

April 15

Unable to conjure an opening for The Phone Call, I revisit the Victim Services website. It lists only one child sexual abuse counsellor for my postcode, but this therapy will be free if I can sort my paperwork. Other than one visit with Frank Somebody, I've never had counselling – but shaky hands remind me, I need help.

~

My appointment is at the Community Centre, a public space. *Will Perp find out?*

The counsellor, Sally, has not accessed my statement, nor my crisis centre file. She's booked the fluorescent-lit, too-cold office for fifty-six minutes. I have to re-tell my awfuls. *Keep going.*

I puff air into cheeks, flint-scrape hands, push through the heavy; the Teacher, rape, out-of-body terror, re-victimisation, head explosions, family friction. Untethered, I shake and cry and forget my mantra. The creeping pull of prickle-skin around my neck signals a tsunami.

Take a breath, pop a painkiller. Ask: 'Can you help me?'

'I'm a Cognitive Behavioural Therapist,' Sally explains. 'Not a good choice for you,' she admits. 'Exposure therapy can re-traumatise.' *Listed under 'child sexual abuse', she accepted my appointment.* 'Have you heard of EMDR?' she offers.

'No,' I say, stumped.

She suggests I find someone trained in E-and-D-R? A kind of eye treatment? She can't help me. Not with The Phone Call, nor therapy. She checks her watch, listening from her faraway chair. She sells her experience in police processes, says she'll help with a Victim Impact Statement. Another statement? What is it? *Do I need one?*

We both express misgivings about continuing but make another appointment. *There's no-one else.* At 10:52 she packs up, suggests I visit my doctor.

'You need a proper diagnosis,' she warns. 'You might have PTSD.'

'Isn't that for soldiers?' I ask, even more doubtful.

Later, I google 'Eye Movement Therapy' and still don't understand what it is.

I try to access resources on the Victim Services website, which don't load. I search nearby postcodes for other counsellors. The website keeps crashing. Brain can't concentrate. Even in the virtual world, I forget where I am. I'm not sure if I *have* a 'case manager'. The process is unclear. I randomly click links, scratch ant-bitten arms. Hopeless. I can't tell if I'm over-hungry or too nauseous to eat.

I am white-privilege-educated. *What happens to those less tech-literate, with more life pressure and dodgy internet?* 'Aurghh!!' I scream at the screen, at the clunky system preventing justice. I rouse on myself, then cry.

Usually an avid walker, rain, hail or shine, I'm now afraid to leave our love-shack safety. I berate myself for avoiding work. I need money, need the distraction, but can't cope with sexually charged teen harassment. Isolated, frustrated, I force myself to do some weeding, but only in shadows, well back from our fence, ready to run. Later, I discover green-ant welts up my legs. I never felt them bite.

Despite not knowing details, Vince sees how desperate I'm becoming. He offers to walk. On a corner near the beach, a car-brake squeal slices through me. Vince watches me crouch-curl, arms over head.

'I could earn a side-income performing at a freak fair,' I joke.

'That's not funny.' He hugs me.

Income

April 19

From habit, I wake and fret-check for a work text. *Has the Department of Education been notified?* The school handled things badly back then. Surely now … *Why aren't I getting work?*

Brain stirs a soup of paranoid wait-worry as Vince prepares for his own work dramas. His bosses refuse to provide HR support. I'm concerned he wants to please them more than they want to take care of him. They've told him to get rid of a troubled employee because mental health issues are 'bullshit'. I wish Vince would realise *it's just a job.*

I check my phone every ten minutes. This is madness.

The Department can't NOT hire me, right? That would be discriminatory.

That school, the site of my childhood sexual abuse, is now my only income. Worthlessness bubbles up, percolates a gritty scum to my surface. Hands shake. Everything awaits The Phone Call.

I spiral into doomscrolls and see the federally funded video for teaching teenagers about consent. It shows a girl smearing a milkshake over a boy's face but does not mention sex.

Maggie rescues me for a mid-morning walk. She listens, does not judge.

'I don't know what will happen when I hear his voice,' I blubber, fear gripping my throat.

'Why do you have to do this phone call?'

'I need supporting evidence,' I flounder, 'especially since my own mother won't help.'

'Mum's struggling, Cathy. Try to understand.' Her hand on my shoulder, Maggie is trying to 'be there' for me, *and* Mum. As she leaves, I don't let her see me cry. Force myself to swim in sea muck, wary of sharks, submerging into melancholy.

Back home, I look up the legal changes resulting from Australia's Royal Commission into Institutional Responses to Child Sexual Abuse. Mandatory reporting laws have been strengthened. It's now a crime to not report suspected child abuse. 'I knew nothing' is no longer good enough. What my parents failed to do forty years ago, through naivete, gender-biased blaming, and 'my lies', would see them jailed today. The new laws are not retrospective, but Mum doesn't know that 'Naughty Cathy' can't incriminate her.

Broody and mooching, I move laundry, from line to basket and back, in brief minutes of sunshine between squalls. As the sun strengthens, I find myself vacuuming, mopping, de-moulding, throwing out, remembering my mantra, burning off chem-fizz.

'Go surfing,' Vince pleads, exhausted by my cabin fever.

I take the forest road to Cressie Bay, where Loggerville's smear has not yet spoiled the northern beaches. I surf until opalescent bubbles waken my heart, filling me with sparkle-stars. Returning happy-tired, recounting every 'woo-hoo' wave, grateful for simply being. Surfing, my green pill, puts me firmly into Body. Joyful present.

I'm offered some school library days. Minimal harassment. I volunteer for Coastcare weeding and chat out my doldrums. Vince arranges a Queensland Covid border pass for his work, and we drive up to meet our beautiful grandchild – a blessing without baggage.

PTSD. What?

It seems I have fallen off the Victim Services system. To continue with the inappropriately matched counsellor, I must re-register. Their website sends me in circles; dissolves me in paranoia, so I call the Rape Crisis Service. Jewel is gone.

'A case manager from Victim Services should be helping you,' Heidi-the-operator says.

'I don't get to speak to humans,' I mumble.

She asks if I've made a doctor's appointment.

'Not yet,' I say, deflated, 'I'll have to go over everything *again*.'

Feeling chastened, I call the clinic. Am amazed that a doctor is available the next day. Having moved so often, I've not had a regular GP.

Dr J's blue eyes are calming. She assures me that Complex Post Traumatic Stress Disorder does not just affect war-weary soldiers. As she lists common symptoms, Body feels disturbing alignments, Brain pockets snippets to google later.

'Symptoms can be severe if the trauma happened a long time prior to triggering, because the denial is deeper,' says Doc. 'Normal memory goes to the frontal lobes where it's time-coded, but when your child-brain switched to high alert, memory storage became secondary to life protection …' Part of me is listening. '… memories can fracture and get trapped in the cerebellum, at the lower back of the head.'

Hot prickles jab my neck, but I know the creature now. I breathe it quiet.

Dr J breathes with me. 'OK?' she checks.

I show her two thumbs up, but don't speak, in case it wakes.

I can't stop the sobs though. Doc passes tissues, continues: 'When trauma is re-visited, stress hormones pump through the nervous system and your amygdala can mistake the past for the present.' Doc explains my flashbacks, headaches, trouble concentrating. 'The freeze response is a failsafe,' she says. 'It slows heart rate, reduces blood pressure, heightens hearing, increases pain tolerance, effectively disconnects brain from body.'

We talk about the amnesia, my out-of-body panic, my aversion to closed doors, certain smells and sounds. We talk about nightmares. Doc tells me I might feel angry, but there's only roiling, numbing sadness.

Doc J briefs me on EMDR; assures me I'll find answers, gives me a list of service providers. I don't remember half of what she says.

None of the EMDR providers are available for months. Some have closed their books. My senses are so dialled up, I can hear a door close up the street. Every noise. Every person in the supermarket. Every passing car. Every child near a road. Heart pounds the danger drum, ears slice open. Vince accidentally cuts himself in the kitchen; I can't even pass the first aid kit. The sight of blood, which used to mildly irk me, now forces recoil. A man near the river is going to kill me. I jump back, run away. Everything that used to be low-risk is now extreme, fire-alarm danger. It's called hypervigilance but I don't know that yet. I don't understand what's going on, inside or outside my body. Exhaustion feels headless.

Googling on my blue daybed, I learn that the inner ear connects to the nervous system. Even before sounds reach the brain, aural perceptions of threat trigger a gut response. *Doors locking.* Body short-circuited Brain before we even sensed trouble.

I think about Dorrigo. *Heartrate increased. Breathing shallowed. Body un-anchored.*

It's like seeing a shark. Everything slows down and speeds up at the same time. Nerd-me thinks Body is cool. Brain is shit-scared because Brain likes control.

Now Brain's think-button is skew-whiff. I forget where to load the Victim Services form, so I call the Rape Crisis Centre. Heidi obliges, does it for me. *Helpful.*

Lianne phones. 'I know you're angry …' she says. *Not helpful.* 'Mum and Dad did their best.'

Part of me, hovering in the distance, disagrees. I scan for anger … cannot find it.

'I'm not angry,' I defend, simultaneously questioning my words, and hers. I dig deeper, trying to ignite the flint-spark that isn't there. *I find only hurt.*

'Be careful.' Lianne raises her loyal flag. 'Mum doesn't need this at her age.'

Guilt scratches neck into a hot ache. Nausea churns through the rain. I sit on my lowest rung, puddling in tears that I deserve. Lianne's words shagpile me to the floor. *I am not a priority.* I am the culprit: the naughty, too-clever, overconfident girl.

Then I google Complex PTSD, am stunned to see myself mirrored in statistics: More than a third of women raped as children experience violent partner abuse as adults. *Not just me.* The duration of abuse determines severity. *Five years.* Dissociation during trauma predicts later-life PTSD … dissociative amnesia is common. *That too?* A child can fear for their safety without realising they're afraid. *Oh.* Recalling events as an adult can trigger intense physiological distress. I nod in recognition. *Police stations aren't ideal for head explosions.*

Staring out the window, I dive into sadness. Our garden, a nest of neglect: buffalo grass strangles hibiscus trees; the mondo path is infiltrated by oxalis. *How can I save what's left of caring?* I walk the beach, draw an Om, try to imagine The Impossible Phone Call.

Some hours – days? – later, Lianne phones again. We gurgle around the same plughole.

'Why can't Mum take one step towards me?'

'Let go,' she urges, as if it's normal, watching your sister drown.

Every single person contributes to this rape culture, unless they actively don't.

I empty out tears and high-volume dance to George Ezra's 'Blame It on Me'. I wash the dishes naked, spooning peanut butter into my gob.

Lianne calls back to apologise, tells me I need professional help.

'There's none available,' I shout-inform her.

She yell-retorts, 'Mum's doing it tough.'

Supportive, then suspicious; round-and-round we go. I understand. The clash of family. Legal and moral obligation. It's complicated.

Actually it's simple. An abused child needs help.

Rising to anger

April 28

Detective Herd calls, has approval for The Phone Call. Guts become cement. Thinking of his voice, a trapped fish darts from my ribcage. A punch of vile air escapes.

'How do I even begin?' I ask.

Herd stalls. 'We can't advise you what to say, Cathy.'

Wait. *What!?*

'Detective Balding said he'd help me prepare?'

Herd follows procedure: 'No.'

Braving up to speak with my abuser after forty years is entirely my weight to haul. A bull shark on a child's line. Panic builds a nest in me.

I walk along cliffs. Swim in grey sea where Dad's ashes cling to rocks. Deep-dive bristling skin into Black Lake. I try to eat but succumb to nauseated exhaustion. I sit in Pebbly Beach car park, watching roaring waves; trying to trust the process, desperately needing a map.

Somehow, I have to trust that I can steer without a chart. Ursula Le Guin's words ground me: 'There have to be long conversations with the dragon I ride. But however watchful and aware I am, I know I can never be fully aware of the currents that carry the boat, of where the winds beneath the dragon's wings are blowing.'

It's OK to not know direction or destination. Ursula soothes, but anxiety is older than dragons.

Lianne has one thing right: *I need help.* I check the Victim Services website for other counsellors, further afield. One, an hour's drive away, is experienced in child sexual abuse *and* EMDR ... unavailable for six weeks. Others are booked for months.

I call Dr J, who finds more names, most not registered with Victim Services. I'd have to pay; *am still paying* for his crimes.

Panic grips me in the rainy night; at 3 and 4 and 5 am. Untethered, I wander the house, gaze at cloud-coy moonlight in wind-battered banksias. Without sleep, teeth clench, ears ring. Depression stalks.

How long can I swirl in this toilet, fearing the flush?

In daylight, Mum invites me for tea. I don't want to go. Shouldn't. But I hold a crushed leaf of hope that she might co-operate.

'How aaare you?' She peers across her patio, beckoning.

'Not great Mum,' I sigh. 'I'm—'

She jumps in: 'I have to go to the dentist on the Gold Coast next week. Could you drive me?'

I ponder a quid pro quo. 'I ... might have more police stuff.'

Mum turns grey. 'You were so *fearless*, Cathy.'

Chin pulls face into neck. Body is affronted.

'Jesus Godfrey! (her favoured blaspheme) I should have locked you up,' she hollers.

Nausea sluices up my throat. Voice does not come: *Who should be locked up?*

She takes a swing at my silence. 'We didn't know it was sexual.'

What did you think 'it' was? I bite down my unspoken.

Mum tosses a litany of my sinful achievements: 'You did so well at school. Won awards. You could do anything.' Harsh light glints off her barbed offerings. We sink into the quiet bog of her strange kindness. Maybe she doesn't want to say the wrong thing and watch me leave. Maybe she believes naughty girls should be punished. I never know with her.

Mum eventually looks at her feet. At the stinking tide of repercussion. *I understand.*

She watches my tears and her face softens. 'It's good to see you cry,' she says, 'to know you're vulnerable.' *Broken.*

Confusion flushes down through floorboards from tingling arms and chest.

Breathe. Keep trying.

'Mum, when I first told you about the rape, you said you didn't act because you were afraid I would "elope".' I laugh weakly. 'I had to look that word up in the dictionary.'

Mum nods. 'Yes, I remember that.' *She remembers.* 'I could maybe write that down,' she whispers. Her tears, like shy fish, almost surface and I see in her eyes something like sorrow.

'It's just …' She closes the moment. 'I couldn't possibly go to that station. Your father's plane. My blood pressure. I'm nearly eighty …' Mum's parade of avoidance pours out, twisting her mouth back to bitter. 'No-one knew anything,' she insists.

My neck ignites but I open my mouth before throat squeezes shut.

'Mum, people knew.' *Louder now.* 'It would be helpful if you could *try* to remember,' I plead, then overstep: 'I know that turning a blind eye was the culture of the day but …'

She pounces. 'So I'm responsible for the *culture* now, am I?'

'You must've had your suspicions, Mum, him always being around … for five years!'

'You were infatuated, *in love* with him, and he with you.'

'And you were OK with that?' Pins and needles rush vomit into legs. 'I was *thirteen!*'

'You were older than that,' she hisses.

'Surely you and Dad spoke about it?'

'Your father never knew.'

I storm home, sealing the steam-vent before it scalds.

Lianne phones, says Mum is distressed at my anger. They misinterpret my silence. Hostility needs a dry run, to build the inferno. Crying girl keeps wetting the tinder. Besides, the little Buddhist in me knows; anger is no antidote.

This too will pass.

'Be gentle with Mum,' Lianne shames me. I want to shove my head into mud. Instead, I wallow out into the sad sea, wishing myself further. But I'm a strong swimmer. I scrape frozen feet home and nude-shower outside, singing: 'Hang these titties out in the breeze.' I eat four slices of Vince's butter cake, each with a swig of whiskey, then fall into bed – but don't sleep.

The next day I'm so fried-wired I cannot find myself in a mirror. I peer fretfully through curtains at a courier van and step suddenly back from the window. *Could be Perp. Perp's brother? What might he do to keep me quiet?*

Rocky calls. 'How's things?'

'Could be better.'

'With the police?'

I sigh. 'And Mum.'

'Oh? How *is* that?' Rocky knows Mum's dark flash of callous.

'She's stuck in Dad's-plane-crash.' I stuff the sob.

'Seriously? That was seven years ago!' He chokes. 'She *still* won't make a statement?'

'I'm not sure I want her statement,' I whisper, switching to speaker phone to wipe tears.

'You've got to be kidding!' Rocky snorts. 'It's bullshit that she "knew nothing". And denying she and Dad ever spoke about it? Utter rubbish!' He shouts. 'She has to step up for *this*, surely?'

Rocky challenges my need for maternal support, lets me feel innocence. I don't believe that Dad knew … that Mum won't assist. Rocky's words bring a fresh breeze; open a window. Then I slam it down on my fingers. *They did not know.*

'She's the only adult left standing,' he rants. 'It's not bloody good enough!'

He's furious. But my stronger habit of silence douses his flame.

'Do you want me to talk to her?' he asks, subdued.

'I don't have the energy for the fallout. They want to protect me.' I try to believe.

'Mum is protecting herself,' Rocky growls.

'I *lied*, Rocky.'

'You were a *child*,' he counters. 'Mum's lying now. You can't let her get away with this!' As if I can change her.

'Maybe she can't actually remember,' I say, suddenly protective. 'She's old and afraid.' Rocky has not seen her forgetful deteriorations.

'Bullshit,' he declares. 'She'll garden all day, doorknock the neighbourhood, join public protests, write letters to the paper, host a Coastcare party, take the ladies to lunch and rip into an off-leash dog owner, but she won't step into the police station for her raped daughter?'

Some part of me talks Rocky down from his beautiful high horse.

'Mum feels guilty,' I defend, kicking the last leg out from under my own chair.

'I could call Uncle John,' he offers. 'Maybe her brother could convince her.'

Off the phone, my ears burn as Rocky journeys Mum to the threshold of remorse. Maybe she'll hear him. She listens to men.

~

The next morning, I get work. Mum wants to talk. We agree to meet by the river on my lunch break. I scan for danger as I walk from school. After Rocky's urging, Mum says she'll 'write something' but insists 'it has to be what's right for *me*.'

Gut spasms.

'Mum, *you're* not on trial,' I try to reassure her.

'Oh,' in her catastrophising voice, 'you have no idea.'

My need for her statement pins me beneath the unforgiving blade: *Family*. I don't want to distress my widowed mother, nor stir old sibling schisms. Numb-dumb tries to convince myself: *They did not know.*

Slow steps

Hours fill with waiting: for counselling; for Mum's statement; for a way into The Horror Phone Call. I ponder Mum's legendary negativity, her challenges to my adult choices. I left the wrong jobs, travelled to the wrong countries, studied the wrong subjects, chose the wrong lovers, painted my walls the wrong colours, planted the wrong shrubs. When I contemplated entering local enviro-politics, she'd warned: 'Tacking Point won't support you'.

Lianne invites me to join her and Mum on a drizzly drive to Black Lake. Ignoring my wiser self, I go. We swim, eat sushi, drive back to the lighthouse as squalls blacken the Tacky sky. In a quiver of rainless quiet I urge my voice from the back seat, towards the *flumm-flumm* of windscreen wipers:

'Why didn't anyone *do* anything?'

Lianne's glare strikes the rear-view mirror. 'Why didn't *you* do anything?'

'What are you after?' swipes Mum.

'Justice?' I suggest.

'Cathy, no-one got justice in the eighties,' Judge Lianne warns, 'and you won't get it now.'

Shut up is all I hear.

'It's time to heal,' Mum simpers. 'Why bring this up now?'

Too gut-punched to speak, I silence the obvious: that reporting reduces the risk of further abuse, that *sexual abuse is not a private matter but a social epidemic!*

Later, when Vince gets home, I'm hiding in bath salts. 'Will you be home for the ant man tomorrow?'

'Why?' he grumbles in self-focus.

'So I won't be alone with a strange man!' I bawl, then brave up then puddle into panic. 'Because I can't handle ant chemicals and might have to go outside, which is more frightening.' Vince sees me unravelling, gives me a hug.

When the pest man arrives the next day, I hunch-hide along the beach path to the café. *Would Perp kill to keep his secret?*

On my third chai, Vince texts that ant man is finished and heads back to work. I rush home, jittery: think about The Phone Call, jump at every noise. Eyes dart to the windows, scanning for tradie trucks that don't belong. Waves of anxiety crash over me. Throat is spasmodic. Something rises from dark water; wants to choke me.

I duck outside with a basket of laundry and startle. Mum's on the back deck.

'How aaare you?' She doesn't wait for an answer. 'You should weed that garden,' she rambles as I rapid-peg things, focused on The Phone Call, on what I should say to a rapist.

'Well, I have a lunch date,' she announces, 'I can't stay.'

Relieved when her skirt swishes up the street, I rush inside and double-check the locks, wondering how long it might take for ants to consume a house.

May 1

Life has collapsed into The Imminent Phone Call. I practise openings, try to think of a reason for calling. A pretext. 'You raped me, you bastard.' *No. He'll hang up.* 'It's Cathy Byrne.' *No. He might hunt me down or threaten Mum.* 'Hey, remember Tacky High? Long time, no sex.' To escape my cynical frenzy, I walk up the beach, away from people.

Not too far away, just in case.

I keep looking over my shoulder. I find a stick and scrape possible words into sand, then scuff them away. I remember trying to speak to him once before, on this beach. I push stick into palm and slap my legs, to stay in Body. Say aloud: 'Feet in the sand. Face in the breeze. I reclaim this place.' I puff out sandy exhales and stare at the horizon for … *How long?* Look down. I've drawn a turtle. Smile; realise I'm breathing, slow and deep.

Then it comes: *I heard your mum died.* That's it! My pretext.

In days that follow, I try to get beyond this opening. I bullet-point myself into a tense ball, draw more turtles, screw up copious notes and panic-puff along the beach. Overwhelmed, I full-body flinch at a hammer-noise from a building site. Body senses danger everywhere.

What will happen when I hear his voice? What power might he still have?

Lianne phones. 'You don't have to do this. Wait until you've had counselling.' She doesn't understand my urgency.

'I've waited forty years!' *Momentum is everything.*

'Take a break,' she urges.

'What, so all the witnesses can die?' I holler.

'There are no witnesses,' she reminds me.

I want it over.

Later, I listen to Vince's work woes: profitability, deadlines, more territory, less support. 'They're assholes,' I affirm. 'There's no justice,' I monotone. He has no idea how close I am to dissolving. He has to leave town again.

Nausea surges when I see Mum walking past our banksia hedge. I step back from the window, call Dr J and get more names. Try the Victim Services website again, which spins its loading wheels and crashes.

I call Detective Herd. 'Can you give me any clue about what to say?'

She hears my desperation. 'I can't give you advice …' The detective holds firm. 'But I think you know what we need.'

Actually, no! I don't, I mind-scream. The creature in my throat begins to squeeze. *Someone. Somewhere. Please help!*

Brain fogs and Body forgets. I find myself floating on motes; in the garage, the supermarket carpark, walking up the school stairs. Before the bell, I search 'help for child sexual abuse' and land on the website for Australia's National Redress Scheme. They have counsellors! *Maybe they can help?* There's nowhere to make a private call. I use the Distance Education cubicle. Kids keep opening the door, throwing rubbish in. I can't get through. A garbled voice-message says they'll call back. School rules say I can't leave my phone on. The day blurs into nausea, extreme noises, mounting terror.

May 4

Heidi from the Rape Crisis Service phones, checking up, caring. She tells me about a therapy group. I dislike group work but call immediately.

Heartfelt House is a non-profit local health service. Founded by a survivor who couldn't find support, its eight-week program starts today.

Six of us meet in a rambling 1950s house with a quiet garden, cosy chairs. A facilitator encourages us to chat, drink tea, share insights. *Not details.* Here, in synchrony with brave, broken women, my rivers overflow. I sob with strangers and another Tacky High graduate. We coax ourselves towards glimpses of light. It's healing, not being the *only* crazy.

Back home, Gemma, my Kal-school-mum friend, calls in for a walk. I tell her I've been to the police, try to explain my head explosion. She listens patiently and 'cannot comprehend' my mother. We drink tea and cackle about the insane world. Laughing helps. Normalcy helps. Connection is a lifeline.

Still, I turtle-sleep.

At some point, Vince returns. I wake at midnight in a terror-sweat, wondering who's beside me. I feel the shutdown alerts. Puff-breathing. Prickling neck … about to freeze, when Vince pats my leg.

'It's OK,' he soothes, 'I'm here.'

I keep a smile handy for Vince, try to maintain our usual amount of sex – fearful of flashbacks. Fearful of telling him too much, in case it overwhelms me. *Us.* I try to live as normal, but nothing is. When we walk, he prattles about his stresses; distracting me from my own. I'm inside-out now. Raw. I practise Phone Call lines. Write and rewrite them and cry.

Fear consumes. Disorients. Disintegrates. Cuts me into pieces that I stuff into ears, behind falling walls. The sound of scissors. The frightening churn burns gut. Throat.

What will Perp do?

Later that morning, my free 'not-a-good-therapy-choice' counsellor says I've been removed from her caseload. I don't know what that means or how it happened.

'I didn't cancel,' I splutter. 'I haven't found anyone else …' She hangs up. And I hang upside down, wriggling on a sharp hook, waiting to be devoured.

Why won't anyone help?

I burrow under blankets, listening for telltale noises. The sun is setting. I hear the wet slap of feet as a surfer jogs past, leg rope clapping at the board, his breath husky-chilled from a good session. I know that sound. Then there's only the rise and fall of my own breath, the sound of sea: slow in, long out. My chest murmurs the rhythm of waves, until even that fades. Time fills the spaces. Everything stills.

I settle, not-thinking, as sleep hovers. Heavy in body, warm in bed, I notice my own presence. Just me. Without warning, my solar plexus clenches, lifting my whole torso up off the bed. Shoulder blades pull back. Rib cage opens to the ceiling. Glutes tighten. Chin juts, baring my neck. *Fish pose.* Then, a choking lump rises through chest, into throat. I expunge an invisible cat-furball that tastes of sour metal.

It will be weeks before I learn about how the polyvagal nervous system flushes trauma-toxins. Today, it's a shock. Brain is not coping. Body is truly weird.

Bruising realisation

May 7

Anxiety rots me. Sleep-deprived, feeling isolated, I re-call every counsellor on the Victim Services website and on Dr J's list. *None available.* I call the Rape Crisis Centre. *Pretext phone call: What do I say?* Heidi is unavailable. I track down an old flatmate who once worked in rape support. She finds a Legal Aid adviser who calms me down.

'Try not to be so hard on yourself. You might dissociate.' *That word again.* 'Do you have a close friend or family member who knows how to help if that happens?'

'No.' I barely understand it myself.

'Don't worry if the pretext call doesn't work,' she says.

If it doesn't work? He'll come for me!

A vice grips my chest. Body must move. *Walk.*

On the beach, Heidi calls back, steps me through Phone Call possibilities, asks me to think about the kind of person he is. *Ego-Man-Boy.*

'What might he respond to? What information do *you* need? Ask what he remembers. Ask for an apology. Be assertive, not aggressive. Have a reason to call. Say you want to chat as an adult, a grown-up.'

Oh. I'm grown up! My air-balloon fills. I breathe more easily.

'Have you found a counsellor yet?' she asks.

'I have an E-DNR? appointment, but it's a month away.'

'Oh no!' She bursts the balloon and my heart jazz-beats a disturbing

'TiddlyBom' flutter that feels like a trapped bird. 'EMDR is not approved by the justice system. Some psychiatrists claim it's like hypnosis. It isn't, but that therapy can be used against you in court.'

Wait! *What?!*

'But …' the TiddlyBom starts flapping erratically. 'A Victim Services counsellor *and* my GP recommended … It's taken ages to get an appointment. You're saying I can't use it?' I spiral towards ear-screams.

'For now …' Heidi tries to dismantle my arrhythmic chest-grenade. 'Cathy, just focus on the phone call. Don't worry about the outcome. Try to eat. Get some sleep. Today, you should do something you love.'

I will worry. I won't eat or sleep. But I know what I love.

I grab my mini mal, drive to Cressie, away from river-murk. There's no wind, but my head is frothing. Distracted, I recite my grown-up lines. *And if he says this? And if he says that?* I stick my head in like a turtle, cooling my neck, trying to calm down, rehearsing counter responses. *When should I say who I am? What if he hangs up and comes for me?*

It's rare for me to be a fizz-mess in the ocean. I try to focus on sun sparkles, on mantra. *Breathe.* Face to sky. Wait for the wave. Turn. Paddle.

I take off near the rocks, cut back to avoid the crowd, and as the wave hollows and speeds up, I shuffle both feet to the nose. Hips forward, chest up, arms out, like a Jesus, I fly across the healing 'woo-hoo' wall of joy! As the wave loses momentum, I descend into bubbles, still standing. Unthinking, I sink slowly into cleansing Schweppes.

BANG! A *craaack*. Face pain.

I scoop for the surface, gasp as air hits my lungs, try to open my eyes, but my right cheek is already ballooning. *What hit me?* Somehow, my board rebounded the sharp fin into my face.

Get to safety!

Clutch leg rope, drag board under me, take the next white-water in. A man looks at me strangely, moves away from dripping blood.

Through my left eye, I see a female longboarder on the beach. Focus on her, hold off dizzy. She sees me, drops her board and comes running.

'Exthcusthe me,' I slur through bruised balloons, '… am I bleeding?'

'Oh yes,' she says, 'that looks nasty.' She watches as I unravel. 'Are you OK?'

It is everything. The timing. The shock. *The Torturous Phone Call.* Everything from the last few months collapses me into sobs.

'Um … I'm … I might be in shock,' I manage, floundering inside my bigger drama.

She drags my board up the beach, offers to drive me home.

Empathy from a stranger!

If anyone is kind to me right now, I will fragile into breakdown. The surfer waves over a couple with a phone, who offer me water. In the time of Covid, I drink their kindness.

They all think I should go to hospital. But I don't want to put anyone out. They track down Vince. He'll come.

They assist me to a picnic table, get ice from the café, show me a photo of my billowing yellow-blue cheekbone, gashed with glistening red.

Blood-shy, I tell them I'm fine. *I'll cope.*

Shaken and shivering, I nod to reassure passers-by. Two fat blokes give friendly advice. Lifetime clubbies, they've seen it all. Another older guy walks right up to me and reaches his hand towards my cheek. When I pull back, he says: 'I'm not going to touch your face.'

Then, as I let my guard down, he grabs my chin in one hand and pulls my face-skin downwards with his thumb. *What the …?*

The blue-ball incident flashes. A surge of panic. *Can't breathe!*

Here in my usually-strong space, I belittle into silence. I want to yell, *'Fuck off!'* But no voice emerges. Instead, I shrink as he manhandles. I hate him, and my little self who disallows her voice. He shirks off without a word, having satisfied himself.

Arrogant men think they're helping.

That's the key, I realise: *ask Perp for help!*

Shock-tears smear iced blood down my lumpy face until Vince pulls up. 'I couldn't bring anyone to drive your car,' he apologises.

I brave up and Vince follows as one eyed, under ice, I drive through pain fog. But I have my way forward, into The Imminent Phone Call.

Mother mess

Soft humidity domes the morning as Mum accompanies my purpling face on a timid walk. Loggerville's brown rain-smear is trapped in the river by the high tide. I envy-watch surfers in aqua tubes off Tacking Point.

'You should give it up.' Mum uses her soft-command voice.

'The joy of my life?' I scoff. 'I've never had a face surf injury before, Mum. I was just distracted.'

'Why?' she asks. I don't answer. She won't comprehend my Phone Call fear.

A brahminy kite (Dad's special bird) glides by, feathering space, creating an amnesty for shared histories. I wonder how long these fragile airwaves can carry the weight of un-remembering. When the next squall comes – and it will – truth will thunder through us.

But I leave that heavy conversation for later. Instead, hoping for mirth, I share my story of yesterday's random intruder: '… then, Mr Man-titlement stuck his hand in my face, without permission!' I scoff, expecting shared indignance, but Mum, stony-faced, stretches the silence; her lips, zip-locked. *Nothing.*

I know she heard me. Sadness drapes over untended wounds. *Outrage is futile.* I let the void gape, hoping she'll sense my desperation for solidarity. Then Mum points out to sea.

'See that container ship?' She closes the opportunity, refusing to acknowledge a man's actions as inappropriate. I shut my crying girl inside.

Another little drowning.

Mother's Day, May 9

Maggie, cooking at Mum's, wants saccharine 'get along' for Mother's Day. I go early to move chairs and tables, chop veggies, make a salad. I take gifts of fruits and flowers from my garden, trying to move beyond yesterday's black hole. It must be tough on her, my mess, years later.

The kettle boils. I tea-gulp painkillers into my bulbous face.

Mum waves a novel she's just finished reading, in disdain. 'Self-indulgent, poorly written ... by a *woman*, of course.' Her anti-feminist jab elicits a puff of stale air from my pressure cooker chest, removing the vocal blockage.

'Mum, why didn't you say anything about the man who grabbed my bleeding face?'

A curled lip. 'Oh, I don't know anything about that.'

'I told you yesterday,' I prompt. She focuses on selecting a tablecloth. 'Your reaction was zero.' I lay the kindling, fuel the fire. 'Do you have a shred of empathy?'

'Maybe he was just being helpful,' she goads.

'Maybe he was giving me "unwanted attentions".' I use her-era language.

'Well ...' She ruffles her skirt, makes suggestive eyes. 'You might've looked like you desired those attentions.' My eyebrows shoot skyward.

'He was just another entitled man doing whatever he wanted,' I spit, dumbfounded.

'I see you're having trouble.' She serves cold empathy. Then, attempting camaraderie, tries on my-era language: 'Maybe he was just an arsehole.'

'Halle-*frickin*-lujah, Mum!' I yell. 'All I've ever needed is for you to see the arsehole in the story.' Then, Maggie's *get a new beach bra* command flies into my mashed-up brain. 'I suppose you also think a woman's swimwear determines if men rape their wives?'

Mum loses anchor, swings out wide. 'Let's talk about women who wear bikinis that show off their behinds!' I look at her, astonished.

I surf in boardshorts. 'It's where my head went,' she excuses, then garnishes with melodrama: 'My blood pressure!'

'Happy Mother's Day,' I monotone.

She gets teary. Her shoulders slump. Head down, watching her pigeon-toed feet, she reminds me of my grandmother. I crawl into my mouse-hole.

'Mum, I don't want to cause you pain. I know the police station is traumatic for you.'

'I just want you to move on,' she pleads. We hug. Then she starts again: 'I don't remember anything … I had three other children … We didn't know it was sexual.'

Afraid I would 'elope'. She contradicts herself, protects herself, from me.

It's Mother's Day. I remember my role. 'Mum, you gave up a lot for us.' I gently hold her shoulders. 'You don't have the energy to deal with my shit. But … I thought you'd stand with me and … make a statement.'

Tears vaporise. Mum's face burnishes with something akin to revulsion. 'You …!' she roars, stabbing a gnarled finger into my chest. 'You were different. Lianne was quiet and shy. Maggie cried, but you …' she spits, 'you always aimed so high, did whatever you wanted.' Her brutality mutes me. A mudlark shrieks me into pieces.

I am cut off, an amputation, tingling with phantom connections.

Fear binds Mother to the teenager she still perceives as me, beyond her comprehension: always too far out to sea, doing too well at everything, learning through curious experimentation. For Mum, life is a *studied practice*. Like meals, her days are a carefully controlled, apportioned balance of flavours, a limited palate. She could never celebrate my 'wild' gobbling of life; my serendipitous mayhem.

Inevitable, that such a horribly spontaneous offshoot must one day bring shame. Just like her own 'wild' sister did at sixteen, with an out-of-wedlock child, adopted out, away from the good Catholics. My abuse triggers old troubles for her, depletes the Mother-Love.

'I gave up everything,' she bitters. 'And You!' she snarls. 'You've been controlling me since you were four years old.' Bewilderment punches breath from Body.

Mother blames *me* for her housewife life? She does not regret for me, but for her own loss? Compassion desperately tries to understand. But can't.

'In my day, there was no choice; you married, had babies, stayed home. I had to stretch a kilo of mince across a week.' She despises women who are not frog-marched on that journey, thinks we can't appreciate her sacrifice.

Is that why Thirteen deserves what she got?

Her melee exhausts me into another dazed realisation: to defend herself, Mother must malign my character, paint me as a provocative teenager, and now, a 'damned feminist'.

Stunned, I walk home to ice reality into my face. I can barely open one eye, but I see clearly now: I cannot rely on Once-Mother. *I'm stronger alone. No-one will help me, but me.*

Back home, I rewrite my notes.

I am ready.

Some Justice

6

The Phone Call

May 11

I get an appointment with another 'free' Victim Services counsellor. Yvonne wears flowy trousers, doodles while I talk. She's not trained in EMDR, which I medically need, but legally cannot do. Her office has real sunlight, a comfy chair and a picture that I chatter about and immediately forget. Clutching my spiky ball, I re-tell my awfuls. Again. Cold and cry-shuddering, I ask to walk by the river.

'I'm more confident now,' I bravado about The Treacherous Phone Call, about asking Ego-Man-Boy for help. *How will I react to his voice?*

Concerned I might dissociate, Yvonne comes to the police station. Upstairs, Detective Balding seems unconvinced when I explain my swollen face: 'My surfboard came off second best.' Focused, Detective Herd says I must be alone on the call. Breath shallows.

'Is that a deal-breaker?' Herd asks, watching me rip off my shoes because my toes are cramping. I clutch at feet, rub my legs. Sip water. *Some men kill to keep secrets.*

'I'll be right outside,' Yvonne reassures. My hands shake.

'I can do it.' Brave Cathy steps inside a crowded office: big chair behind a giant desk swamped with files; a cabinet stacked with boxes; a whiteboard crammed with names and court dates.

Robert John Cunning is not written there. Not yet.

Something is writhing inside me as we stand around a device on the desk.

Detective Herd presses 'record,' reads out a surveillance form, asks if I want to contact the accused.

'No!' shouts Thirteen. Herd looks at me patiently. 'I mean yes. Sorry.'

'It's OK,' she reassures, re-records.

Nausea burbles. Throat clamps. *Once I say my name …*

Through teary blur, Detective words jumble into jibber.

'Do you understand the document?'

'Yes?' I mindlessly sign three pages, giving some kind of consent. Herd invites me into the Big Chair. Blu-Tacked to the wall, a newspaper clipping shows Herd on a small boat, holding a large fish. I time-waste talk about Vince's boat while Herd attaches the recorder to a No-Caller-ID phone.

'No-one answers calls from unknown numbers,' I protest.

'That's all we have,' she says firmly. 'Shall we proceed?'

Pause. Breathe. Nod.

'Let's catch a shark!'

Detective Herd dials the number, presses record, leaves the room. *Click.* Door closed. Fear avalanches down Body, into gut. The call goes to voicemail; Perp says his name. Phooff, air is thrown from lungs. Blue spikes press into clammy palms. We try again. Voicemail. I go outside and pace, practise abdominal breathing but forget I even have a mantra. Yvonne is nowhere. I sit in a café, order a scone that I don't eat.

Go back.

This time he answers. 'I'm in class!' His growl chases my mind down confused hallways. 'Who is this?'

Shoosh-shoosh. Danger! Do not speak your name.

'You're … in class?' I'm alarmed. *Still has access to children?*

Body prickles as Brain re-wires packets of panic; synapses plug into weird slots, sparking neon-blue pulses behind squeezed eyes. *Say something!*

'It's about … your mum,' I stutter. Hand grabs throat.

'Well, you're calling from a private number, and you didn't leave a message.' He's cross. 'I'm on playground duty in forty minutes. Call back then.' Mr Angry hangs up.

Ants scurry from my gizzards, into pores. Solar plexus knots. Head pounds. Furball-*phoofs* launch from my throat.

Herd steps in, takes the recorder out, as I sit, bouncing legs. Both detectives return. 'He's in class!' I shout. 'I thought that taskforce confirmed he wasn't teaching?'

Balding frowns. 'What taskforce?'

I take a deep breath, bridle-bite my words. 'Years ago, my brother contacted a police taskforce, established after *The Teacher's Pet* podcast. They confirmed Perp was no longer teaching,' I hiss. 'Well … he's teaching!' I jump up, gun-click my right index-finger knuckle and stomp twitchy legs.

'Teaching in Queensland,' states Balding, as if border-crossing transforms a pedo.

'It's concerning,' offers Herd, a mother. 'You're a teacher, Cathy,' she refocuses. 'Should we call while he's on playground duty?'

This is my only chance.

Brain interrupts. 'He'll be surrounded by noisy kids. He won't have five minutes, won't admit anything,' I fluster, guarding embers of hope.

Balding smothers the fire. 'If he mishears anything it will be dismissed in prosecution.'

We arrange to try again at the end of the school day.

I can't go home because I don't want to scald our visiting granddaughter's tender skin with panic. I walk the river path, contemplating this ridiculous process.

If I say my name, I'm a target. He knows Mum's house. This is madness.

One woman is killed every week by a current or former partner. I don't know if Perp is still the porn star of his own horror show.

I have laid bare my truth and trauma, to police, to family (again), to various counsellors and to my doctor. I have submitted a formal statement and waited sixty-three days in increasing distress. Now, I'm supposed to get him to talk. It's ALL up to the victim: the least valued object in the justice equation.

My only chance.

I go back to the station and wait. Ask: 'Why can't *he* be brought in for a mediated conversation, so *I* can be protected?'

Balding reminds me: Perp's innocence is assumed; the child rapist has a right to privacy.

'Ten minutes in a room with a non-uniformed counsellor. I'd get him to confess.'

'It doesn't work like that,' Balding says, clicking his tongue.

Then make it work better.

~

At 3:30, we try again. Five times. No answer. The No-ID phone is a waste of time.

'We'll try again,' encourages Detective Herd. I'm not sure I can.

I drive home nerve-weary; watching cars, wondering if Perp already has my address. I shake out my whole body, slough off the yuck, before opening our front door. A sleeping-baby cuddle is restorative.

I have tea with Vince's older girls, Lee and Mikah, who've generously driven the precious bundle from Brisbane. Vince has probably told all three children what little he knows. Kal's texts 'just to say hello' have become more frequent. Thankfully no-one asks for details. We're all dog-tired. I hot shower and sit outside, watching stars spin in a bigger drama: universe creating, destroying, twisting forever, as Vince snores.

Married to fear

I lock my doors and double-check. Paranoia peers through the banksias, stains my curtains, creeps into every sinew. *Was I this afraid back then?* Body's thermometer is erratic. I boil, then freeze-boil. I flinch when a car brakes, when a knife scrapes, when a pressure hose starts two houses down. I am a crazy person; waiting, jumping, hosting hostile ants. And there's something else now; a sense of inevitable, inexplicable doom. *It's waiting.*

I'm relieved that I know how to play dead. Maybe that's how I've lived my adult life. Standing in the shower, eyes closed, I startle when Vince steps in.

After, we stroll the beach path. A car door slams and I cower, cover my hearing ear, taste sulphur. Vince gets me home but has to travel for work. I cheery-fake wave him off, already rationing food so I won't have to shop.

I step back inside, check the locks again. Alarmed. Overwhelmed.

How did I get so damaged?

Between sunrises, only half my brain sleeps, like a dolphin. I spend a few days in panic-prison, prepare for another night alone; descend into semi-waking nightmare …

I'm in Perp's third apartment, under white ceiling, brown beams. The wedding has finished, and there's leftover wine. He's at the fridge. Perp? Where is Vince? Whose wedding? I'm on that couch, looking across at the man with a white shirt on, a bow tie. I can't breathe. Can't see who I married.

I've dreamed this before. On my real wedding night, twenty years ago, I woke, sweat-staining my actual marriage bed. Confusion weighs my chest. Who *did* I marry? I fall deeper.

I watch the man turn slowly. Am petrified-desperate to see. Vince did not wear a bow tie. I never married Perp, did I? Who is it? Let me see his face. Then, an umbrella pushes under my ribs, blocking air. White shirt and … a sucking noise as the umbrella pierces my sternum.

I explode off the bed, legs kicking free.

'What?' Vince asks, sitting up suddenly.

It's morning. I'm home. He's home. It's 2021. I married Vince. Only Vince.

I sob all over him.

'You need help,' he gentles, holding me. 'Talk to me.'

Over breakfast, I finally tell Vince … about the Unsuccessful Phone Call; the Victim Services' paperwork debacles; my shocked nervous system, the lack of support from Once-Mother. He's furious, but mother-and-son-in-law flare ups won't help. 'I'll handle Mum,' I warn and shuffle him off to work. I get a late work call. Need the distraction.

As I sign on, I get a call back from the National Redress Scheme. I'm grateful that it exists, but like any community service, it's over-subscribed. Underfunded. Libby, a legal adviser, asks questions as I sit in the very un-private staffroom. *He used to work here.* Throat chokes as I whisper-spell Perp's name: 'Rob-ert J-John … *Cunning.* C-U-NN-ING.' *Phooopth.*

I'm confused when Libby says I'd be 'better off in a *civil* case' because 'they're resolved faster'. I don't understand; I'm deep within a *criminal* process. The bell goes. She'll call later.

Back home by 3:55, I step in and lock the door. My phone rings.

Check the door. Answer the call.

'Is this a good time?' Before I respond, Libby introduces a counsellor on another line and asks: 'Do you have a current will?'

'Are you asking because he might kill me?'

They weren't expecting Ms Paranoid.

'Oh, no!' Libby explains. 'The question is for the purpose of financial compensation.'

I haven't thought about that.

'The police won't be able to protect me once I say my name,' I yell.

No response. *Don't they have other cases like mine? About life. Not money.*

They try to calm me. 'You should discuss the phone set-up with the police,' says the counsellor, as if I haven't tried.

No wonder people discontinue legal processes on rape and domestic violence.

The systems aren't designed to protect. All effort, all risk; it weighs victims into silence.

~

I call Detective Herd. 'What if, when I say my name, he hangs up and comes for me?'

'I've never had anyone make contact from a pretext call,' she tries reassurance, 'and if he does, we'll take care of it.'

How? If he appears on my deck with a gun, can I call the station and 'Press five for emergency-teleport-away-from-murderous-arsehole'? I imagine starting a survivor vigilante group. *Machetes and machine guns*! This predator has lived without consequence for his crimes. I have paid, over and over, with my terror, grief, re-victimisation, inability to deal with confrontation, changing jobs, loss of income, running, hiding, staying quiet. I buried myself in a glacier that's now thawing, exposing me to threat. After years of taking the blame, I have finally done the 'right' thing and stepped into the ice-bath. Now, I am tired beyond belief, hideously nauseous, anxious to the point of insanity, shaking with fear.

The ultimate karma of the risk-taker?

No. Justice is not worth dying for. I should shut up while I'm alive.

Dadirri

At group counselling, I tell other survivors that my face is only a surf bruise. Our session opens with a beautifully slow video from the 2021 Senior Australian of the Year. Dr Miriam-Rose Ungunmerr-Baumann presents the Indigenous concept of Dadirri, Deep Listening: 'A quiet awareness that connects us with nature and nurtures wellbeing.' Dr Miriam-Rose teaches us to be patient in sorrow, to wait for the right time and allow plenty. 'Even though the tree is scarred, and the leaves scorched, its roots can be reborn. Grief ought not be hurried. Healing comes when it is ready.'

At home, I watch and re-watch the video.

Keep going.

May 14

Dr Miriam's words rinse me as I recite lines for the Try-Again Phone Call. 'We cannot hurry the river,' she reminds me. I walk calmly beside Tacky's dark ebb. It washes away my desire for an outcome as I focus on breathing; on simply being present.

Look up. A sliver of moon floats above pink-orange sunset dollops and gently bobbing boats. Armoured in Dadirri's quicksilver, I step into the station.

Detective Balding sets me up at the big desk. This time, the phone has an actual number. He dials and leaves the room. Time telescopes, bending hope around me and I'm slow-motion paddling when a dark shape looms. Hand squeezes blue spikes.

Alone with the predator.

~

[*The following conversation is reconstructed from detailed notes. The transcript is protected due to privacy laws.*]

'Hello, this is Rob.'

'Rob Cunning?' asks Big Brave.

'Yes, who's speaking?'

Careful.

'I was sorry to hear about your mum passing.'

'That's OK.'

Slow exhale.

'It's Cathy Byrne.'

'Caa-thy! How aaare you?' He's pleasantly surprised, as if hearing from a long-lost friend. I want to vomit, but I breathe the river.

Use your notes. Ask Ego-Man-Boy for help.

'Actually, I'm not doing so well.'

'Oh, why not? What's haappened?' *As if he cares!*

'I'm having some anxiety issues related to what went on between us … I was hoping you might be able to help?' My voice kicks up at the end, a terrified mouse squeak.

'Oh …'

'I had to lie to everyone, so you're the only person I can talk to … I was hoping we could speak freely, as adults, so I can move on with my life.'

'OK.' A gut-wrenching pause. 'I'm so sorry.'

Stick to purpose. Don't alarm him.

'I was worried … about the photos you took. Do they still exist?'

'No, I lost all that when I went overseas.'

'Lost? Or …?'

'I took care of them.'

How? *Don't get distracted.*

'Well … that's good to know. Was it a polaroid camera, or …?'

'I would've taken the film to the chemist.'

Someone else saw. Suppress vomit. *Keep going.*

'I remember at your parents' that first time …' *you raped me*, I want to yell. *Don't accuse.* '… we had sex, I bled on the towels. You wrapped them up. Did you have to lie to *your* mum?'

'No.'

'What about your friend in England? Did you lie about how old I was?'

'No. Why would I? He was in England!'

'Weren't you worried you'd get me pregnant?'

'That was never my intention. I cared too much about you.' Choke the puke. 'That's why we used protection.' *We.*

'Not for a while we didn't, not in Boundary Lane.'

'Was that the little side street?'

'Yes. I took so many risks … I was so stressed.'

'I'm sorry, it should never have happened.' *No.*

Keep going. Breathe the river.

'What about sex at Back Beach? I was so late home, had to tell so many lies. Do you remember?'

'I don't remember that, but I remember Limeburners Beach.'

School musical camp. What happened there? *Stick to your notes.*

'You came on a family camping trip. We went for a walk to see the moon and you told me about "blue balls", that you'd die if you didn't have sex.'

'It's a real thing, you know,' he insists, even now.

Revolting. I press *my* blue ball into thighs.

'Do you remember holding my head? I couldn't breathe.'

Should I mention the horrible gag reflex I've had all my life?

'I'm sorry. I don't remember that. I'm not denying it happened, but …' He clears his throat. 'When my wife tries to pleasure me like that, she always asks "Why don't you come?". It might have something to do with …'

It haunts him.

Be careful. He'll find you.

'At least I got to tell Dad. He was horrified.'

'I thought your father knew,' he says. Vomit surge. *Clench muscles. Lift frosted feet.*

Dad didn't know. *Stay focused.*

'I thought that's what you wanted,' he justifies. Gut lurches years of metal-sweet bile.

Breathe.

'What do *you* remember?' I ask.

'I remember it all went to shit after that phone call.'

'What phone call?'

'At the soccer club awards night. I won "Best and Fairest" for …' He says some club that I don't catch. 'I drank too much, called your house and spoke to your sister, Lianne? or Maggie? I thought it was you, said how much I loved you. Everything changed. Your parents came to see my parents. I was supposed to back off.'

My parents knew? When? A flicker of outrage gets coated in numb. *Keep going.*

'You say you cared, but you kept hurting me. What was I to you?'

'I don't know. I can't explain it. I'm so sorry, Cathy.'

'What are you sorry for?' Guts writhe.

'The whole affair. It should never have happened.'

'I was so young,' I whisper, careful not to say how young.

'Yes, and I was an immature young man.' *An excuse.*

His was not a one-off error of 'immaturity'. It was the premeditated grooming of a child. An elaborate manipulation of me, my parents, teachers, siblings, friends, for years.

Body freezes into a stiff board. The sex position. I manage to emit small nose puffs so Grown-Up can keep moving her mouth.

'Do you have children?'

'Yes.'

'Can you imagine how you'd feel if this happened to them?'

'I can, yes, because … my daughter was raped when she was twenty.'

He knows what he did.

Sympathy shoves me as the shark-shadow circles. *Stay still.*

'I sometimes wonder if it was like that,' he confesses, 'with us.'

Throat corks acid-vomit; decades-old truth. *Raped.*

Then Thirteen explodes from my chest: 'That's *exactly* the word I'd use!'

'I'm so sorry,' he repeats quickly; his voice urgent. *Suspicious?* He wants to get off the phone. I want him to realise his damage.

'So, after forty years, I get an apology?' Throat seizes.

'Yes. Good luck.' He hangs up.

~

I lurch for the door, heaving furballs.

Detective Balding offers to drive me home. I'm gripping the dizzy-wall, shaking my head. 'I need to walk.'

The river slow-breathes me as silken water rinses my expectations. Dadirri.

I walk until I'm calm enough to drive. Somehow, my car follows its headlights home. Time does its accordion trick as Body stares down darkness in the garage. Vince doesn't come to the door. He's drunk his usual whole bottle of shiraz and passed out in front of the TV.

'You OK?' he burps, passing me in the dark kitchen.

'Don't know,' I manage.

I take a long, hot shower. Vince is snoring when I climb into bed.

May 15

I dream on Saturday morning, a repeat of a meditation vision from my mid-twenties …

A black stone, circular medieval tower, tapers to a metre-high crumbling turret. I kneel beside it on icy ground, scraping rubble. The mortar has thinned to dust, but the stones are heavy and my bleeding fingers sting with frost. I clear enough to find a person huddled inside, covered in blood-stained bandages. I unwind disintegrating cloth to discover my 13-year-old self, then I flood with overwhelming compassion. For me.

At 25, when I was still overseas (not coming home), a meditation master helped me to find my damaged child. Then, I'd stopped self-medicating with alcohol, tried to become the most compassionate, ethical person I could be. I shaved my head so the light (I knew was inside me) could better feel the sky. After a few years of meditation and yoga, I remember the feeling, arising unbidden; real forgiveness, for the unforgivable – for him. It came with a strong sense of knowing that I was bigger than any crime against me and that my own perspective helps create my future.

I thought I'd freed the waif. Back then, I didn't understand how deep my loss, how Body hid shame and fear. I left my mute child-self down in the ice. Got on with life.

Now, at 53, I realise I still have rescue work to do.

I wonder if we're ready. If I'll have the strength to carry her. Her me?

~

The morning after Perp's confession, I lie in warm sun and sense my younger selves. Thirteen was blamed. Fifteen was trapped. Eighteen left town. Twenty-Two escaped the Sydney Beast. But Thirty-Three came back to Tacky Point, got married, had a child, tried to rebuild a life.

I'm guilting myself for waiting so long.

'Tea?' Vince invites me into the day. We stuff our backpacks and walk north. We're training for a Tassie wilderness trek. Something to look forward to.

I'm imagining all this will be over soon.

Am I safe?

By midday, the humidity feels ominous. I hang the laundry haphazardly, fighting obedience. Body scans for intruders. Brain is jittery.

I call the station. My temperature plunges. Teeth grind and chatter.

'Was the phone call enough?'

'Be patient,' says Balding. 'We need approval to arrest and extradite.'

As if Queensland is a remote country. As if Perp is not merely hours away.

'Am I safe?' I panic-ask.

'He didn't sound the type to track you down,' says Balding.

Pedophiles don't look, sound, or act in-type. No-one knows what they're capable of.

I trust nothing. No-one. Vince notices my sensitivity; to noises, smells, raw meat, TV violence. I avoid sex even more than usual.

On Monday, Vince has to leave town. I could whiskey myself under, but I'm on crimson alert. Instead, I stay at Maggie's. She kindly cooks, acts normal. We chat of nothings.

Back home, I'm constantly scanning. Every noise, every passing vehicle. I'm wired so tight, the metal in my veins slices my ear canals into hot-fuzz headaches. Calls from numbers I don't recognise. I switch my phone off. Plug my ears. Hide inside.

I watch an SBS documentary, *See What You Made Me Do*, trying to understand why I couldn't get away from the Teacher, and the aftermath. I'm shocked by the show's answers.

'After the first time, actual violence isn't necessary, just the believable threat,' says the investigative journalist, Jess Hill. 'It's called coercive control.'

Perp's power was established that first time, when I was frightened, literally out of mind and body. After that, a slight change of tone was enough for submission. The confused child becomes the puppeteer's plaything. But his power over me was ignored, his threats unseen by others, and myself.

The documentary explores re-victimisation, suggests adults are more likely to experience sexual assault if they've been child-victims, because *that* trust-breaking is so fundamentally disempowering. Victims can be oblivious to the abusive nature of interactions, even the second time around. Perps sense this vulnerability, like sharks.

~

The Beast was my first professional boss …

At 21, I started 'on trial' as an assistant editor with a children's publishing company, one of two graduates competing for the dream job. We launched 'the Crazy Chicken' food chain; ran a red-carpet event for the new *Batman* film; developed stories about the ozone layer, recycling and tree-planting. *My thing.* We won a contract to produce an airline's kids' magazine, which 'might involve travel'. *Adventure. Saving the world.* I was hooked.

Within weeks, the boss requested assistants take turns working after hours. He was overweight and moustached, like the Teacher. I didn't make the connection. On his hotel bed, he ate chips and watched TV while I worked until midnight.

One night, he said: 'I don't think you're the one I'm after. You won't take a chance.'

'On what?' I asked, confused.

'You limit yourself.' He shook his head, disappointed. '*Tsk-tsk.* I need someone who can step into *any* role.'

'I can do that,' I protested.

'Show me,' he said.

'OK,' I replied, unthinking.

'You must be able to respond *immediately*, no matter how complex or simple the task,' he challenged. 'It's about trust.' He leaned closer, his breath metallic. 'I need someone *special* ... Absolute trust,' he repeated, needy.

'I can be that,' I said, naively.

'I could ask now ...' he taunted. *Cunning.* 'But you're not ready.'

'Ask what?' I baited my own hook.

'What colour knickers have you got on?'

'Um ...' I went to peek down my skirt.

'No looking!' He grinned, had a habit of licking his lips.

'White,' I said, assuming that would do.

'Prove it,' he challenged.

I hesitated.

'I don't care if you do,' he said 'but showing me means you *trust* me. Your undies are irrelevant. I need commitment.' I didn't realise what he meant. 'I can only choose one assistant,' he clarified, and waited.

'If my undies are irrelevant, you don't need to see them,' I blocked.

He shrugged. 'You don't get it.'

So, of course, I flipped my skirt, flashed my shiny whites. It was nothing, like he said. It was the beginning of him knowing he could ask me to do anything. The traps proved I trusted.

Stupid. I walked into them.

He asked about my life. I confided about Teacher-Perp. He knew I was damaged, found out I was a hard worker. In hindsight, he was just another egomaniac I didn't see coming. I suppose, after the Teacher, I wanted to feel worthy.

We flew to Darwin for the airline magazine, where the Beast took my passport and plane ticket, violently raped my dead body, reminded me I had no value, but I *might* be chosen. All office calls came through him. I didn't realise he'd prevented other job offers.

Five years with the Teacher had instilled misjudgement of myself. I didn't want the Beast's thing in my mouth. Wouldn't lick his anus. He made sure I understood commitment. When I refused to eat oysters at an office party, he publicly embarrassed, then privately hurt me. He controlled my income, leaving only enough for 'our' apartment I should never have rented in my name. *Damaged Goods.*

The 'chosen ones' moved to a new company where the Beast's charisma drew a well-known publisher, TV sponsorships and high-profile projects. For nine months I sacrificed my sad self to his 'greater good', telling myself I'd find a way out.

Strong Cathy can cope.

But the Beast pre-empted my escapes; forced me to sell my car, demanded the money. I vomited for days but he refused to take me to hospital. By then, death threats were normal. 'Your body won't be found,' he warned, raping me with a knife at my throat.

Slut-child thought she deserved it. Didn't know how to get away. But when I saw him backhand his wife into blood-bruises, I knew I had to run. I tried to convince the mother of his young children to get out. Then I told the Beast's boss about the violence.

'I very much doubt that,' said the respected publisher.

'I could submit a sexual harassment claim,' I warned him.

'That would be unwise,' he countered. He'd 'managed' the Beast before.

I would not get support, he told me. I was a lowest-rung nobody.

I hunker-hid at Maggie's, but the Beast extracted her phone number from a colleague. When I heard his voice, I was almost slurped back in, until Uncle John phoned: 'Get to the airport. I've arranged a ticket.'

A few years after my escape, the Beast was jailed for sexually assaulting a minor, and his 'very-much-doubting-that' boss was awarded an OAM.

~

'It's not usually a case of "once bitten, twice shy",' says Jess Hill on the documentary, 'but, ironically, once bitten, twice as easy.'

Hugging Kal's knitted blanket, I cry in sorrowful recognition.

My self-respecting boundaries were never built. Patterns of fear-filled submission were imprinted on Thirteen, then Twenty-One did not recognise the warning signs, 'as if the victim has been brainwashed into blindness' … unable to gauge if a predator's intentions are malicious.

No wonder my family don't understand. I still don't.

Victims of prior abuse can be attracted to people who hurt them because stress hormones, associated with fear and aversion, are misinterpreted as 'familiar'.

The Teacher and the Beast. My first ever experience of sex was rape. All sex that came after was tinged by it. Hiding from it. Escaping it. Being immobilised in it. Copying it. Reliving it. Never understanding the need for it. In my mid-twenties, women were safer. Until Vince.

Body justice

Fear knots me. Five days after The Phone Call, I've barely slept or eaten. *Go to group therapy.*

To release bio-chemically charged trauma, we practise mindful breathing, body tapping, ear pressure-point massage, humming, painting. We acknowledge our pain, seek something better. I share some rescue remedies: long walks, immersion in the sea, frosty showers. Some denounce my cold therapy as insanity. It's winter. We try to laugh.

I google nerve-repair exercises, try cooking, naked dancing, barefoot walking into storms. I reignite the chanting and meditation of my twenties. When that isn't enough, I Tibetan-stomp our Tassie-oak floorboards, shaking out cold feet and vocalising nonsense '*zee*' syllables.

I continue hatha yoga, a weekly class I've done for twenty years.

As I enter the hall, Once-Mother puts her face too close to mine: 'How aaare you?' It switches me to vomit mode: no 'downward dogs'.

After, she offers to buy tea, lists her health concerns and commitments for the week. 'I'm willing to write a statement,' she confides, 'but I'm not contacting the police,' adding: 'I couldn't *possibly* rearrange my schedule!'

I numb-hope that the police contact her. I'm tired of asking nicely.

At home, I find some online videos describing Trauma Release Exercises (TRE), which include the instruction to NOT try them alone. *How hard can it be?*

'Lie on your back, knees bent, heels together ...'

Something twinges in my lower ribcage, sending my entire thorax into painful spasms. For days after, I have trouble breathing and my neck is a hot brick.

Once-Mother sends me 'Are you OK?' texts, not wanting to hear that I've not slept, not eaten, feel constant pain, fear and nausea. My misguided attempt at TRE tightens a thick rope around my ribs. Breathing is excruciating. Every nerve is threaded with razor wire, firing hot shocks into skull. I sip agonised air.

Vince rubs me with Tiger Balm but my calves, thighs and glutes burn. Heels are painful to walk on. I visit an acupuncturist and a masseuse, but relief is temporary.

I find a local Buddhist TRE practitioner. Sarah is caring and Irish-hilarious. Using tapping, meditation and alternate nostril breathing, I finally become present. After a few minutes, my chest involuntarily heaves up off the floor and, from deep gut, I cat-furball coagulated horror. Hot tingles flare, feet to scalp, releasing pain from my ribcage. After the session, for the first time in months, I don't feel nauseous.

Later, I learn that the vagus nerve connects the voice box, neck and upper thorax.

TRE helps un-silence me! But without work, I can't afford more sessions. I check the Victim Services website for Trauma Release Exercise therapists. Sarah is not registered 'because the paperwork is a mountain of ridiculous'. Like EMDR, TRE is a somatic (body) therapy, 'unscientific', thus illegitimate in the justice system controlled by mostly male medicos who prefer drug-based psychiatry. Anything non-western or female-focused is ruled out.

I need help *now*. I need to trust my body, the place that stores and still fears rape. Body can help me recover. *If only it would sleep.*

Dead baby

May 23

Patience. I wait for police, for criminal justice. I haven't slept properly since the Possibly Useful Phone Call. Nausea is vengeant. I taste bile as I count 255 steps up the street, to where Once-Mother does not open the screen door. She's afraid I have news.

I'm not sure why I'm here.

I ignore her un-welcome and ask if she wants tea. She unlocks the door. I put the kettle on but can't stomach her offer of stale rice crackers.

'The police will probably contact you soon,' I say nonchalantly.

'Ho, I'm nearly eighty!' She gazes through ghosts in the garden.

I sense something calculated in Mum's frailty but can't interpret her glances. Throat spasms, as the shallow-trapped possibility of truth breaks the surface, swishes its tail, and is gone. *There's something she's not telling me.*

'How aaare you in there?' asks Once-Mother, peering.

'Actually, I'm a bit down …' I begin, as a mudlark lands on her patio.

'Oh, that silly bird!' Mum flings the screen door open. '*Shoo!* That one made a mess on my table, remember?' She overdoes her avoidance dance: 'Youuu won't remember. Your memory is worse than mine.'

I raise my eyebrows. Once-Mother thinks I play a zero-sum game; if I win, she loses.

'We should be friends,' she says.

A friend would speak up.

'We'll need each other in the future,' she pleads, worried about ageing alone.

I need you now.

About to cry, I unmask: 'I'm grieving, Mum ... for the child I lost.'

'This again!' She locks her eyes to mine and raises a gnarled finger. 'I lost a *real* child.'

I swallow my own sad, make space for her long-kept grief.

'At eight months,' she explains. 'That baby lived for one day. Your father buried her while I was in hospital. I didn't get to say goodbye.' *She had no say.* 'He went ahead with the New Year's party and the priest came to the door to check on me.' *Shame.*

'I'm sorry that happened, Mum.' The reality of her trauma brims my heart, and *my* grief feels ephemeral in comparison.

'Young women these days want In-Vitro babies, mental health support, equal pay, cheap daycare. They should stay home!' she rails. 'I dealt with it ... and so should you!'

But she hasn't. She hasn't processed that child loss, nor my child abuse, nor her daughters' homosexuality, nor her son's teen struggle with alcohol, nor her sister's teen pregnancy, nor her husband's shocking death. It's all bittering in there.

'You could access counselling,' I remind her.

'I don't need that rubbish,' she snorts. 'I know more than any psychologist. I've read all the books. I don't need to go over that.'

'Go over' ... her trauma, or mine?

'I don't need to give a police statement,' she clarifies.

Sharp rib pains make breathing impossible and I have to lie down. Trying not to cry, I squeeze myself down through floorboards. *To shallow-buried memories.* When she found the cemetery crucifix from her child's grave, she brought it home, stashed it under her house, in ant-sand. When Dad died, she dug that cross into her garden.

Outside, a mudlark pierces me into remembering: Mum telling my school friend, Garry, to 'be careful' of me, because 'you don't know what she is.' Not *who*, but *what*. I recall the feeling, hearing those words, shrink-spinning down into a headless René Magritte figure, looking up through skull, at sky. When I introduced Vince for the first time, she thanked him for 'taking me off their hands'. *A burden.* Once-Mother needs to believe I'm fundamentally bad. She must blame me, or she'll glimpse the role she played.

I slowly, painfully sit up. *Come from compassion*, I tell Buddha-self.

'Mum, have you told any of your friends what I'm doing?'

'Why would I do that?'

'You might need to talk to someone.'

'Nonsense,' she spits. 'We couldn't have done anything. You were *infatuated*.'

'So, tell the coppers that,' I plead.

'Don't be ridiculous,' she dismisses.

Once-Mother doesn't get it; a teen crush is not a crime.

We sit in sticky silence. Uncomfortable, Once-Mother wants idle chitty-chat. 'It's *your turn* to talk,' she squirms. 'And don't be boring,' she instructs.

I feel heart muscles rip; manage to crouch-stand under the ceiling spin. Then the screeching begins. Not the mudlark. It's the high-pitched dentist drill. Push finger into ear.

'It *is* my turn,' I exhale. 'The police have evidence now. They *will* be calling you.'

Two hundred and fifty-five steps home, into untrustworthy sky, the wind snap-crackling through me.

A win and a warning

Tuesday, May 25

Ten days since *The Damning Call.* Rib-pained, I try a hot bath, long chant, chocolate ice-cream. Nothing relaxes me. Vince's flight is delayed. He won't be home until midnight. I pace, lock, check the doors. Watch unsettled seas. Wait.

At 6 pm, Detective Herd calls. 'He's been arrested on eleven charges; he's in the lock-up.'

Relief escapes in a deep moan. 'Thank you!' I punch the air. Something like victory percolates.

'He knew it was coming,' she adds. 'During the arrest he told his wife "It's happened."'

I text Once-Mother and my siblings: The TEACHER was arrested!

Rocky responds: Outstanding! I'm applauding!

Maggie: Proud of you for being so brave.

Lianne: I want to give you a hug.

Once-Mother: Got it. Read it.

I stare at the ceiling until Vince flops into bed, then I fall into nightmares. Of Perp getting out. Me being hunted.

Thursday, May 27

I wake shiver-sweating, heart hammering, make a hot water bottle for my neck. It's 2 am. My heels and thighs prickle-burn. I hobble to the guest room to let Vince sleep, but I'm awake again at 4, sweat-drenched, with a raging headache and snotty dream tears. I switch thermo-strategies and wedge ice packs under skull.

At sunrise I cold-shower outside. Rattled by nightmares, I call Detective Herd.

'What happens next?'

'There'll be a mention at Loggerville Court,' Herd explains. 'He might make a statement. Don't be surprised if he gets bail,' she adds, off-handedly.

Panic crushes thorax. *Bail?!*

'Perp thinks he has a reputation to protect,' I protest.

'I doubt he'll make contact,' she tries to reassure. 'He doesn't seem the type to do anything silly.' *Silly? He didn't seem like a rapist, either.*

By day's end, it's local news.

'A man was extradited from Queensland over the alleged historical rape of a student …'

Deep calm

Thursday is group therapy day. I'm struggling to get there because Brain is disintegrating, missing data. I'm late or early, speeding along the frosty highway, staring out the windscreen. Then, Miriam-Rose's 'Dadirri' video soothes my ant-chem skin. We focus on reasons to keep fumbling towards self-belief. Footholds.

At some point, in the comfy, well-worn chair, crocheted rug over knees, I'm describing other people's expectations about 'moving on', why it's important to acknowledge what we've left … *WHO we've left behind.* And there it is: recognition of my fractured child-self, waiting in the rubble; my crystalline understanding of Thirteen, still crouched in her cold turret.

I realise how deep my terrorised child-self dug down. Tears pour off my face. In the group, no-one judges or blames, or rushes to comfort. I am gifted a safe space, to grieve.

I will not abandon you again, I promise.

I feel a subtle letting go as we amble about the sunny garden, shaking out limbs and clap-stomping, Tibetan style.

Afterwards, I join a group TRE session with Sarah, who helps me recognise my rational controls. 'Cathy, I can see your thinky-face. Allow your nervous system to do what it needs.'

Eventually, belly-breathing calms me enough to allow, and observe, a shudder from knees to shoulders. The skin around torso tightens as another cat-furball hauls my chest off the floor. *Phoopthhh*, stale air explodes out. Then, more tears.

I leave the session drained, physically, emotionally, peaceful. Somehow, my back and chest are not in pain. Dadirri breathes me. *I'm not expecting an outcome.*

The calm stays, even as Detective Herd tells me: 'He got bail at $5000. Had to surrender his passport, can't be around kids under sixteen, can't go back to teaching.'

'Where is he now?' My surface ripples.

'He must remain at his Queensland address.'

The wave crests. 'He could easily drive here!' I yelp, crumbling my shoreline.

'He didn't indicate he'd try anything,' Herd says confidently. 'Don't worry.'

Don't worry? 'What about his statement?'

'He chose not to make one.'

That he has a choice is ridiculous. It took me weeks: to track down old addresses; find photos; put myself through the grist of remembering. He pays his paltry bail (less than the income I've lost). All my efforts, all that police time, barely worth a sideways glance. Moreover, his presumed innocence implies that *I am lying*. Society needs better justice.

'What happens now?' I try to re-anchor.

'He'll attend a court hearing, late July,' Herd says.

'That's two months away!' I blurt, suddenly adrift.

She pauses. 'There's one more thing.'

'Oh?'

'Your mother is being ... difficult,' she says, 'about giving a statement.'

No time will be appropriate. No arrangement acceptable. Once-Mother *refuses* to remember.

'Maybe Detective Balding should try?' I offer. *Once-Mother might talk to a man.*

Kerfuffle

Friday morning, still strangely grounded, as if my feet are deep in a forest, I open the door to Once-Mother, who wants tea. *Breathe.* I tell her how calming the TRE session was. 'I drove home under the speed limit.' We laugh.

Seated on my deck, she assesses Vince's peanut biscuits.

'Tasty. Not too dry,' she approves as I hang laundry.

I watch her nibble another. Her impish eye-glint and half-hidden smirk. *She wants to tell me something.* My surface ripples. I'm tired of her games. 'What is it, Mum?'

'I had a most unsatisfactory call with your detective,' she reveals.

'Unsatisfactory?'

'She got me at a bad moment. I was kerfuffled.'

Here comes the parade of excuses.

'I *am* old, you know. I was late for my walk. I was putting my shoes on.' She builds pace into agitation, her face marbling. 'I'm still troubled by that station. I will *not* go there. It will end badly.' *Shame is frightening.*

I drop the empty laundry basket and step onto my deck, facing her as she stands, defying the tide. 'I have to get my hair done … I can't miss yoga on Tuesday … and coffee …' She gives me the 'so sorry' eyes. Pleased with her performance, she dusts biscuit crumbs off her skirt. 'How old is that detective?' she asks.

'Detective Herd can probably visit you, Mum.'

'Oh, yes, that *girl* said someone could come today, but I can't rearrange my lunch.'

Throat spasms.

'I said I'd think about next Friday, but she doesn't work Fridays. It's most unsatisfactory.'

Calm evaporates. 'Detective Herd works part-time because she has children.' I defend my kind detective who has listened to – and believed – me; the only adult ever to act on my behalf against the pedophile.

'There should be considerations for the elderly,' Once-Mother blusters. 'You were so *powerful,* Cathy.'

I step inside and close the screen door. From behind security mesh, I'm able to speak: 'Imagine,' I say calmly, 'how it felt Mum, for me to feel so *powerless* I was unable to move.'

Once-Mother picks up her hat.

'Well, I can't be late for the ladies,' she says. 'My community duty.' She stabs a look at me. 'I won't have some young, *female* detective arranging *my* week.'

Sharpness pierces my chest and nausea floods upwards.

'Don't *youu* call her,' Once-Mother sprays her suspicion; that I'm controlling police scheduling. Then, with a wry, determined grin: 'I want to see what happens next!' She victory-marches up the street.

Paranoia, gossip, shame

By nightfall I'm convinced Perp is coming to silence me. I call the station in panic. Herd is not on duty. Balding tries to reassure me. 'His bail conditions include not approaching *any* witnesses,' he says. 'He didn't give any indication he would. We've no grounds to be concerned for your safety.'

No-one knows what he might do.

Maggie texts me: Stay off the internet. I sense the Isle of Lies, in a Facebook feeding-frenzy, speculating about who the as-yet-unnamed Perp might be.

Sunlight wades through heavy air as I haul laundry off the line. Fold it. Unfold it. Try to un-remember. Neck pain sizzles into headache. Tea goes cold. I file my nails in the dry bath. Play Brazilian Samba and stomp-dance. Nothing feels real. Numb. Waiting.

For what? Once-Mother? Justice? Death?

I lie in bed with my iPad, avoiding news. Fog-Brain is trying to understand the National Redress Scheme. *Should I get a lawyer?* No, that's civil justice. In criminal justice, the police represent *me*; the State of New South Wales is my lawyer. *Right?*

To distract, I doomscroll news. The National Redress Scheme is criticised for being 'incredibly slow, overly complicated, re-traumatising'.

Rocky calls. 'Is Mum still being weird?'

'Detective Herd said she's "being difficult", but I think Mum's afraid.'

Rocky is angry now, for me. *At me?* 'She's afraid they'll ask what she knew,' Rocky seethes. 'She's afraid to tell the *truth*.' Body senses Rocky's spotlight on stormy water, where Fifty-Three flounders. 'Cath, if she can't step up for this … it's disgusting. It's a blatant lie that she remembers nothing!'

The power of his voice reaches deep inside my hollow. His words, a rescue rope I can't quite grasp. I'm sinking further, into denial. *She didn't know.*

'The bastard got bail,' I manage.

'I know.' His words shock me into alert.

'How do you know?' I plead. 'They can't publish names.'

'He's named,' says Rocky. 'It's in the news.'

'Shit!' Every cell in my body hits the flush button. Toxicity surges down my legs and all over the bed covers. It's in my bedroom, a poisonous flood invading sacred space. The stench of my history, oozing into the marriage that, until now, I've protected.

'Your name's not published,' Rocky rushes to reassure.

'The whole town knew it was me!' I cry-shout, hang up and fling the iPad off the bed. *Everyone knew.*

Eventually, I look at news: *Tacking Point Teacher Robert John Cunning accused of historical rape* ... The image of him sears my chest. *The former teacher was granted bail due to health concerns and 'strong ties' to the community* ...

I gulp Panadol, shrink-wrap my head in shame, slide back into bed. Once-Mother calls: 'Just get on with life, Cathy.'

'I'm trying to *get on* with criminal justice,' I say, 'but I need your support.'

'I have to make some other calls,' she diverts, hangs up.

Maggie phones. 'How are you feeling?'

'Trepidation. Mild panic. Relief?' I search for the answer.

'I bet he got a shock when he was arrested,' she says.

'Yeah, I'm trying not to think about *him*,' I say.

'Good,' says Maggie. 'Take care of you. And ... avoid Facebook.'

Why? What's there?

Lianne phones, asks how I'm doing.

'Well, it's tough that my mother won't stand with me.'

'Mum and Dad did their best,' Lianne absolves the then-adults.

'It's not about back then,' I argue. 'It's about what Mum's not doing *now*.'

'You participated,' Lianne hisses the poison. 'Mum shouldn't have to go to court, at her age!' She raises her voice. 'Mum doesn't need you being angry, she needs *support*.'

I search for angry but sink into hurt.

'I can't support Mum through this,' I tell Lianne. 'She'll need to talk to her old friends.'

'Yes, someone reached out to her.'

'Good. Who?' I ask.

'Meg Morrell, she worked in the school canteen. She called to comfort Mum, told her she knew Mum tried to get you away from him.'

Another adult knew something.

'Cathy, what do you hope to achieve?' asks Lianne.

They all want me back in my silence. Still blame me for 'my part' in it. Blind to the child who never wanted any of it.

'You were so cocksure. Move on, you don't want your whole life to be about this,' she reprimands.

I close my eyes and imagine Rocky's rope ladder. 'My whole life has ignored his crime,' I say, feeling conviction seep into my throat. 'I can make the hurt worth something.'

My hand senses the rope ladder; its strength.

'They did their best,' Lianne repeats. She fears my fight for justice will besmirch my parents' reputations, does not understand my promise to myself.

'There is no justice, Cathy. *Be careful* how you proceed.'

She hangs up. The rope sways out of reach.

Falling deeper

May 29

Mum drops in after her Saturday walk. 'Are you making tea?'

I unlock the door and she sits at my dining table. I put the kettle on, continue the dishes. We eye each other as water boils.

'I hear Meg Morrell phoned,' I mention. She narrows her eyes as I repeat Lianne's words. 'Meg knew you tried to get me away from him. You could write that in your statement,' I suggest. 'Or ask Meg to write something?'

'No!!' Once-Mother flings horror across the bench. 'Meg doesn't need that stress in her life. You don't know what she's going through … her blood pressure!'

Everyone else's pain is important. And I'm almost there, at the point beyond trying.

I fill two cups, let them steep.

'Is there *anyone* you'd approach on my behalf?'

'Who?' She's aghast.

'Other teachers … old friends?'

'No-one knew.' She swats the idea away.

'Lots of people knew, Mum. It was a very public relationship.'

'That's absolute rubbish,' she retorts. 'I didn't know it was … *sexual.*'

'Well, you knew *something*. Others suspected.'

'I didn't suspect anything,' she insists, gulping her too-hot tea.

My head is a spiked ache.

'What will people say?' she voices her real dilemma; her fear of gossip; of being savaged by 'unrespectability'. 'I suppose you'll be putting an ad in the newspaper, asking every busybody to come forward? Ho!' She snorts derision at me.

I hadn't thought of that.

'You can't change the world, Cathy.' She dismisses my social activism. But then I glimpse real fear in her eyes: an ugly family secret is 'out there' now, exposed on 'the internet' – a place she doesn't understand.

'What will people say?' she repeats.

I sigh and sip. I get it. I know how trauma hunts. Once-Mother hides from horrors she cannot fathom.

'Promise you won't contact Meg,' she demands, clunking her teacup down and standing to leave. 'Don't youuu dare!'

Ribcage drops into guts. Disappointment cloaks me. She has no idea how close I am to drowning. She desperately needs to denigrate my truth to keep her own inner-world from imploding. Compassion stirs.

'It's OK, Mum.' I shuffle her out and re-lock the door.

Slowly, I turn towards familiarity, the only place I have left. Darker and colder than abandonment, despair drags me by the ankles and sweeps me under turgid currents. Beyond threat, this airless estuary has no sharks, no waves of terror. An unbelonging that feels like comfort. *Almost.* There's a stench of decay, of knowing that the fight is lost, an end must come. Here, I submit to worthless lethargy. Everything is still in place, just how I left it.

Move your body!

I shove phone into backpack. Head north and keep going, towards cliffs. I've lost something since I was last here. That 'confidence' they keep talking about.

My headless outline blurs into smudgy rain. On a dangerously high, rain-slicked edge, I lie down on vague grass, reach out to a clump of wildflowers.

Reach a little further.

I've turned on my fully charged phone inside my pack and shoved it up the knoll behind me. I've texted Maggie so there'll be a ping on the phone when they start the search. It means nothing now, to let the grey sky, grey sea, empty, rip and tear asunder. For me to fall.

Eyes closed, images of Kaleidoscope and Vince and a grandchild haul me back from the edge. I cry out like a wounded dog, crawling back to the path.

Brain navigates. Body carries me home.

Into nightmare

Rocky has spoken with Detective Herd. He calls and we both cry as he reads his statement …

> There was special attention and singling out of Cathy. He provided opportunities in musicals, in school band. Motorbike rides, to and from soccer, rehearsals.
>
> When Mum turned 40, we had a party. Perp played his fancy guitar. Cathy would've been 14. Family birthdays were usually for family and close friends. This man was neither. He latched on to our family. Perp and Cathy were inseparable. Why wasn't he hanging around people his own age? It always struck me as very strange.
>
> Perp tagged along on a family camping trip. As a 10-year-old, I never understood why he was invited. I resented his presence.

I have a clear memory of Perp and Cathy at a waterhole, swimming alone together. It felt weird.

After Cathy went to university, something big happened. I was about 16 when Cathy showed a letter to Mum and Dad about what went on. Mum and Cathy had a stand-up shouting match while I imploded at the kitchen table. Something earth-shattering had happened between Cathy and Perp. Those revelations created immeasurable pain for Cathy and great stress for our family; it's gone on for more than 40 years. I've raised it with psychologists.

In 2017, I was triggered by *The Teacher's Pet* podcast. Cathy wasn't ready to do anything. She had a child still at school. But I couldn't bear the thought he might still be teaching. There was a taskforce, and a police hotline. I reported what I knew, to flag this dangerous predator. They confirmed he was no longer teaching.

My instincts told me that the grooming wasn't normal then, and it's off the chart today. 25-year-old teachers should not hang out with young kids. I have a 13-year-old daughter. If a male teacher started visiting, it wouldn't be tolerated. Not for five minutes, let alone five years.

'Is that OK?' asks Rocky.

Gratefulness opens my chest, pushing aside the chasm of misunderstandings between us.

'Thank you,' I say, wiping my face.

Rocky and I haven't surfed together for years. His approach to difficult conversations has been to avoid conflict, wait for a miracle. Now, he sounds strong, like he's holding onto something worthwhile. The belief that being a responsible parent takes courage. The idea that love is stronger than fear.

I will be forever grateful that he reached for me, just when I was sinking.

Knock knock

I'm excited. Maggie is giving Kaleido a lift home, for university break. In Kal's old room, with the deep blue wall, I clear the desk of ugly paperwork. Vince's warm scones fill our love-shack with the anticipation of buttery jam and sweet company.

At some point, up the street, Mum receives a phone call from my brother, and another, from hers. I suppose they – Rocky and Uncle John – coax or bully her.

I don't know any of this. Until she calls me.

'Hey Mum,' I say happily, standing in the sparkle of nearly finished cleaning, of knowing Kal is coming. My head isn't aching.

But Once-Mother's chastened spirit is not for niceness.

'Now,' Mum booms, 'you *behave* and be quiet!'

I'm stunned at her growling command.

'Get me that detective girl's number.'

I shrink into a smaller version of myself. 'Um, well—'

'Right now!' she yells.

'I don't have her mobile number,' I say, confused.

'Don't give me that,' she spits.

'I usually just call the station.'

'Well, give me that number. *Right now!*' she demands.

My skin hot-prickles and the back of my head mushrooms into throbby ache.

'Well?' she blasts. 'I have a pen ready.'

'I need to look it up,' I say, feeling sliced open. I take a slow breath and ask, 'Why are you angry, Mum?'

In a hiss that suggests I must already know: 'Your brother's been on the phone, and my brother as well. I don't know what you've been saying. They ripped into me about this statement. I *was* going to …'

She thinks I'm pulling strings.

Rocky and Uncle John's intervention backfires into my chest. I hang up, text her the number and, despite her nastiness, invite her for scones.

She calls me straight back, pronounces: '*I'm* providing Maggie lunch ...' Mum likes to control the catering. She declines scones and 'will wait for Maggie, as planned!'

Whatever!

I deep-breathe myself back to calm, think about what lovely Kal and I might do: visit the art gallery, shop for house plants, invite friends for sleepovers. We'll watch re-runs of *Doctor Who*, eat cake and ice-cream, and walk the beach. Craving comfort, I'm delighted by Kal's text:

Nearly there! :)

I hear a *knock-knock* at the back door and a deep voice. 'Helloo?'

Maggie's husband! I walk past the laundry, behind the dining table, into the hallway, and ... feel my heart pound. *Bah-Boom.* There's a man standing on my deck, at the screen door. I don't know him, can't see his face, silhouetted against bright sunshine. Not Maggie's husband.

Brain and Body separate. Skin prickles. *It's just a man, answer the door!* Stay calm.

He's here to kill you.

Legs are heavy, pushing treacle. *Bah-Boom. Danger!* Brain stalls. Body can't run. My command centre hacks itself. Dissociation is a felt thing. Connections sever. Synapses unplug, *pop-pop-pop.*

Nine more steps to the door.

Eight ...

I stare at the man. He's heavy-set, wears a leather vest. Boots. Facial hair. A biker?

Seven ...

A pounding *shoosh-shoosh* flushes through my ugly underwater ballet. My frontal lobe watchtower is infiltrated by a conspiracy wack-nut.

Perp's brother? Here to kill?

Six ...

When a shark swims under your surfboard, time stretches, everything slows. Adrenaline floods the long space between breaths. Awareness expands into every cell. Every molecule. *Baaahh ... - ... Booom.* Heart is engorged, ready to burst. *Stay still.*

Five ...

'I'm looking for Cathy Byrne,' says random biker man.

Brain screams RedAlert. Head is a monster-ache. Iwantto shutmyeyes. Thenthe *Baahh* ... - ... *Booom* stretches again, too far between breaths. *No oxygen.* Chestexplodes. Ears Scald. RingingClose.SoVeryclose. *Move the body.* Step.

Four ...

This is when you know that time is infinite and space could bend you through the universe and suck you away, and that's what you want, because you are, for certain, about to die. Brain is desperately trying to be grown up, to answer the man. I have seconds.

Three ...

'What's it about?' I peep.

'Is this 22 Pebbly Beach Road?' he asks. *Checking his target?*

'I'm looking for Cathy Byrne,' he continues. 'I'm Detective ...'

Suspicious, Brain glazes over his name.

'... from River Region Area Command.' He flashes what looks like a police badge.

Where is my Tacking Point Detective?

Two ...

The screen door is not locked! Then I see the gun.

One.

Reach and click the lock. Launch out-of-sight.

'VINCE!' I yell, hearing only siren-scream. Brain is nuclear fission. Body is stumbling, falling. Throat spasms, then clamps. *Can't breathe.*

Vince comes. I'm gripping the wall as Fake Detective repeats his routine. 'I'm looking for Cathy Byrne?'

He shows his fake badge. Real gun. Bizarrely, Vince accepts gun as proof.

'What's this about?'

They step outside and I stretch hot listening ears.

'It's a police matter, regarding the alleged offender, Robert Cunning.'

'Yes?' Vince waits.

'He's dead.'

Shock slams violence into me. A howl launches from my shut-off throat. I collapse under surging sobs; the child who loved and hated the man, the student confused, the teacher aghast, the mother, appalled. I instantly assume suicide: I have been robbed by him, again. First my innocence, now, my justice. So much to carry, and now, a life.

I am the 53-year-old who caused a man to suicide.

I grieve for the waste of it, for his own family, for my only chance.

Vince holds me. 'It's not your fault. It's not your fault.' But all I can hear is my heart, pulsing the poison: BLAME. BLAME. BLAME.

THE ONLY ONE WHO KNEW THE TRUTH OF WHAT HE DID.

HE'S DEAD.

Facebook Justice 7

The killings

May 31

It's a too-bright winter Monday, so sparkly-sharp the sky hurts my eyes. But my skin will not warm. Something devours me, leaving strange puddles where I walk.

I revert to laundry, pegging Vince's clothes higgledy-piggledy, trying to ignore his salmon linen shirt, which punches images into me. *Perp had one the same.*

I ponder the word 'suicide'. A kind of freedom?

A car door slams across the street, flinching me into hiding between washed sheets, which billow into waves. Let dampness smother me.

Once-Mother is suddenly at my garden steps. She thinks she's free now, but eight weeks of the lie has cracked me. *She is not my protector.*

'I'm soo sorry! Let me give you a hug.' She holds out false arms.

'No,' voice squeezes out.

'OOOhhh,' she melodramas, releasing tears that no longer stain me.

'What was that phone call yesterday?' asks Big Brave, defending yesterday's child. 'You spoke to me as if I was a naughty teenager. I had no idea Rocky and Uncle John called you. But you assumed *I* arranged it, that *I* was in control.'

She stares, fawn-eyed, not denying, not stepping closer.

'Why?' I demand.

'Well …' she starts, pulling herself up out of old-lady sandals.

'You told me to *behave* and *be quiet*,' I interrupt. 'Why?'

She slump-acts the frail old thing. I soften, offer water, but don't invite her in. She crumple-martyrs in the sun: 'This is … such a shock.'

Perp's suicide? Or my sudden ability to speak?

'It's been terrible,' she performs, 'for me too, you know.' Once-Mother muddies into self-focus. 'I was angry with the over-confident child we had to deal with, years ago.'

I stare, confused, careful of the danger of her. She sobs. I offer the shade of the balcony. But she prefers the harsh light of centre stage.

'He was helping your career,' she sniffs.

What?! Even Thirteen knew I was no great music talent. Once-Mother is grasping.

'I probably shouldn't have spoken to you like that.' She quietens, huddling onto the steps. I kneel beside her, put my hand on her shoulder, but her almost-apology lasts barely a second. 'Cathy, you were impossible! What could we have done?' *So much, you could have done.*

'Can I at least have *my* truth now?' I beg. *Do I want truth … or freedom?*

'Can I at least have tea?'

Once-Mother wants to see her grandchild, to pretend things are fine. I am instantly protective. 'Kal is sleeping.' I deny the honour.

Yesterday, Kal saw my distress. Brought me tea, and storytelling cuddles. Probably heard that Once-Mother is 'being difficult'.

Once-Mother's eyes narrow through sour suspicion. 'Well, you won't need my police statement now,' she declares.

'I have no idea, Mum.' *Does she sense her exit?* 'I'm not running this circus. I asked for your help, and you refused. It's too late …'

'OOhh!' she diva-howls. And then, like an axe-chopped snake, she spits: 'I bought you all those shoes!'

Stunning! Her switch from suicide to shoes throws me, way back. Barefoot me hated wearing primary school Jesus sandals, and high school blacks, and strangulating girlie click-abouts. Once-Mother coaxed my tomboy hairiness into moustache-bleached, shave-legged femininity and corporate wardrobing.

I should be glad I'm free from that, but the behaving-daughter evaporates. *Phoofff.* The last of something scours me, seeps out through nausea into sadness as it leaves.

THE ONLY ADULT WHO MIGHT HAVE SPOKEN. SHE IS DEAD TO ME.

~

'I'm going inside.' I shoo the ghost, knowing I'll never be free of my love for her. *Knowing that I must protect myself.*

In a last-dash move to regain control, Ghost-Mother declares: 'It's over now. *I'm* not holding guilt. *I'm* moving on.' She sets off, waving to the neighbour as she swishes up the street, satisfied she's had the final word.

June 1

Body wants yoga but cannot face Ghost-Mother nausea. Instead, I see Victim Services counsellor Yvonne, who reminds me Perp's suicide is 'not my fault'. Today's talk-therapy does not relax me.

'You were sexualised at a young age,' she says. 'Part of you probably refuses sexual sensation. We should work on that.'

I don't want to. Below the waist is purposely blank. I don't make another appointment. Don't want to ever enter those unknown parts.

Instead, Kal and I go plant shopping and visit my nephew and his shy dog. Maggie (nephew's mother) comes too. The poor pooch is more skitty than I am, but we calm each other with ball-retrieval pats. Animal therapy.

When readying to leave, Maggie yelps: 'I have to tell you something!'

I wait in the ominous.

'It's not just one suicide.' Her words implode me: 'His wife … also suicided … with him.'

Disbelief. Confusion. Horror. Dog barking.

Wait … *What? Why?* This extra life on my blame-bonfire sears my tether. I float into dumbfounded responsibility.

Kal drives me home, finds me fizzy water. I scroll the news: *Tacking Point teacher in suicide pact; Teacher on bail dies with wife after sexual assault charges.*

'It's not my fault!' I clutch the echo and call Detective Herd. 'So, it's all over now?'

'Unfortunately, yes.' Justice is beheaded. Cold blood pools into my feet. I grip the bench. 'There's no-one to prosecute,' she says bluntly. 'It's a shock to all of us, Cathy. He didn't seem the type.'

No-one ever understood what 'type' he was. Did he kill her? Her him? How? Why?

'The main thing now,' says Herd, 'is to deal with what's in your head. Take care, Cathy.'

And just like that, I am ejected from justice, as if no crime occurred. As if the trauma stampede did not crush my life.

~

A few days of headaches later, Ghost-Mother 'needs to walk'. Body wants movement but I don't want to need her. Ever again. Desperate, I wrap myself in wary: 'Just walk, no talk,' she promises. So I hunker into my thick purple raincoat, remind myself of boundaries. At my mailbox, the Ghost mime-zips her lips shut.

I focus on the beach soundtrack: birds and waves. Enjoy not-listening to her prattle, though she barely contains herself. Her mouth wants to flap.

We take the bay boardwalk, alongside low-tide scum. Nausea holds breath against rotting, rubbish-clogged mangroves. Ghost-Mother hands me a note:

I avoided the police statement because of the deep shame and remorse at having to admit publicly that I (we) failed in our duty. I was angry with the child we were dealing with. I would now like to let the child go.

I'm 53! The note slips her 'no-talk' promise into mud; forces me to speak. 'It must have been a powerful fear of shame to make you abandon your adult child.'

'Yes,' she replies, chastened. For once not defending.

'Maybe you were afraid I'd end up like your sister, a pregnant teen; a spectacle? Or maybe you've always been challenged by my adventurous nature?'

'Yes,' Ghost-Mother admits. *She's been coached.*

Careful, do not resurrect her.

The moment I hand the note back, she erases its intent.

'We tried,' she splutters. Cannot sit in her sorry. 'We didn't know it was sexual.'

Perhaps.

Then she delivers her killing blow: '*He* never lied to me.'

My inside fills with tears. *He lied to us all.*

I stand there, holding my child by the throat. Wind-whipped by confused compassion, I drink the sour stench of mangroves; realise there's nothing left here to sustain me. It's too late. I'm old; Mum's too old. I don't know why I bothered, with any of it.

There's only one killing left in me.

Weariness rides my bones to the breakwater. These past few months I've learned that speaking up is terrifying. Silence is less painful. Forgiveness can fail. Compassion is irrelevant. Justice without truth is empty.

Sad eyes watch the reeking, slick-yellow river.

How might it feel to let these heavy boots drag me under?

A chat with Dad

'*I thought your father knew?*' Dead Perp's words haunt me as I hot-pack my neck, drinking ginger tea. It doesn't settle my writhing stomach. I conjure Dad: hard working, clever, gentle. Encouraging. He taught me how to love the ocean. A sudden memory surfaces: a chat with Maggie and Dad. We're in the TV room. Dad on the green lounge, Maggie on the ottoman. I'm cross-legged on the carpet, facing the mini family conference.

'You're *so* smart,' says Maggie, in her school uniform. 'You're better than him, you can do *anything*. Go to university, anywhere. Don't waste your talents.'

When was this? Maggie was two years ahead. *Fourteen? Fifteen?* Maggie talks about Perp targeting Lucy. *Trying to help me see that Perp is … too old? a serial threat? Dad's hoping Maggie can convince me to move on.* He asks: 'What do you think will happen next?'

Next? After what? What initiated that chat? His drunken soccer-night phone call? *Awards nights were in September. Before my birthday. Which club did he say? In '82 he played for Loggerville. I was 14. In '83, he played for Tacky. I was 15. My sisters had both left by '84, so …* Ants prickle skull as I ignore what memory tells me. They knew before I turned 16.

'What do you think will happen next?'

'I'll marry him,' the child-bride parroted the abuser's answer.

Big Brave wants to vomit. Numb pours cold into bones. They don't ask how the 'path to marriage' started, or how long Perp pretended to 'wait' because I was nearly the 'age of consent'. *Except I wasn't!*

I google 1980s law. Back then, 'carnal knowledge' of a child under 17 was 'statutory rape'. 'Responsible adults' (like teachers) were restricted until the child turned 18. My parents hid behind blinkers, galloped sideways, chose to see a naughty not-child.

Brain argues: *Nearly 16 is NOT an adult.* They didn't know it was sexual. What *did* they know? *When did my parents visit his?*

I call Detective Herd. 'Can I get a copy of The Phone Call?'

'There are privacy issues,' she warns. *He's dead!* 'You'll need a lawyer to access the recording,' she continues. *I can't get a copy of my own conversation?*

I scour the internet to make sense of this ridiculous, and there it is: a person has a right to privacy for *thirty years* after they die.

Numb-cold, I can taste mud. So I haul myself into a frosty outside shower and dry-retch. Body scrapes itself out. Throat is acid-scalded. I clamber inside. Under soft blankets, cat-furballs wrack me as I purge his face from my mind.

I wallow in the detective's words: *Deal with what's in your head.*

Not just my head. It's in my whole body; my relationships; my beach; my lovely house; my real marriage bed; my laundry; my nightmares; deep under my skin and in every breath. The criminal justice process reignited my awfuls. I never wanted to go to court. I wanted him to understand the damage. His paltry $5000 bail was granted because he had 'hypertension' and 'community ties'. *What a coward! What a farce!*

He's gone, but I'm still smouldering. Fuming. Society deserves better.

The cures

Isak Dinesen says salt water – sweat, tears, or the sea – is the cure for anything. So when Gemma offers me her half-renovated apartment near Cressie Bay, I immerse in frosty south-westerlies. Walk. Swim. Run. Lull into evening. I mourn for gone things: my child-self, my chance at justice, my idea-of-mother. I paddle a kayak beyond the headland, hoping for turtles, wary of sharks. I surf, chant and meditate, eating just enough to dampen nausea. I practise abdominal breathing and do my own yoga. I wear warm snuggly clothes and no bra and hug myself through the fear of being alone. Through frenzied calming,

I enter peaceful exhaustion and actually sleep. Truth is all effort. Freedom feels possible.

I could 'move on' and survive.

On my third sunrise, a stout kookaburra sits close on the balcony rail. Strong, bold, brave, clever. She cocks a sharp eye as I stroke her feathers. I reach again but she holds her boundaries, flies away. Confident, mirthful, beautiful. *Free.*

Gemma comes to walk the rainforest loop and laugh me into sunshine. 'As a friend,' she says, 'my job is to help you see when to let go.' I'm not there yet.

I drive to Sarah's group TRE session, try to allow nervous system release. Just as giving birth requires submission to ancient wisdom, this therapy requires trust.

Body knows what to do. Don't analyse. Enable.

At first, I have trouble with others in the room. Then I question if I'm faking – making the shudder happen. Eventually, deep breaths carry me into a state of not-wanting, not-processing. Simple presence. On my back, knees bent, feet together. I slowly release hips, like a clam, knees opening to the floor. Deep abdominal breaths, long-exhales. When I feel ready, I engage pelvic muscles and, very slowly, raise knees to close the clam, feet flat, ankles together. The posture seems simple, but the effect is phenomenal.

The tremors build to a steady knee-knocking rhythm. Ripples of energy shimmy up through torso. Cat-furball knots explode in sudden *phooff* exhales, chest-lifting me off the floor. *Just breathe.* Each time, I begin again, without focusing on ant-skin or heatwave gut.

Allow. Don't think.

Chest vibrates, throat spasms. Arms flex involuntarily in a whip-like cactus arm flick that starts at my shoulders and ends in a loud knuckle-crack. My whole face scrunches as my head turns side to side. It's a full-body shakedown with an after-calm that lasts for hours.

Vince phones and I answer, crying. I don't-explain.

So much crap can never be resolved.

'I understand,' he says. *How can he possibly?*

I read an article quoting clinical psychologist Professor Ian Coyle, who has reported on more than five hundred survivors; only three escaped drug addiction. 'Child sexual abuse is a life sentence,' he says. 'Very, very few people ever fully recover.'

Sipping salty tears, I acknowledge I'm not a drug addict. I don't yet realise that hyper-achieving is a common response by survivors trying to prove themselves worthy; it's just as destructive as addiction.

On my last day in Gemma's haven, the TiddlyBom bird returns, flapping wildly in my chest. I try to find her boundaries. Freedom is inviting, but ... Truth still wants a chance.

I'm not done yet.

More panic, more to pay

Dr J tries to find a Victim Services therapist, to help my nausea, headaches, noise-flinching, paralysis nightmares, insomnia, twitchy ants. Now that criminal court is off the agenda, I could try EMDR, but they all have wait-lists.

Doc asks if I have family support.

'For Mother ... I practise compassion.'

To get some rest, Doc suggests Valium, but I'm a medicine minimalist.

'Try melatonin.' It makes me even more nauseous. *Impossible.* I throw it out.

Floating in bilious fog, I don't know how long I've been in my garage. *Five minutes? Thirty? Is it safe to drive like this?* I go inside. *Was there a form I had to fill?* I start cleaning house but notice the coffee pot is spitting. I pour some. It's just hot water. I roam about, trying to remember what I'm supposed to be doing, find my groceries by the door. I stare at the clock, knowing I once knew, trying to figure out what time means.

Move your body!

I should hang the clothes, but there's electric wire around the laundry basket.

I walk to the beach through stifling air. The slam of a car door catapults me back home.

June 8

Libby from the National Redress Scheme calls to ask if I've chosen a lawyer. I'd forgotten about the Scheme until they sent a parcel. One document discussed 'possible financial support' while panic attacks prevent me working.

Libby's high-pitched chattiness annoys my ears. She asks if I had any luck with the call.

'*Call?*' I grasp for meaning.

'The police phone call,' she clarifies. 'Last time we spoke, the No-ID set-up …' Her perspective thrusts me underwater. '… Maybe when you try again—'

'There won't be a next time,' I interrupt. 'He's dead. Suicide.'

'Oh, I …' It's her turn to flounder. 'The police should have notified us.' She starts again: 'You'd be better off in a civil case anyway … they're faster and give better outcomes. Redress takes at least nine months … and won't account for lost wages or medical expenses.'

I want it to be over.

Why am I being encouraged out of the Scheme? Was I ever in it? I need assistance, but if I initiate a civil case against Perp's employer, well … that's *my* employer. The Department of Education might never offer me work. The State of New South Wales is no longer my lawyer! His actions robbed me not only of my past but my income in the present and maybe into the future.

'What should I do?' I ask Libby.

'We can't advise you,' she replies unhelpfully. *Who can?*

I can't seem to communicate, even cogitate. Yet here I am, attempting significant decisions. *It's hopeless. I'm hopeless. My confidence, that problematic thing, curetted.*

'We sent you an information pack with three law firms to choose from,' says Libby, hooking me back into now. 'Have you made contact?'

In the last few days, I've waded through thick words, forms, explanations. Fog-Brain can't comprehend a paragraph, let alone a page.

'I'll make contact,' I say and hang up, then lie down.

Eventually, I call a small firm in Brisbane.

'Can you provide details of the abuse?' asks Lawyer 1.

'I made a police statement,' I say, assuming she'll have access.

'Could you send me that?' she asks.

'I don't have it. Can't you ask the police?'

'The police should have given you the final document,' she says.

'Well, they didn't,' I say. Skin stretches over a hand-grenade in my chest, and a piercing alarm starts in my head. *Again. I must do the work.*

The room swirls as I find, then photograph and email, twenty pages of my scribbled-on draft statement. It takes all day to do something I used to do in minutes. I let Lawyer 1 know that Dead Perp made admissions in the Useless Phone Call.

'Can you send me that?' she asks.

'They won't give it to me. The detective said a lawyer has to request it.'

I'm floundering in civil injustice.

Lawyer 1 calls back. 'Can you send your sisters' signed statements?'

'I wasn't even supposed to *talk* to my sisters.'

'Could you ask them for a copy?'

I call Maggie and Lianne. Neither were given copies. Panic percolates. Legal administration by a person in trauma-shock is inadvisable.

Lawyer 1 needs my sisters' permission to access their statements but is reluctant to spend time on my case: 'The request could take weeks. We're not even sure if this gentleman has assets worth purs—'

'STOP!' Voice cuts her off. 'Please. DO. NOT. refer. to. Perp. as … a gentleman.'

Voice feels like someone else. *Someone strong.*

'I'm not after his assets. I don't want to hurt his children!' I hang up. I still want justice, but its pathway confuses me. Eyes swim down the lawyer list.

I call a big Sydney firm instead.

'We're trauma-informed ... Yes, we can access statements. Yes, we'll request the phone call transcript.' Then, Lawyer 2 'must advise me of the fees, costs and risks involved.'

I have no income. *How can I 'move on' with my life when I don't have one anymore?*

Re-reading the Redress Scheme documents, I slowly understand that a 'no win, no fee' agreement does not mean 'no costs'. It seems 'costs' are different to 'fees'. A semantic trick.

All risk is mine.

I call Lawyer 2 back.

'So, if *you* lose my case, *I* have to pay for this man's crime?'

'Someone has to pay,' she says.

'I've already paid.' I sob her off the phone and pace the hallway. *He never paid.*

Each time I pass the laundry, I shove the growing pile in and shut the door. Avoiding.

June 9

Weeds have overtaken my garden. I spend the day inside, interpreting thirty pages of off-putting cost agreements. In a daze, I sign various authority forms. Then I re-read Lawyer 2's letter: *There appears to be grounds for a claim against the Department of Education for failing to remove you from your family earlier.*

WHAT?!

I call Lawyer 2. Unavailable. The receptionist says I may speak with a paralegal, charged at $250 per hour. *Am I incurring costs?*

The paralegal apologises: 'It was a form-letter for Aboriginal clients.'

How do Indigenous survivors cope? What happens to those with less resources? More severe trauma?

Ms Para sends the corrected document. I use the last of my ink to re-print and re-sign, then I notice my birthdate is incorrect on every form. She resends. I am stunned to learn that 'charges are structured in six-minute units plus GST' and 'hourly rates may change without notice'. The paralegal took thirty-six minutes already, fixing her faulty files.

Ch-ching! My head aches. I barely manage the drive to town for more ink and paper. Then I make tea, try to read critically, like I once could. About to sign, I re-read this:

We may require prompt payment of disbursements, regardless of the outcome. Brain is boiling. Further in: *payment of disbursements is conditional upon the successful outcome.*

Contradictory! shouts Brain. And … are disbursements 'fees' or 'costs'?

Section 3.3: *disbursements include search fees, court filing fees, process server fees, fees for clinical records, medical reports, non-attendance fees, witness expenses, travel, transcript expenses and barrister fees.* Google says barristers cost $10,000 a day. I read that the firm can make *a payment on my behalf* but *charge me interest* for the time it takes for them to resolve the matter.

Conflict of interest! yells Brain.

The document includes an estimate of $67,000, and a further $25,000 if the matter is 'litigious'. I google 'litigious' to find: 'argumentative, combative, belligerent, and' – *yeah, I'm starting to feel* – 'hostile.' I thought the Redress lawyers would fight *for me,* but I'm a revenue stream *for them.*

My potential cost is $92,000. More if it takes a long time.

We'd lose our love-shack, Kal's university fund, our Tassie trek! I might lose my husband. Should I proceed with civil justice?

I scan through blurring words and discover that I must sign before they'll even assess my chances. I cry indecision into a hot bath until Vince comes home.

We cook as he rants about his work. 'They want *more* revenue,' he moans as I stir veggies. 'Their systems are dodgy. Their CFO is clueless,' He flips his steak. 'We just won the biggest supplier in the country, but they won't let me pay industry rates.' He glugs more wine. 'Our best guys will leave and I'll be blamed!' He clunks bottle-to-bench. We eat, exhausted, do the dishes. I step around the alcohol conversation, head for the TV. '*I* might not have a job next month,' he muses, puts on *Vera*, for me. I wish he didn't flee into booze. I avoid angry. Now, shiraz-morose, he slurs: 'Howwosh*your* day?' Then he snores.

Should I proceed?

Justice is gone and truth is not worth the risk.

Five A's and forty-eight hours

Our group therapy facilitator explores 'discomfort,' suggests we 'sit with it': 'By listening to gut instinct when our body flushes with fear, we can redirect habitual neural pathways.'

We discuss boundaries; being clear with ourselves and others. We breathe and repeat: 'What *I* need doesn't have to make sense to anyone else.'

Nothing makes sense. Do I really need more legal stress?

During a visualisation exercise, I become Joan of Arc. Having rescued my damaged child from the stone turret, I pick up my sword and smite the heavy vines of others' limitations. In chainmail and cape, I am our glowing protector. My skull fizz-tingles as I rewire. Re-connect. Child-self feels stronger. Sensation translates into words: *We can take as long as we need. We will not go back into silence.*

I want my truth spoken, in family and community.

Later, Lianne phones. 'Why are you contacting lawyers *now*?'

I was told to.

'It's the only path left,' I defend, gripping my sword to draw a ring around my many selves, '... to *some* justice.'

'Didn't you get that already?' she says, carelessly.

I feel the flush of betrayal, but don't 'sit with it'. 'His suicide was cowardice, not justice,' shouts my inner Joan. 'He made sure no-one got the truth. Justice requires remorse, not escape.' Lianne sighs. My sword-tip touches the floor. I sigh.

'I'll probably just go through the National Redress Scheme.'

'Cathy, be careful,' Lianne warns from her usual hideout. 'Redress takes a long time.'

'Forty years is a long time,' I reply.

~

It was a mistake to tell anyone I might get a victim-recognition payment. Ghost-Mother says I should refuse *any* payment, because 'society can't afford it'. *She thinks I don't need help.*

The crying girl hates needing anything. Anyone.

At the blue-walled desk, I open the journal I've been using as an anchor and float across my '*5A's of Justice': Admission of crime. Acknowledgement of harm. Apology from all. Accounting for impact. Access to recovery.*' I never needed to punish the perp.

I google 'child sex offender suicide risk.' Caucasian male professionals, perps who create indecent images, those married with children, with broad community networks, without prior criminal record, are at extremely high risk, especially within forty-eight hours of becoming aware of an investigation. Offenders who rationalise, who think 'it's what you wanted', suffer massive cognitive distortion. Their ideas about themselves as 'upstanding citizens' are so challenged by the threat of public shame that it outweighs their fear of death.

Robert Cunning fit the extreme risk profile: Arrested Tuesday evening. Named in the media on Thursday. Dead Saturday.

The police knew he took photos, was a community ego, was married with children, still claimed 'blue balls' was a thing. They allowed bail.

How different would the path to justice have been if we'd had a mediated discussion? I might have gotten acknowledgement of my damage, a fully-informed apology. My family and community might have learned from their mistakes. His children might still have a family.

Now, a civil case will maul my parents' reputations, trigger me into panic, waste more of my life on a pedophile's idiocy. Any compensation will be inadequate. Besides, in some unsatisfying way, I'd already forgiven him, back when I'd meditated a path to my great, and singular, Self.

TiddlyBom flutters. *Why aim for truth when I can have freedom?*

Because society does not understand the true cost of child sexual abuse. Reluctant to admit, educate, prevent or heal, society silences victims. Because society 'can't afford' to repair the damage it creates.

Society makes choices about what it values, I tell myself. *Silence is not neutral.*

School phones to offer me work. We sorely need the money, but I can't. Just *can't*.

Out on the deck, I finally talk to Vince about lawyers, about financial risk.

'If you don't try, you won't know,' he encourages. 'I'll support whatever you decide.' He pauses, adding: 'We could sell the boat.'

We gaze forlornly at the boat trailer choking in buffalo grass.

'You used to enjoy it,' I say, sad.

'We used to enjoy our garden,' he responds, sad.

'Let's go to Brisbane,' we both say.

We navigate the Covid paperwork to visit our three children, cuddle the baby, fill awkward silence with delightful coos.

I visit Uncle John and Aunty Marion, who might help me decide how *and if* to proceed.

'Don't feed the lawyer-vultures,' John warns. 'It could take years.'

I sigh. 'I'm told the Redress Scheme takes longer.'

The sun reflects in their garden pond as Marion makes tea.

'It might not feel like it, Cathy, but his suicide is a good thing,' John reasons. 'Can you imagine your mother in court?' He shakes his head, horrified.

I envisage Ghost-Mother, enfolding judge and jury in kerfuffle. She would have endured the shame of it; relished the game of it.

Marion wonders aloud if court 'will focus on the promiscuous young teen?' She moralises that modern justice 'should be better'. But we all know I'm kidding myself.

'Were there … others?' Uncle John asks.

Other victims? Is he trying to make sense of Perp's wife's suicide? *Aren't I enough?* I want to shout but can't.

This implicates me!

June 11

Teacher-Beast still hunts my night shallows. I wake in throbbing sweat, legs frozen, stinging.

Ghost-Mother comes to my front door, wants tea. I offer Vince's fresh ginger biscuits.

She has no-one else to talk to. *What harm, to let her ramble?*

'What can I do to help you move on?' She takes another biscuit.

I fill the sink to wash dishes. 'Well …' *Breathe.*

'I'd like your statement.' The words fly out: 'I might pursue a civil case against the Department of Education.'

'Why?' She fires acid-blame. 'What happens when the lawyers say the school wasn't at fault?' she splutters. 'Then *I'm* in the firing line! This implicates me!' she shouts, standing up. 'I'm getting ready to *die!* You'll be after money from my house next,' she accuses.

From behind my kitchen bench, I see how terrified Ghost-Mother is; trapped by the myth that women use rape allegations for 'getting back' or 'getting money'. I see my reflection in her eyes; a tiny upside-down me.

Ghost-Mother imagines I want revenge; that I could toss her from the family home.

She does not know me.

I pull the plug on the dirty water, take a slow breath, deep into abdomen, out through a straw, through thick waiting.

'Don't you dare involve Meg,' she barks. 'She's dealing with enough.' Meg, who remembered that Mum 'tried to get me away'.

Hand is on spasming throat.

Mum's fearful eyes soften. 'What can I possibly do?' she asks, sitting back down.

I breathe through revulsion, plant bare feet firmly into *my* floorboards. 'Will you write your statement?' asks my stronger voice.

'I will, if' – she jabs a gnarled finger – 'if you promise *not* to contact Meg.'

'That's your deal?' I ask, bewildered, tasting sharp blue cheese.

'Yes.'

Desperate, I accept. 'OK.'

'I won't type it,' she defiantly stands, 'and I certainly won't email it!'

I wonder what scrap of paper might come my way. 'Do you want to just give your statement over the phone? My lawyer could call you?' I offer.

'No!' she blasts. 'I won't have a lawyer call me!' Ghost-Mother is afraid to document anything. Afraid of everything.

She stops by the door, howls: 'What could *anyone* have done?'

Throat spasms violently. *You could have reported your concerns to Regional Office*, I don't say. *Could have banned him from your house*, I don't say. *Could have found someone for me to talk to*, I don't say. *Could have told me I wouldn't be in trouble*, I cry inside. *Could have reported, when you did know, to remove the risk, reduce my damage.* I feel vibrations through my ground-down teeth. Demolished boundaries.

I do it to myself. This silencing.

'Why drag all this to court *now*?' she shouts as I kneel to buckle her shoes, so she doesn't fall down my steps. 'Move on,' she instructs.

I hold the door open and try to refocus on 'the deal'.

'You'll have to type it, Mum,' I say. 'I can't type it for you.'

'I'll do what's good *for me*.' She swirls away.

A heavy cloak shunts my eyes as I lock the door, gripping the frame.

Head spinning. My legs disappear. I'm swallowing watery air, *phoopthing* spasms off the floor.

I can't possibly proceed.

Intruders

Mid-June

I'm skirting around a bigger problem. Something I can't even whisper. It hits me, a bomb-slap. Sometimes on waking, sometimes during the day. A hideous image slinks behind my eyes. I can't cry it away. I walk and long-breathe and try to stretch, but the vision stalks me, confronting the core of goodness I thought I could cling to. This Me-Perp thing I cannot speak. *Telling would prove that I'm rotten. Just as they all think.*

I write-pour horror into my journal, but these invasions revolt me, into shuddery mess. Brain says these imprints never happened. Body's not so sure. Disgust festers in skin with sticky dead ants. Evil slides behind the dunes and waits. I try to vomit it out of me. But icy fingers probe my chest. I am convinced now; I am very badly broken, unworthy of justice. Unworthy of anything good.

~

Lawyer 2 puts me off with inept mistakes and needlepoint focus on cost–risk. I go to Brisbane to meet Lawyer 1 but haven't committed to a civil case yet. The visions seem like a warning not to. Vince offers to come, but I still don't want him in on ruinous details. Don't know what might surface.

I drink all of my water bottle, waiting in reception. I need to be hydrated, not stressed. Then I *am* stressed, because I need to pee. Reception has a brochure on 'Pets for PTSD' which redeems Lawyer 1's 'Pedo-is-a-gentleman' faux pas. And now she's here, shaking my hand. Lawyer 1 is Amanda Steel; fit, honey-blonde, dressed in no-fuss navy with sharp heels.

Ms Steel leads me into a meeting room, quickly explains that 'vicarious liability' might be used against me because most of my assaults happened off school grounds. Her assistant takes notes. Brain struggles to follow. Body fidgets, awash in chemicals. Steel says I'll need to show 'public knowledge', doesn't understand Ghost-Mother's 'reluctance'. 'Can you contact other teachers? … classmates?'

I make a list.

After forty minutes I really need to pee, but don't want to interrupt. I start to panic because myphone isrunning outof charge andVincewon't knowhowtofind meand I needhimjust tocrossthe roadbecause I havetoholdmyEars.

Steel asks if I'd 'like to proceed? … with a case.'

Drowning in second thoughts and eyeball urine, I tell her I'd like '*some* justice'. Then the enormous risk takes a seat beside me. '… but IhaveNomoneyforthisman's crimebecauseI've paidsomuch already.'

Steel sits back. 'Our costs have to be covered.' She places hands on the table. Assistant puts pen down. They watch me, hawk-eyed. *All my risk.*

'Costs can be minimised in Queensland,' prompts Amanda Steel, sensing my dismay. 'We have compulsory mediation.'

Brain cannot grasp the words pulsing chilli-sauce through my skull.

'We try *not* to go to court,' she explains.

Good, I think. Head hurts. Ears ring. Phone dead. Now I justneedto emptybursting bladder. They give me documents to 'read and consider'.

Outside, I flit in desperatebursts betweencar and freewayNoise. Can't find Vince. I tightenthighs and eye-scan-search SouthBrisbane, hopingVince willrecognise mycrouch. *This is ridiculous.* He could be anywhere. Then Vince pulls up beside me.

'Toilet!' I blather-cry. *Stressed people do odd things.*

Days later, Steel emails a cost agreement, the same as the Sydney lawyers'. Vince offers what's left of his superannuation. Exhausted, afraid and angry, I dump the paperwork on a shelf. My teeth metal-ache.

June 16

Vince has gone early. Oceanic gusts swirl outside as I wander from kitchen, to guest room, to laundry, unfocused. Body carries buzz-Brain. *Oh.* I hang the clothes I'd forgotten. A magpie demands tidbits of my cheesy crackers. She has babies to feed. Their squarks remind me; I'm supposed to be hunting truth, that shallow-trapped fish, of who-knew-what, when.

Back inside, staring at my laptop, I find a contact for Garry, the sweet boy from school whom I did not treat well. He stole my abused heart from the Teacher. Could have saved me from the Beast, but I was too numb to give him a chance. Deep breath. Send the text:

> Hello Garry, it's Cathy Byrne. Sorry I've not been in contact. I suppose you've heard about Cunning's arrest and suicide? Just wondering if you'd be willing to chat with my lawyer? I'm seeking truth.

Garry has no reason to help me. After all these years, I'm not expecting anything. I go to make tea, but a *ding* sends me straight back.

> Absolutely, no problem, replies Garry. That situation is why I left school early. I'll call this weekend.

My face is awash with relief. *I am not alone!*

A few minutes later Georgia, a student-friend of Maggie's, calls. She'd been monitoring social media when Perp was arrested. 'I can give you names of people who said they knew, if that's helpful?'

After months of isolated desperation, my thorax umbrella pushes up, allowing a deep breath. Something lifts off my shoulders. I sit taller as gratitude snot-spots my sleeves.

I've not looked at Facebook since recoiling from his image, months ago. Anxious as I click Tacking Point's 'community' page, Perp's photo tosses a *phoopth*-grenade into chest.

I hate Facebook!

People have commented; they 'knew this was going on', this 'whispered secret'. Another 'knew he was creepy'. Nothing reliable enough for court. Someone declares: 'historic cases are irrelevant … he was a good teacher'. Another: 'The story wasn't *simple* … he and his wife took their lives because no matter what, he'd always be judged'.

It's a crime to have sex with a minor. Simple as that. A child cannot consent.

I sigh myself away from ignorance, notice the light drop as clouds thicken. My neck prickles but I force myself outside, to move half-dried clothes back to the deck. My fingers freeze-grip the laundry basket too tightly. I cannot move. Cannot feel the rain. I don't know how long I'm there – until the neighbour's door slams, and the gun-shy rabbit bolts.

Inside, I sit very still, don't close my eyes … *Breathe* until the terror passes.

I check the Bureau of Meteorology: no rain is forecast. Nothing is trustworthy. I step outside and stare at the sky as if I've glitched my processor. I'm missing something. Go back. *Keep going.*

A Facebook novice, I discover a link to 'private messages'.

Breathe in. Click. From Tilly, before the suicide:

> Cathy, I heard about Cunning's arrest. Many of us from school will back you. I saw Garry's friend Scott a few times. He hated what Cunning did. I'm here for you.

From Tilly, after the suicide:

> I'm so sorry, Cathy. What a coward! Your 'relationship' was joked about at school. It's impossible that teachers didn't know. Yours wasn't the only one. Other teachers socialised with students, with alcohol. We were all kids, but everyone knew something disturbing was going on. Reach out, Cath.

I forget to exhale.
From Sam:

> Cathy, the relationship between you and Cunning was common knowledge. I hope you're OK?

From Kristen:

> Hi Cathy, when I heard Cunning was charged, I instantly thought of you. Fucking coward! I'm so sorry. I often think I could have helped you more back then. Dad was a Head Teacher and might have some insights.

I exhale-type 'thanks' and ask what those insights might include.
There are more messages.
From David:

> Cathy, I hope you're OK? I recall the unusual closeness between Cunning and yourself, how you arrived at, and left school with him. It was common knowledge something was going on. Stay strong, we're all supporting you!

From Jonah:

> Hey Cathy, I've been on the verge of contacting you but was unsure how you were coping. I remember Cunning 'grooming' you at Pebbly Beach and the increasing amount of time you spent together. It's my clear recollection that your 'relationship' was common knowledge. I'd be willing to put this in a statement. Hope you're OK.

'Support!' I whoop. Yes! The sun is back out. I re-hang the laundry without freezing up. Chuffed, I put the kettle on, check my laptop. There's an email from Carol, the girl from my year who'd yelled from the school bus. She writes:

> *I'm so sorry you were abused by Cunning. I remember you being unusually close and him treating you differently. When my sister told me about his death, your name came immediately to mind. I'll help any way I can.*

Students knew it was wrong.

These old classmates, who I've not spoken to for thirty-five years, offer concern, solidarity. I stay afloat in their empathy, thank them, ask if they'll write their recollections.

I bounce around my living room, shouting, 'I love Facebook!'

~

In group therapy, we do superhero stances to enter our inner strength. We Tibetan-stomp around the garden, deep-hum ourselves into our extremities. My chest blooms with hope for the first time in months. I remember my mantra. *I can breathe!*

I offer to visit Ghost-Mother and 'not-talk'. I buy her two locally pottered teacups and think about how difficult things have been for her. A few sniffs of my Vicks menthol inhaler dampens my intense nausea and I shield myself in lemon-balm tea steam as she edges around me, tries to be pleasant. I hold myself in a fragile cup.

The sun is still out when I get home, coating the sky in silver shimmer. I bring in the laundry as if I'm not afraid. I find the legal agreement and attempt to understand 'vicarious liability': an employer is not necessarily responsible for *all* the actions of its employees. I doubt that my schoolmates' support will prove the Department 'knew'.

I take a call from Kristen Rolfe, whose father was deputy principal back then. She tells me her father was 'aware that Cunning had an affair with a softball-team girl at Loggerville High' before he came to Tacking Point. 'Dad said the parents condoned it …' She pours these strange words into my silence. 'I don't even know what that could mean,' she adds.

Brain spins into question-mania: *Someone before Lucy? Was Perp's first wife a student?* That would explain the lacy bridal underwear. *Did the Department move him on?*

'I'm sorry,' she says. 'Dad won't make a statement.'

Nausea coats guts with realisation: Kristen's mum, Janet Rolfe, was Lucy's 'suspicious' PE teacher, Tacky's PE mistress who refused to let Perp coach our girls' soccer. Perp got so angry about that. Now I know why. Janet had also taught at Loggerville, knew of Perp's prior 'relations' with a student. I feel both betrayed and validated. *Teachers knew it was wrong.* Ms Rolfe might have helped back then but she died a while back. And now, Kristen's dad is afraid.

Truth has a use-by date.

I hold head in my hands. Should eat, but stomach is cement.

Maggie calls to say that Lucy won't make a statement. 'She's sorry, but she's dealing with too much in her life.' I pull spines of disappointment from my chest.

'Tell her I understand,' I say, but don't feel.

I breathe-walk myself past doorways, muscles twitching. I'm avoiding something but can't pinpoint what. I check the wall calendar, worried I've missed an appointment. I sense a replica inside the zombie that lives my life, avoiding spectres behind closed eyelids. I can't scratch them out. Head plonks on the dining table. I cry and cry, blotting the legal agreement.

I return to the blue wall and stare blankly at my laptop. An unread Facebook message from Maree, another Tacky student:

> Cathy, thanks for speaking up. A similar thing happened to me by another Tacking Point teacher. Because of your courage, I've finally reported to police after 35 years. When I read about Cunning, it affected my whole body. I knew I couldn't move forward

> without doing something. I'd blocked it for so long. Thank you for showing me the courage to speak my truth.

I'm proud-horrified that I've enticed another survivor into the trauma-layer-cake of police reporting. Nausea surges. Head is a fire-ant nest. Why drag my parents' names through mud? my husband into financial ruin? my family into fracture? my school community into 'irrelevant' history? myself into a fight with my own employer? Why can't I escape that pedo-rapist-coward's mess?

I contact Maree, who tells me of other 1980s cases. One teacher was discovered altering the exam results of a senior girl he was abusing. The girl did not get help and ... ended up killing her own child.

Horror swamps me. And recognition. I tip-toe through the house, stepping around the question: *Am I becoming monstrous?*

Revelations

June 20

Sunday is squally-cold. Ghost-Mother texts: How aarre you? I can't stomach answering. Vince is cooking bacon. I can't turn the phone off either because I'm waiting for Garry's call. I open windows, sit at the dining table and google 'central nervous system and nausea'. I learn that the distasteful chem-gut-flush is a dopamine-apomorphine cocktail, injected into a cavity near the brainstem where the vagal nerves prepare the body for an emergency.

I've been living in my emergency for too long.

I spread out legal documents, but my eyes blur until I'm staring at other paperwork: my senior school subject selection forms. I'm in my school uniform. Mum and I are fighting. I'm being sixteen-sarcastic, threatening to select Perp's music class. '*He said I'll get good marks.*' She's threatening to move me from Tacking Point High to

Saints College in Loggerville, to 'get me away from him'.

Teachers suspected. My parents suspected. They never got HIM away from me.

Garry calls. I go to the guest room so Vince doesn't have to hear my awfuls. Strips of muted light reach through the blinds as I hunch on the futon. I hear that Garry suffered too, having to leave school before final exams. He felt used by me in the cover-up 'relationship' but feels guilty about not doing anything when I told him later about the rape. So long ago now.

We apologise for our various failings.

'I saw Cunning a few months ago,' Garry tells me, 'at Scott's funeral.'

'Wait … *What?*' I stutter. *Perp and Scott stayed in touch?* 'Sorry, I … didn't know Scott died.' I remember Garry's best friend.

'Cunning got invited to Scott's funeral by mistake,' Garry explains, 'but he didn't dare come to the wake. There were lots of people from Tacky High. I told everyone that Scott's death meant one less person to testify against the prick. Scott hated what Cunning did to you.'

I'm time-warp-shocked that these two 'loves' from my early life met recently. 'When was the funeral?' I ask, looking through the blinds at gathering clouds.

'March 9th,' says Garry, still grief-stricken.

'That's the day I called the police.' I'm stunned by synchronicity.

'Scott would've been proud of you for coming forward,' Garry says sadly.

I'm quiet. Absorbing. Remembering stepping into the police station.

'I was sick to the stomach when I saw Cunning,' Garry continues. 'I refused to shake his hand, and the coward didn't understand why. "History," I said, but he had no moral view on his past actions.'

'I know,' I reply, breath shuddery. 'He justified his abuse on a police phone call, said he thought my father knew.'

Uncomfortable silence slides down my throat as the last strip of sunlight fades. Gun-metal clouds loom in from the sea.

'Is someone with you now?' Garry asks carefully.

'Yes.' The incoming squall clatters the blinds. I slide the window shut and pull the blue-swirled futon-cover around me.

Garry takes a deep breath. 'This information will be difficult.'

'OK …?' After the past three months, I can't imagine anything more difficult.

'In Year Ten, Scott spoke to your father in the playground. I've never forgotten. He said: "Rob Cunning is screwing your daughter." Your father just walked away.'

Phoofff. The vacuum sucks lead into empty lungs.

'We were expecting something to happen once your dad knew,' Garry continues, 'but nothing changed.'

Body becomes both heavy and light. Not breathing, I dizzy-float over waves.

Dad knew.

'Scott and I couldn't believe the adults never stepped up.' Garry pauses. 'Cathy? Will you be alright?'

'Ahhh … *Phoofff.*' I clutch Little Brave, sip in air. Nausea claws my throat. 'I have to go.'

I hang up and stumble out to Vince, howling turmoil out of my chest.

'Dad was told! … but did nothing. *Nothing!*'

Vince hauls me into him. 'I'm here,' he says. 'Who was that?'

'This world is sick,' I whisper, 'I can't be in it anymore.'

'No. No. No.' Vince holds me as my legs crumble.

~

Why proceed with a civil case now? I answer the blue wall: 'Because Thirteen is still waiting. Because children deserve better.' *Truth matters.* Accountability is needed.

I sign the cost agreement and send it to Amanda Steel who promptly informs me that 'student support is not enough … You need a teacher who acknowledges the public nature of that "relationship".' Ex-Teacher-Ghost-Mother will not.

I feel the important, impossible choice. The call of river mud.

Community Justice

8

Weeding out the Queen

On Doc's advice I send my police statement to old family then shallow-breathe the hours, wondering how they'll respond. I juggle to thirty throws, then forty.

Ghost-Mother pinches her mouth in distaste; she's come to help in my garden, 'not to talk about *that*.' She points at a clump of false shamrock. 'You have to dig oxalis deep, get to the root of it, underneath the corm, or it keeps coming up,' she lectures. I swallow the irony as she demonstrates with recycled chopsticks.

'I'm sad that you blame me,' she bemoans.

Sigh. 'The one to blame is *dead*, Mum ... but you had your suspicions.' I hold her in it. 'You went and spoke to his parents.'

'No. I'd remember *that*.' Ghost-Mother shrinks away to poke at stubborn weeds.

Does she forget? Or avoid remembering? Truth keeps weeding its way up.

Visiting his parents might've been Dad's idea of protocol. Perp's father was a senior teacher. They chose to protect fraternity.

Ghost-Mother can't help herself. Steps back towards me.

'How *aare* you?' she asks, 'I mean … inside.'

'I don't feel I'm being heard.' To avoid her eyes, I step sideways, dust my gloves.

'I'll never convince you that I didn't know,' she says quietly.

'I haven't accused you of knowing, just of not acting on your concerns. And not supporting me recently. That really hurts,' says Big Brave.

'Your *new* story doesn't erase our experience of how you were back then.'

Not a new story; the truth of the old lie.

Reporting *should* change everything. Should ignite compassion for the manipulated child. Ghost-Mother does not understand the price I paid. I ask what she could have done differently.

'We could have restricted your activities. No surfing, no music, no outings. We could have banned you from riding your bike.' She'd *still* punish the child. 'By not doing a statement, I protected *you*,' she adds.

'From what?' I snap.

'Your deceit,' she bitters, twisting chopsticks into sand. 'I wasn't going to lie *for* you.' She tosses shame into my naughty-girl bucket.

'I never asked you to lie,' I choke out.

'When I was a child,' she steamrolls, 'my father went to court and was ripped to shreds.'

'That's horrible, Mum,' I empathise, 'but it doesn't justify your recent inaction.' She confuses 'recent' with 'back then'.

'We didn't know,' her voice raised '… about the rape.'

Rapes. Multiple. Child non-consent. Over and over and over.

The rare sunshine chokes in clouds. I slow-breathe, watching three noisy miners hassle a kookaburra. Ghost-Mother walks to the other end of my path and, separately, on our knees, we rip up dirty clumps of history.

Relentless, she circles back. 'We're all hurting,' she says, 'but you *refuse* other perspectives.' Her gnarled finger prods my shoulder. 'Pull yourself down a peg and listen for a change.' Ghost-Mother demands humility from the 'uppity' girl.

I exhale sour milk through cotton balls.

'The last time I dealt with police, it was horrible,' Ghost-Mother justifies. When she'd peeked under the station fence to see Dad's crumpled plane? Or ... was it making that character statement for the community worker charged with having kiddie porn?

I remember. After Dad died. She'd typed two pages for a local politics string-puller. Asked me to proofread her righteous 'Letter of Support,' for someone she thought was being 'unfairly harassed because he's a greenie and a homosexual'. She'd come that far at least.

Truth shimmers here, white-hot sparks under eyelids. She'd defended that 'upstanding' man ... *but not the confident girl.*

I float on a cold gust from the south. Then, like Irish weed, Ghost-Mother rises, tugs me back, her voice triumphant:

'In our day, your father and I, we took two years to go from dating, to kissing, to sexual intimacy. I ... We ... didn't know.'

Furious, I pull my gloves off. 'The fact that an *adult* was having a relationship with your *child* should have been enough.'

'Oh,' she ramps into her superior tone, 'I know of other relationships – young students with *teachers* – that worked out. The Queen was only thirteen when *she* was married off, and *she* had a long, stable relationship!'

Her royal misinformation astounds me.

'I'm tired,' I say, heading inside, not inviting her.

Mother's statement

Late June

Ghost-Mother phones. 'It was an effort, but I've typed it,' she bemoans. 'I'm not welcome in your house ...' I don't correct her. 'So, you'd best come up.'

Astounded, I gobble ginger bears, sniff my Vicks menthol, and brave the 255 steps up the street, counting in tens, deep into nausea.

It takes only a minute to email it to myself. Stuff the rules of justice.

Then I get the pottery cups and ask: 'Mum, what do you love about me?'

She pauses: 'You travelled …'

'That was ages ago. What about *now*?' I persist, risking the mother-love myth. My ears burn in the hush. Shadows shift in her garden. I sniff Vicks. Watch the leaves. She diverts to her sister's husband's skin cancer. I rub sharp pains in my abdomen and walk my shredded expectations home to read her one-pager:

> Our four children were encouraged to achieve academically, were involved in after-school sport, musicals, bands, gymnastics. Both of us were working. We had one car and a motorbike. The accused made himself useful with transport. Part of the grooming process.
>
> Cathy was always strong, confident, determined. A high achiever. Happy. Healthy. She played representative soccer, travelled to Japan. We had no reason for concern. She seemed in control, of everything. These traits are why this crime was not outed years ago. Cathy thought she could deal.
>
> She was initially infatuated and I thought she might run away with him. He rewarded her with placements in the band, roles in musicals. He made her feel special. He was involved in soccer coaching. I never saw anything to make me think the relationship was sexual. We tried to deal with his being around so much. Tried, but not hard enough. I'm so sorry. We failed in our duty as parents, to protect our daughter.
>
> If we'd been told of this sexual assault and Cathy had been prepared to talk, we would have reported the matter. I now understand Cathy was under his control, that she lied to cover their tracks.

Sometime after January 1987, Cathy told us he'd raped her. It had to be after this date because he was at Maggie's 21st. We were so shocked. We knew nothing until then. Then she went away and we couldn't do anything because Cathy was off exploring the world.

In 1989, I was teaching at Saints College, Loggerville. The accused came up to say hello and I just looked at him. He knew that I knew what he'd done. He hurried off and I never saw him again.

Recently, Cathy brought this issue to the police. I now see the devastating effect this is having. I'm mortified that we were groomed and used. We are all victims.

There it is, like a sliced-up photograph: a truth that took one hundred days of asking.

Her insistence they 'knew nothing' sits at the black-hole edge of my blame-fuelled nausea. Even later, when they knew, they didn't report.

They were all still teaching!

I send Mum's statement to the lawyer and, risking email-overload, to my siblings. Cold seeps into sleepless bones until worry wakes, to war:

'*Stop this email shit. You're driving a wedge into this family*,' Lianne reprimands, reminds me I 'participated'. Rocky is 'disgusted' Mum took so long to write a statement, wants to '*burn the family veil of secrecy*'. Lianne is 'disgusted' with Rocky's version of my story (which might include his own paranoia about our parents). Lianne says attacking Mum is cancel-culture and '*You can't rewrite history, Cathy!*' She insists Mum and Dad '*tried to discourage it*'.

Discourage what?

'*Children keep quiet when they feel blame, Lianne, like when you hid your homosexuality*,' I poke.

Maggie is 'dripping sweat inside her Covid clinic gear,' and 'loves us all'. She has real emergencies to deal with.

Family. The obligation wraps so tightly around our necks we strangle each other. Lianne calls. Hasn't read my statement. 'Should they have put a 16-year-old in court in the 1980s?'

'Dad was told,' I protest-swivel the spotlight, trying to find my big sister.

'Told?' she hollers into the phone. 'That's schoolyard gossip.'

Testimony, not gossip. Throat spasms. Body scrunches into a tight ball. I taste the sharp bile of my obsession. Hang up. Pour whiskey.

A civil case, now implicating my parents, will decimate us.

The waterfall

La Niña taunts the coast. Everything is slick-sticky. I walk along the sludging river, earplug guarding against sudden noise. It's no barrier to the shrill inside my head or the images that bully me. Back home, I juggle, counting the throws to empty my mind, but it doesn't, so I force myself back outside, chance a swim in the murky sea.

My saltwater self-care routine is becoming sporadic, its effects short-lived. I spin into sleeplessness and vertigo. Days sway with nausea, sound sensitivity and panic about what is real. It rains and almost clears. Rinse. Repeat.

When the sun finally peeks through, I step out with wet laundry to find Ghost-Mother on my deck with a bag of 'healing lemons' from her tree.

'I chose the bag especially for you,' she chortles, waiting for me to turn. I don't.

'It says "Your Family Butcher",' she hollers.

I peg towels in the thick soak between us; a waterfall behind my chest. *What happens if I pull the plug?*

'So … I'm the Family Butcher?'

'Gaawd, I can't say anything right.' Mr Hyde simpers back under old-lady skin. 'There's a note inside.' She waggles the bag, trying to redirect my frozen stare, but I don't move. Enthralled with her own performance, she reaches into the bag, flourishes a scrap of paper and orates: 'We should be on the *same team* against the rapist.'

Only now, joining my team? What does she want?

'You forgave the rapist. Can you forgive us for who we were then, and now?'

What's left of my tiny Buddhist stretches gossamer-thin, afraid to breathe.

'I forgave him too soon, Mum,' I whisper, 'and he wasn't really sorry. He said it was what I wanted; that he thought Dad knew.'

She holds the scrap of paper like a code breaker, seeking a clue, a way forward.

I will never be free of her desperate need for absolution.

'I need a walk,' she gripes.

'I don't feel like walking.' I sigh, running out of hanging space.

She shrugs and swans off down the road, swaddled in breezy nonchalance. Neither of us realise ... we must forgive ourselves.

Recognition justice

New South Wales Victim Services emails. I *won't* be reimbursed for the medical expenses *they advised me to claim*. I call the Rape Crisis Centre. Heidi urges me to try again.

'They just have to click one box on your file.'

'Who clicks the box?' I ask.

'Your case manager.'

'I don't seem to have one.' I flounder between phone calls and webforms.

Someone at Victim Services says: 'You need a medical certificate saying you're unfit for work, from the act of violence. It must be physical harm, from the time of the act.' BodyBrain's psycho-physical harm, from the violence of 40 years ago, surfaced only months ago.

'So, historic cases can't get PTSD support?' I ask. *I can't work.*

'You need a letter from a clinical psychologist saying you're unfit for duties as a direct result of the violence.' But I can't get in to see a psych. Can't afford one.

I'm told to fill in another form.

Bureaucratic box-ticking palaver frustrates me into doomscrolls. I find medieval misogyny: female soldiers forced to march in high heels; a women's beach volleyball team fined for wearing shorts instead of skimpy bikinis.

Get out of the house.

~

Rain threatens again as I drive to meet Maggie's friend Georgia, who's trying to find me a psych appointment. I tell her I wish it was all over.

'PTSD can take years, Cathy. Your nervous system is inflamed, with deep wounds. You wouldn't expect to heal broken bones so quickly,' Georgia chides gently. 'Give yourself time to recalibrate … try dancing,' she suggests.

'I've been dishwashing to "Dancing Queen", and I tried a drumming class at the community hall,' I tell her, 'but they asked me to leave when they found out my age.'

Georgia raises her eyebrows.

'It's for pensioners.'

We laugh. Georgia tells me I am not responsible for Ghost-Mother's fears.

Validation without judgement feels good.

I drive home under oppressive clouds as the radio pushes words into ears: 'South Australia's Opera Chief … jailed for eight years … sexual relationships with teenagers … no remorse, no insight into his gross breach of trust … victims accused of being "flirtatious, willing participants".' The judge argues they'd been 'manipulated into his adult secret'. 'A schoolgirl crush would come to nothing,' she reprimands, 'if teachers respected professional boundaries.'

Understanding! I wind down the window, let rain sting my face.

'It broke me inside,' says a victim. 'I pretended to be grown up, but I was vulnerable, groomed by a predator.'

The judge rules that 'The protection of children is paramount.'

Responsibility! The acknowledgement unblocks my chest as I drive; the wall of blame cracks. My waterfall thunders out and I pull over in surrender, sobbing until I'm empty-hearted and snot-sodden. I'm still wiping my face when Lianne calls.

'I read your statement,' she says coolly. 'Nothing we didn't already know.'

What was she expecting?

'No wonder he was arrested.'

Does she doubt its completeness? Its validity?

'You should have gone into law, Cathy.' Her snide remark squirms in my eardrum. 'You showed no outward signs.' *She doesn't understand. Broken inside.*

'Truth isn't simple, Lianne,' I defend, voice shuddery.

'Cathy, there *is* no truth. Everyone has their own version. Mum and Dad did their best, while you were sneaking off having sex.'

Oh! *Phoofff.* Body stiffens. *She thinks I enjoyed it!*

Unable to speak, I hang up, drive home and haul my dripping up the stairs.

Tacking Point lies

July

An email from Victim Services declares: 'Ms Byrne was a primary victim of an act of violence.' Someone clicked a box. I'm eligible for a Recognition Payment, a *kind-of* justice.

A quick calculation reminds me I've lost more than this amount in teaching days given up for the police interview, hunting old addresses, attending appointments. Recognition helps, but having no income tightens my panic. *How can I find a brave teacher?*

I ring Amanda Steel and tell her I can't ask ex-teachers about their knowledge because another 1980s Tacky High sexual abuse case is being investigated. Maree's safety might be jeopardised. I won't risk that.

'Keep trying,' Steel urges.

Justice feels impossible.

~

I'm staring blankly at my laptop when Facebook suggests a birthday wish for Karen Schiller, my junior-high soccer buddy, whose father taught maths.

She responds immediately:

> Hey Cathy, how are you coping?
>
> Getting over the shock, I reply.
>
> I knew it was you, she says, even though the media withheld your name. Dad told me the maths master reported Cunning, and your father was called to the principal's office.

Seriously*?!*

Blood drains into legs. Chest implodes. I fight the chemical choke-drowning; the hot patch behind skull; the skin-ants.

Dad knew. The school knew. But Confident Girl was not worth saving?

Brain wants information but Body urgently needs a lie-down. I *zhee-zhjou* nonsense words, vomit air, in anti-gulps. Close my eyes as *phoopthhs* launch me off the bed until my breastbone aches.

Squalls rumble through spaces that used to contain memory, filling me with the squelch of greasy ocean chop and hurling rain. That night, I try to scream from inside a fish-trap. No noise exits my mouth.

'Nothing untoward'

I message Karen. But 'No,' her teacher-dad, Bert Schiller, 'does not want to comment'. 'What could it possibly come to?' he'd asked. 'Cunning is dead. The principal is dead. Cathy's dad said there was "nothing untoward" going on. What does she want … money?'

Karen apologises for her father's obstruction. Says she understands I want *finality*. Yes, and to escape this constant nausea.

I doomscroll to a study that says 'many people still think sexual assault reporting is motivated by revenge or greed.'

Why not truth?

I track down a contact for Mr Donnelly, my once-favourite maths teacher. He was community-minded, fun. He has children. Girls. *He will help.*

'I know why you're calling,' Donnelly says. 'I had a call from Bert Schiller, who remembered when your dad was called to the principal's office.'

Oh. 'What do *you* remember?' I hold every muscle in abeyance.

A weighted pause. 'I found it hard to reconcile our teacher training with what was going on. We were taught that if you even looked sideways at a senior girl you'd be transferred' – he hesitates – 'or sacked.'

Transferred?

'You and Cunning were a topic of conversation in the staffroom. People were concerned. It *was* reported to the principal.'

'Would you be willing to put that in writing?' I hold a hope-filled breath.

'I …' A sharp exhale. 'I don't want to get involved. The Department has the report. You should subpoena that document,' he advises.

Can a document be subpoenaed?

'Couldn't you just write down what you remember?'

'I don't want to go to court,' he admits.

'Neither do I.' *No-one has to go to court if you just write down what you've told me.*

Donnelly sighs. 'Well … I'd feel gutless not saying anything,' he raises my hopes. 'Let me think about it.'

Think about what? Why are they all afraid? My head is a babbling switchboard. *Was the maths master's report the reason Dad chatted to me with Maggie? When did my parents visit his? When did Scott speak to Dad in the playground? What did the principal say to my father?* And then, the lightning, waiting for the thunderclap: *What was Dad's reply?*

~

I track down another maths teacher's address. Trying to calm-breathe as teeth grind, I walk the thirty minutes to his house. Back then, we called Mr Marsh 'Walrus'. Long socks, brown shorts, camel-coloured cardigan, creepy moustache. He's outside, walking his dog. Same cardigan.

I wade through nausea, take a deep breath. 'Mr Marsh?'

He looks over, squints. An effort to remember my name? or calculating his escape?

'Cathy Byrne,' I remind him. 'I'm trying to contact Mr Trotter, the old maths master.'

Marsh seems nervous. 'You're not accusing *me* of anything, are you?'

'Not at all,' I respond, confused.

He shakes his head. 'Where will it end?'

It should end the sexual abuse of children, I don't say.

'I had a relationship with a student and we got married,' he admits.

You probably didn't rape her when she was thirteen, I don't say.

'We heard a sixty-six-year-old had been charged, then Bert Schiller called, asked if I'd been up to my old tricks,' Marsh chortles, 'So, *I* said …' I stare-wait for his punchline. '"I wish I was only sixty-six, so it can't be me!" Heh heh.'

The void between us balloons in slow motion. Gum trees in the breeze. Pelicans in the creek. Me, not-breathing.

'Well, if it was *horrific* …' He looks away. 'Something should be done.'

What child abuse is not horrific?

People sense wrongness but the choice, *to not act*, becomes a habit of 'unseeing'. The child 'seems fine'. The lack of care, then and now, by adults who failed me, drags a heavy blanket. The shadow encroaches.

Walrus says he doesn't have Trotter's contact. 'I'm more interested,' he wavers, 'in why your father crashed his plane.' I am astonished by his flippancy. 'It's a bit gossipy, I know, but there's a rumour these stories are related—'

'They're not.' I cut him off. 'If a report was taken to the principal, but not the Department, that's *negligence*.'

The word alarms him. Walrus backs away, tugging his dog leash.

'What can you hope to achieve?'

'I want the truth,' I mumble.

Go home, Brain commands Body.

Distractions

Vince has to drive to Childers for work. I have to escape Tacky sludge. He drops me at Noosa and I carry my board to Tea Tree Bay. Paddling with friendly locals, floating on serene green, I stretch arms wide and suck the sweet mango sky into belly.

Joy comes in waves; in healing walls of ocean. *This* therapy helps me to keep going. Happy-exhausted, I ride a final 'Jesus-wave': feet on the nose, hips, chest and arms out, skimming sparkles all the way to shore where I step onto sand, laughing like a sugared-up kid.

The high lasts all day. I fit in a long chant, yoga, a bath, then cocktails to celebrate Vince's big contract win. I get the best sleep I've had in months.

Heading home, Vince takes a call from his boss. Despite the win, they still won't hire support staff. 'They're assholes!' I voice his outrage. *Buoyancy is fleeting.*

Ghost-Mother phones, ridicules my 'wasteful spending'.

La Niña flings another rain bomb through Tacky's turgid lies.

July 5

Radio news announces Queensland's 'Failure to Report' law. 'It's now a punishable offence for an adult not to report any sexual misconduct by an adult against a child.' New South Wales passed this law in 2018. *Are the old teachers afraid the law is retrospective?*

Soon, people will cease gossiping about Perp's double suicide. Relevance disintegrates. Soon, another retired teacher will die, their recollections lost forever. I can't find Trotter, the maths master. I phone Donnelly, leave another message asking for a statement.

Trapped in churning water, wanting surrender, I wonder how long I'll keep paddling? *How long can I keep wishing truth from other people's hearts?*

Mid-July

I haven't heard from my lawyer in a month. Stalling, I juggle until I get to seventy-five throws, until breathing calms me enough to politely email-prod Amanda Steel. Her assistant phones:

'Ms Steel will make contact when she has news.'

A caged lion, I flit from deck to office; from laptop to kitchen; from blue daybed to blue screen. I shouldn't use Facebook until Maree's made her statement. I drink forgetful tea and stomp about barefoot, wanting to let go. But something grips my intestines. *Someone.*

I try Donnelly again. He doesn't respond. Chooses 'gutless'.

To access the report Donnelly mentioned, I'll have to proceed to court. *It's all up to me.*

Amanda Steel sends me more 'authority-to-access' forms. Why has it taken this long? My case is bottom-shelf unimportant.

I listen to 'Nothing Ever Happens' by Del Amitri as evening sea mist stalks the garden. I flick aimlessly through Tacky High's 1988 yearbook. In the dimming light I read that Perp and his stage band appeared on national TV, on The Ray Martin Show. Gut clenches at the words: *Band leader Robert Cunning raised the standing of the school.*

Wait ... *When?* I switch the light on, adjust my glasses.

1988!? Even after concerns about an inappropriate relationship – in *1983?* – the predator kept touring! With busloads of children! To eisteddfods in '84, '85, '86! In 1987, his school band, now including my brother, was awarded Tacking Point's Young Citizens' Award. They travelled to the USA so the man-child could 'play at Disneyland'. He was lauded. Applauded. Protected? *Why didn't I report?*

I rapid-fire desperate Facebook messages to Isle-of-Lies retired teachers, avoiding Maree's perp's faculty, asking for recollections. Then I vow not to open Facebook for a week.

My Dadirri connection feels broken but I'm trying to un-want an outcome. Surrender is difficult. *Why won't teachers speak up for me? Was I horrible?*

I swirl-wake early into snot-oyster headaches. *Do something!*

I drive to Loggerville, dry-retch as I pass the house of ruin. *Keep going.* I visit Loggerville Library and scroll newspaper microfiche until my eyes burn.

When did Perp win 'Best and Fairest'?

At Loggerville High, scanning yearbooks, I find PE teacher, Ms Rolfe, and Perp's father, and the softball girls Perp got too-friendly with. No pics of Perp. *Did the Department shift him?* Heart wants the truth of when my parents knew, but Brain disintegrates.

Garry texts: Hire a private investigator.

I don't have the funds, I reply. I just need an adult to be an adult.

I get nowhere and barely get home before another storm engulfs the coast in black sky. Vince is away again.

Why won't anyone help? I. Am. Worthless.

Rain-imprisoned, tired and tense, Body gets ready to walk. But Brain knows what I'm planning, so I throw my raincoat down, run back inside, lock the doors. Throw juggling balls at the ceiling. I sit in the dry bath and cry against the clamour.

July 19

Maggie listens as we lean into wind. 'I know it's difficult to understand, but my trauma is not forty years old. It's raw and recent.' She tries to comprehend. 'He's dead, but I'm still startled by every noise, afraid to leave the house, unable to eat or sleep. Reporting punched me into old fears.' I don't mention the visions or the cliffs.

'What do you need?' Maggie asks sincerely.

I need a teacher to admit awareness of the 'relationship', I don't say.

'I need Mum's old friends' affidavits. Mum could contact the canteen lady, Meg Morell.'

'Sounds reasonable,' says Maggie. 'Have you asked?'

'Mum had a meltdown.' I drop my head in dismay, hug Maggie off to work and head out for a cold float in the rockpools of Dad's ashes.

Can he see me now, cradling respect?

~

When I get home, Amanda Steel's email asks for the maths master's contact.

I'm trying to find it! I e-fluster.

Steel calls to tell me I can't access the police phone call without Perp's next-of-kin's permission. 'I don't want to harass his children,' I yell.

Steel says the 'defendant is not responding to requests'. Realisation cements my gut: *The New South Wales Education Department.* I'm no longer fighting for truth, or justice, or anything noble. The 'defendant' used to be the Teacher-rapist. Now, the 'other party' is a law firm for an international, shareholder-profit-driven insurance company, acting for a state government agency, fighting to protect its assets. *A faceless behemoth.*

'It's just about money for them,' Steel reminds me.

The Department will hide behind a team of lawyers. The longer it takes, the more the lawyers get paid. *Cruelty has no credit limit.*

'How long can they stretch this fight?'

Her lead-words plop into my gut: 'It might take two years.'

Heaviness drags me, into groin, knees, ankles. Brings on dizzy. I hang up. Lie down.

Horror thoughts barge behind my eyes. Something soft-innocent, tossed from a balcony.

No! *I would never do that.*

Time oozes, drip-feeding blood-hungry sharks.

Hours later, Body faces the blue wall. Brain floats across lines of text, re-reading the legal agreement I shouldn't have signed. Can I back out? *Plead insanity.* They can stall until my witnesses die, until Vince and I run out of money – or willpower. I feel vomitous.

Gemma rescues me for a beach walk, away from squeaky brakes, barking dogs, and retired teachers who won't make eye contact. It's windy. The ocean booms.

Gem sees I'm frazzled. 'I don't know if I'll know when I've had enough,' I confess, swallowing tears, scrunching sand between toes.

She looks at me carefully. 'You need sleep.'

'Yes. No. Yes. No, I'm fine.' I try to convince us both.

'At some point,' Gemma says, 'seeking truth might take too much. Are there positives to letting go?' I consider her words.

'Well …' I scoop dry sand into each hand and face her. 'I could drop all of this,' I say, pouring left-hand sand into her palm. 'I could abandon my fractured child and pretend that's OK, but I'd disintegrate. Or' – Gemma peers at the grit in her palm – 'I take on the fight' – I raise my right, warrior-hand – 'keep my head above the shit, subject my adult-self to *more* fracturing, and' – I toss the sand into the breeze – 'still disintegrate.' I noisily exhale, dusting both hands. 'I don't know if either path frees me.'

I close my eyes, try to un-see unspeakables. *No-one will get to me in time.*

When I open my eyes, Gemma is looking into me. I pull a clown face. We both laugh.

'Which way are we going?' she asks as we turn back.

'Does it matter?' I play the metaphor.

Attempting EMDR

I'm about to break my vow – to not check Facebook – when Dr J calls. There's an EMDR cancellation with a counsellor who's not a child sexual abuse specialist.

Her bright office buzzes with sharp fluorescent light, smells of disinfectant, and the requirement to re-tell my story, again.

'Your case is complex. So many layers.' She acknowledges my trauma cake, then white-boards the nervous system, showing how EMDR can re-categorise memories.

We make an appointment to begin treatment. She's all I've got.

Mid-August

Back in the buzz clinic, the counsellor passes me two egg-sized hand-vibrators and explains their brain rewiring function. Then she asks me to recall my rape. Just like that.

She won't know how to save me from head explosions.

I dive in anyway … into his anger as he storms from beach to bike, into the sound of doors locking. I hear his slurpy breath, his words. Mine, ignored. His smell. My blood.

'*I'm so stupid*,' little voice cries.

'Tap your feet,' says the counsellor. 'What comes to mind?'

'I can't … tell anyone, *ever*.' Thirteen uses my mouth. Body locks up, then-now, in this too-bright room.

'What do you notice?' she prompts.

'Be.Very.Careful,' warns Thirteen through slimy gums. Then I notice I've disappeared my middle: 'I'm cut off at the waist!' Cat-furballs spring from upper chest. My sternum hurts. 'I might throw up,' I mumble.

She passes her lined office bin, into which I dry-retch, burp and 'sorry' about my tears. I sense other versions of 'me' watching. So many selves. Waiting. Wondering if memories will shuffle into their proper places now.

Was that EMDR? Did it work? Am I fixed?

I drive to get groceries, gripping the steering wheel tighter than usual.

Noisy bright lights hunch-slump me over the trolley. I put my earplug in. Re-adjust the Covid mask, but smell-swarms trip me into shallow-breathing. My ears bleed a fire-alarm. Ants surge. I see things I don't want to see. Some are memories. Others, horribly red-wet, axe-sharp. I squeeze eyes closed through flashes. Head in hands, body swaying, I barely make it to my car.

Back home, I juggle, brave up and open Facebook. No-one made contact. I go to make toast but realise I didn't buy groceries.

I've missed two calls from Lianne. Shouldn't lower that draw-bridge, but I do.

Worried, Lianne thinks I need a proper psych.

'They're all booked for months,' I exasperate. 'I can't get in until October.'

Lianne tells me she recently lost two friends to suicide.

'That's awful. I'm sorry.'

She wants to help, 'but not with bits of paper'.

Truth, like laws, can be written.

'What are you doing now?' she asks.

I mention my Facebook plea and immediately wish I hadn't.

'You shouldn't be collecting evidence.' She contradicts my legal advice.

Should I go back to the shops?

'You need *professional* help!' She raises the volume.

'It's not available!' I shout.

Lianne roars louder: 'You don't have to do this now!'

Actually I do. My life has collapsed into this muddy black hole and my many selves are sinking. I have to finish what I started. The rescue.

But I don't want Lianne to worry. 'I'm taking care of me,' I reassure. 'I surf and beach-walk,' I say, glimpsing slippery cliffs. 'I have to aim for *some* justice.'

'What does that look like?'

'I don't know,' I flounder. 'I never imagined I'd have to be the investigator, the family mediator, the financial risk evaluator, the legal administrator … *on top* of being the unemployable abuse survivor,' I blurt out. 'I have to do it all,' I whimper.

'You could let it go, Cathy,' she reminds me. 'I understand your anger has to park somewhere, but—'

'I'm *not* angry,' I shout. 'I'm *hurt!*'

'You had us convinced you were *in love*, Cathy. Have you ever tried to stop a teenager having sex?' She dives back into misunderstanding. *Surviving sex.* How can I explain 'peritraumatic amnesia' when I have no words for this myself? How did I fracture into screaming bits and hide quietly under teenage bravado?

'You buried it back then,' Lianne accuses. 'So bury it now,' she commands.

'No!' I howl.

'There are other perspectives.'

Perspectives on child abuse? No. Perspectives on *me.*

'You were an over-confident teenager. Mum doesn't want to change her statement.' The words are poison-tipped. *I did not ask. What has Ghost-Mother been saying?*

'You're on your own now, Cathy.'

Another piece of me shakes loose, falls. Such a regular, ordinary thing.

I slide into whiskey.

Until the end of time

I need a teacher to admit knowledge. Ghost-Mother 'urgently' needs me to collect her from her mechanic. I agree without looking in the mirror.

She's waiting, umbrella-ed on the footpath. The *scrape-scrape* of my broken windscreen-wiper pounds my whiskey-addled head. Ghost asks to be dropped into town, suggests I could take 'better care' with my 'appearance'.

We sit in drip-wet, parked near the river, in stultifying stand-off.

I want to love her. The chip-cracked daughter heart aches for some Mother-hug that maybe never existed. Perhaps she really doesn't remember. If so, how hurt and afraid she must feel, watching me pleading from across the void.

'Cathy, it's *my* fault,' she blurts. 'There's no point blaming anyone else.'

'The school had a duty of care.'

'Ho!' She readies her tirade, but I interrupt:

'Mum, the maths master reported it. Dad was called to the principal's office.' Heart beats a TiddlyBom.

'No. That didn't happen. I'd remember *that*,' she dismisses with a wave of her hand. 'I suppose you got that "convenient" gossip from the internet?' She glares.

Then she cries and I feel her pain. *I never wanted any of this.*

'What do you expect *me* to do?' Ghost-Mother spits.

'I already asked you' – I heavy-sigh with tiredness – 'to ask your old teacher-friends, to write down what they remember. How hard would that be!?'

Ghost-Mother will not be mocked. It triggers her inner attack-dog.

'Ho! I won't be involved in rumour mongering.' She jabs a gnarled finger into my arm. 'Think of an eighty-year-old's blood pressure!'

'What about *my* meltdown, Mum. Do I count?'

Suspicion sours her face, then she shrinks back. 'It's all *my* fault.'

'That leaves me nowhere, Mum.' I sleeve-wipe fog from my windscreen, try to flick a trapped fly out the window. 'You say you want to help,' I plead, 'but you won't.'

She flips. 'Alright, I *will* contact them,' she growls, 'but not with *you* in the room.'

'Why?' I ask, bewildered, eyes flung open.

'So you can't control what they say.' *So you can?*

'I remember how it was.' She hooks me back into the humid space, wounded fly still buzzing. 'Confident Cathy, controlling *everyone*.'

'Really, Mum? There's so much you refuse to remember!'

'Rubbish!' she spits.

'You don't remember Dad being called to the principal. Or visiting Perp's parents?'

'No,' she adamants. 'And so' – in her supreme logic – '... it didn't happen.'

I tap fingers over the bird in my chest, try not to fade through fog.

'What about my letter ... and the argument we had when I told you I'd been raped?'

'I don't remember a letter,' she blocks.

'So, because *you* don't remember, it never existed?' I pick apart her logic.

'Now you're accusing me of dementia?' she booms in horror.

And then I see: I'm being cruel. She does forget. She's afraid of the missing bits.

I know how terrifying that can be. But ... *Go on. Voice it.*

'Mum, your statement said you saw Perp at Saints College, *after* you knew he raped me.'

'Yes, that's correct.'

'And you still did not report him?'

Hold that silence wide open. *Will she see?*

She nods. 'You were gone.'

'He was still teaching!' I yell, revolted by her inaction. 'That's why people keep getting hurt. Why we must *do something*, to stop this!'

Ghost-Mother glares darkly. 'What makes you think *you* can change the world? Men are men. Rape will happen until the end of time.'

Some words should not be spoken. One hand smothers a violent cat-furball. Ice-white knuckles clutch a steering wheel. It's her or me. Hurt or be hurt.

'You should go.' I wind down the windows, to exorcise her foul words. She will deny them soon enough.

'Can we be friends?' she asks, leaning in.

'You're my mother,' I half-choke.

'What does that mean?' she asks as I drive into rain.

~

Mid-morning, still with bed-hair and twitchy eyelids, I see Dr J about throat spasms, vertigo, ear screams. She says my efforts at compassion might block important processes.

'Protecting your mother is *not* your first priority. It's OK to feel angry.' She gives me another list of counsellors. Then explains 'allostatic load' – a toxic body-flush from repeated, prolonged stress. 'The body can get stuck in the "on" position, "survival mode".' She offers a pamphlet about how PTSD is linked to autoimmune and bacterial inflammation, poor insulin regulation, erratic hormone production. Effects can include ringing ears, abnormal responses to sounds, cold hands and feet, mood swings, allergies.

Hello me.

I sense the enormity of my damage. As a teenager, the stress of 'hiding it' became my normal. Later, I was easily bored, frequently burned out. Doc says that 'stress hormones in traumatised people sometimes never return to healthy levels.'

Is this why I changed jobs every year? moved house so often? Had mystery food allergies, weird stress skin-ants, gut aches? Why I can't relax? And never sleep?

'You have an exaggerated startle response,' says Doc, 'and low tolerance to high pitch and volume. Let's be careful this doesn't develop into full-blown sound phobia,' she warns.

Doc gives me a referral to an audiologist, but remembering my childhood hearing tests, I'm already avoiding those screaming headphones. I delay following up. Instead, I get acupuncture, learn that liver channels store emotion, which can cramp the guts; that liver nerves wrap the throat, blockages cause gagging and spasms. *Cat-furballs.*

Meanwhile, Sydney re-enters Covid lockdown. Vince and I cancel our Tassie trip. My head feels foggy. We run out of teabags. I cry.

I phone every number on Doc's new list. None available. Another cold front thumps towards Tacking Point. Nausea builds.

I go to my final group therapy; the program has been de-funded. We talk about what we've learned – from each other, about ourselves. How to listen to Body, how to stretch a glimpse of joy across a day. The facilitator asks us to leave our burdens in the garden.

'Can I bury my nausea?' We laugh.

I could try to stay connected to these brave-broken women but wonder if I should. We say goodbye, each of us afraid of coping alone.

Come what may

Without thinking, I walk into threatening sky. Pins and needles burn the base of my spine, and I have to concentrate to not fall over.

I should not be walking north.

I pass the campgrounds where I last saw my father alive as the heavy blanket lumps onto my shoulders, forcing me to squat, head between knees.

Push on, I have a plan.

I step off the path and head for ocean, thick with scum from the Loggerville hills.

Oyster-grey squalls devour morsels of sunlight as wind slaps rain into my face and putrid-logs stench my nostrils. Along the greasy tideline, someone steps over dead, puffed-up things. And now … I'm above booming cliffs.

This place knows me. It offers a grim, glistening freedom.

Far below, phlegm-coloured swells crush the myths of a martyring Ghost-Mother and a righteous Dead-Father onto rocks. And the Naughty Girl – *Boom. Crash.* She'll be gone soon.

Something brews in me. Something demonic. I'm not sure who I might be hiding. Afraid I'll slip into my headless body and hurt someone.

I am Impossible. Deserving of nothing.

I lean over treacherous waves, tempting vertigo. The salt breeze refreshing, then not. Even the air around Tacky lies. I don't know if I'm hot, cold or crazy-feverish. Mouth is a slime-sweet cotton ball with metal teeth.

There is no point now. Everything will rot soon. I'll become a pink-stained bubble of sea foam, whipped away by a random squall. I gaze down into thunder as a brahminy kite flies invitingly, below my feet.

Hello Father.

I am not sad now. Not worth anyone's botherings. Not even my own. Absolute worthlessness feels empty. Soul-less. *Free.*

I may as well, so everyone can 'move on'. Ghost-Mother into guilt. Maggie, distress. Lianne would red-swallow tears. Rocky would fume angry at them all. Vince would slide into melan-alchoholia. And my treasure, the rainbow Kaleido?

Kal would miss me.

And I would miss their stories, still unfolding.

Love catches in my throat, clutching broken pieces. Broken selves. Urging us back from slippery grass. Holding off the dark blanket. Clinging to threads. One of us lies down, then another, forming a chain through time. I try to grab hold. *Too fast.* I slip.

Again. More slowly.

Pattering rain eases into light mist on our face, and I curl my fingers gently around hers. We chest-thrum an echo back to sky. Tapping fingers over the slowing, above the roar of the sea, along collarbone, to our heart. The fluttering rests.

Just being, not thinking. It takes time. I don't know how long, but clouds finally clear, out to the horizon. Thirteen connects us all, uniting us into something lasting. Sounding. Powerfully surviving.

Survival

9

Trapped

August

The sun hides behind sheets of wet grey. The Education Department ignores my lawyer. I avoid Facebook, wade chest-deep through the hours, wonder if any teacher will extract that rotten tooth. *Truth.*

Vince needs help with a video project. It's an income.

At his factory, I overhear that Covid border closures stop his workers from getting to sites, from returning to families. Vince's eyes are red and glassy. I recognise his drowning, but I'm hanging on too tightly to myself. I go to pick up new nausea meds: Esomeprazole Mylan.

Radio news says Brittany Higgins' accused rapist denies everything. Meanwhile the Prime Minister installs another accused rapist, who can't be tried because his victim died by suicide, as Leader of the House of Representatives. The PM refuses an inquiry. Grace Tame comments on Australia's 'chilling apathy'.

By the time I get back from the chemist, Vince is home, pacing with anxiety.

'I had to leave the factory.' He slumps into a deckchair. 'I felt pins and needles and heart palpitations.' He's pale and shaking. 'I stood up for my workers.'

'Good.' I nod.

'Boss says to fire them.'

'Bad.' I hug him into me. 'You have to get out.'

'I'll be OK,' he convinces himself.

He doesn't look OK. His brother recently had a heart attack. 'See a doctor,' I urge.

'Let's sell the boat,' Vince detours. Rain has turned the boat floor mouldy. We've barely used his desperate attempt to relax.

Vince heads to work earlier, stays later and complains of *shooshing* in his ears. 'They'll get rid of *me* next.' He sounds angry, looks frightened, says: 'I feel trapped.'

Then, we *are* trapped. Covid lockdown means he must work from home.

'At least you *have* a job,' I grouch. The new medicine saws my guts. I snap at Vince's bacon-stenchy kitchen mess, his annoying TV-channel hopping.

He barks at my 'naggy-nitpicking', slams the door, drinks more than his usual too-much. I sneak-pour his wine down the sink. He yells that I 'treat him like an idiot'. I shout at his 'unwashed blobs on the cutlery'.

'You're so negative,' he says, '... just like your mother.'

~

I hide in the bedroom, try TRE. Unintentionally, I'm inside my teenage beach dissociation, reaching for that silver string. A sharp pain shoots from coccyx to outstretched jaw and the howl drags rust from my throat, snorts from both nostrils, reclaims space inside. When the tremors subside, I'm calmer and crave custard. *Don't overanalyse.* Go to the fridge.

Later, Ghost-Mother texts: I'm negative!

I know, I laugh ... until I realise she's referring to her Covid test result.

I die today

The rain is light. Tide is high as I drive to Back Beach. Within the lockdown zone. Murky swells roll in, but I'm desperate for a wave. I do my stretches, rub suncream off my hands with sand, like I always do.

Suddenly, ice claws my chest, fear-squeezes my throat with clear knowing: *I die today.*

I breathe in menace. Will it be a shark? A surfboard to the head?

Doom feels familiar. Certain.

Every cell screams: 'Don't enter the water.' Brain yells 'Don't be absurd.' Body mallet-pounds my heart into shallows. Guts churn.

Seriously? Panic in my sacred place?

Then the heavy blanket crushes me into shell grit. Blood runs instantly cold. My cheeks puff out and I straw-breathe imminent catastrophe.

He cannot have surfing. Not this too!

When I close my eyes, I see something worse, and squat back on my heels in the maul of it, then the *shoosh-boom* in my ears, the life-sucking fizz of clawed sand.

Can't breathe. Can't move. I must be dead.

~

Pure blue opens my eyes to feathery clouds and seagulls. The weight of emergency slides off my chest as I try to find the good that I hope I am. *Breeaaathe*, back into Body, pulsing with ants. *I should go home.* Everything sounds muted. Far away.

No. I push my head-clogged self to standing. *He cannot have this.*

Bashed by the brightness, I breathe into belly and paddle out, ignoring the shadows below. I deep-hum a different mantra: 'Nam Myōhō Renge Kyō ... Nam Myōhō Renge Kyō.' *Devote yourself to universe and Buddha emerges.* Try to remember; Nothing is Permanent.

I curl freezing toes to avoid cramps and pull my hands through motley water. Out the back, I long-breathe. Wait for a wave.

A smiling woman paddles over. 'How do you know if sharks are coming?' she asks, in her Spanish accent.

My faraway voice talks about bait balls, baby whales, muddy water. 'It's the predator nobody sees that causes the most damage,' I warn.

We share a knowing glance and I catch the next wave.

But I don't paddle back out, so I'm cross with myself. *Surfing is my therapy.* I gave up my yoga to escape Ghost-Mother. I barely walk outside now, avoiding sharp noises and retired teachers. Life expects my 'normal person'. But I'm skittering, upside down, wearing the ant-infested skin of a not-me. *Barely a person.*

I have to tame this fear, or I may as well hold my own head under.

Driving home, my ears pop and I hear the world again, the news: 'Trade in online child-abuse material.' The Australian Centre to Counter Child Exploitation is investigating 1,248 offences by 121 men. Fifty-one rescued children will 'struggle to live their full potential'.

Society is de-evoluting, into brutality. This must *not* continue 'until the end of time'. Children deserve a life beyond mere survival; we want the ending to be more important than the beginning.

At home, I open Facebook, check for teachers' replies. Vince storms into the kitchen, growling down his phone. Something is wrong. I'm moving, to check on him, when I glance back and read:

> There's no doubt there was knowledge of your 'relationship' with Rob Cunning. It was part of the school's culture of silence at that time.

Mr Quinn names the evil.

My chest balloons with relief. *Finally, a teacher with nothing to hide!* I add Quinn's comment to a document of witness contacts to send to Amanda Steel.

September

Steel calls: 'One teacher's support is not enough to proceed to court.' I'm gutted. She tries to reassure, says I'm booked in for a medical exam in December and the Department's lawyers are 'taking instructions' for doing the same.

'I have to do a medical *twice*?'

'That's fairly common,' she says, as if it's no big deal, surviving a volcano.

Determined to distract myself and earn some cash, I head off to film Vince's construction video in 30-degree heat.

After two days with little sleep and constant nausea, my skull is on fire. Every sinew, a razor wire. *We both have to work. This has to work.*

It doesn't. Vince comes home brutalised. 'I can't do it anymore.'

'I understand,' I say.

He shakes his head and cries, 'I'm having chest palpitations!'

'It's just a job,' I tell him. 'It's not worth *dying* for.'

Tired of the fighting way, we laugh and let go.

'You and me against the world!' we say.

Vince does a grocery run and hands me a surprise. After twenty years of legal poisons, we eat marijuana gummies, sip Mary J tea and watch the sun go down. It eases the stress. We watch bees on the rosemary and rainbow lorikeets in the grass. We walk along the beach, into a kaleidoscope of butterflies, fluttering seawards.

Their journey is impossible. They keep going.

In the euphoria, we relax into gentle, loving sex. No counting to ten, no flashbacks. Happy-sleep carries us into morning and I spend the next day wasting time.

As if I'm allowed.

But doob doesn't disappear the world. I ask Ms Lawyer for an update and get no response. Vince's doctor diagnoses him with PTSD. He can't go back to work but can't quit. Everything gets medical, legal, financial, stressful. Our options liquefy beneath us. Both sliding, we step on each other's frictions. Vince tells me what he's going through. I tell him I've been there for months.

We sell the boat. I don't celebrate turning 54.

Inequity

Vince's doctor navigates him through recouping lost wages and superannuation. Vince's 'psychological injury' form for New South Wales WorkCover is similar to one I filed for Victim Services. But Vince is offered support: a statement fact-checker; a psychologist, coordinated by his GP; a vocational social worker; salary replacement; and a case manager!

Wow! I'm stunned by the inequity. On reporting my injuries, my income disappeared. I pay for my medicals, had no coordination.

I'm glad he's getting help ... he's been under pressure for a year. I held tight for forty.

'Society can't afford it,' Ghost-Mother had said.

Indeed. Sexual abuse trauma is costly.

Support for work-injury victims exists because employers pay insurance, creating a pot of 'care' money. The National Redress Scheme is an attempt to create something for child abuse victims, but perpetrators are not financially held to account. 'Justice' would redirect perps' assets, arguably the 'proceeds of crime', to a survivors' fund. *But no.*

My skull surges with marching ants. I email Amanda Steel for an update. Then text Donnelly, again. Neither respond.

Within weeks of submitting his 'workplace injury' form, Vince has his medical exam. *Efficient.* I overhear Vince shuddering through difficult thoughts about 'feeling worthless'.

I want to tell him how much I understand but I'm afraid to open my own floodgates.

More rain, more greying mud at sea. *Waiting is not justice.*

Turtle food

Standing at the blue-wall desk, checking news: A Queensland woman is charged for failing to report child sexual abuse. In the eighties, only teachers, doctors and registered nurses had reporting obligations. Not psychologists named Frank. The new law requires *any* adult to report. Even suspicions. *Hoo-bloody-ray!*

In strange synchrony, Amanda Steel asks my permission for the New South Wales Department of Education to access files from the Queensland psychologist I saw once, in 1989. Frank did not keep records of our conversation, about a teacher who raped me. He did not encourage reporting. This lack of action allowed Perp to resume teaching.

Didn't I give permission for this access months ago? Exhausted, I sign again.

Jaw aches. Skull burns. I need ocean therapy, but the sea is an oily-mud slick. I cold-shower, then ice my boiling neck. It helps.

Vince says he's struggling; describes his anxiety symptoms. I reveal some of mine. As we walk the beach path, I teach him breathing exercises and ask him to find 'one-good-thing' he can see – a strategy from group therapy.

On the breakwater, he spots a huge leatherback turtle, one of my favourite ancients. These magnificent creatures can slow their breathing and heart rate, dropping their body temperature to avoid sharks. Courageous, self-reliant and free. *I want to become that.*

We wave encouragements for its seaward journey.

'Go you great being, flee, far from here!' I shout.

'Follow the moon!' Vince yells, theatrically lifting his hat.

Laughing together, we dance the majestic being into the deep, not caring how crazy we look. The rare sighting, and our spontaneous parade, revive hope.

October

With Covid still surging, we can't re-book Tassie. Vince mows the yard. I do home yoga. We laugh over Wordle. He tortures me with Van Morrison. I make him dance to Elvis. He gets therapy, self-medicates with shiraz. I still wait for a psych appointment and pour whiskey into fragile bones. 'Go surfing,' says Vince.

I drive to Back Beach, defying fear. A birthday group have let several balloons fly into the water. I'm angry at the adults' disregard. The surf is grey chop, but I decide to retrieve their rubbish. As I paddle out, jellyfish balls tickle my fingers. I scoop a handful of the lolly-sized creatures. Clear, with a speck of purple at the centre. No brain, no heart. Turtle food.

I sit up near a balloon, but the gusty wind twists it away. I can't reach the long, silver ribbon twirling into the breeze … 'Oh! No. No!' I'm spliced back in time.

When am I? Thirteen?

I'm terrified I might split permanently into back-then. In silent-scream panic, I grab the silver lifeline and frantically exit the water.

On the beach, a young boy stands beside a teacher I vaguely know. Still shaky, I hand him the balloon and mention the rare leatherback.

'We need to keep our rubbish out of the ocean.'

The boy does not hold the string tight. Within minutes, it's back in the waves.

Crying in powerlessness, I walk away from the heartless, brainless humans.

That night, black horizontal rain wakes me into awareness of painfully rock-hard guts, visions of slicing metal, clotting red. *Innocence brutalised.*

'Get out of my head,' I whisper revulsion. 'Get out!'

Vince leans over. 'What's the matter?'

'Horrible,' I say, curling up in tears. Vince rubs my back. My leg muscles twitch. I shower outside in freezing rain but nothing erases the image. *I need help.*

Unexpectedly, I get a psych appointment.

10 Somatic Justice

Meeting Apple

October 22

Apple wears a gentle face, an Om necklace and comfy clothes. A psychologist experienced in child sexual abuse trauma, she has a quiet art-filled office nestling three dark blue sofa chairs. A cuddly-toy koala sits in one, wrapped in a sky-blue blanket. There's a glass of water, fancy tissues and natural light. Not cold, not hot. Just right.

We sort administrivia. Apple is not registered for Victim Services because 'the paperwork is absurd.' The floor melts as she offers to refer me on.

'No. Please! I'll ... find a way to pay.'

Apple says I can choose *what* to talk about, *when* and *how*. There's no rush. Her purpose is not to 'move me on'. Slowly, patiently, she ekes out my story.

'A child cannot consent,' Apple checks my perception of guilt. Part of me scuttles off behind the chair. *She noticed.*

Apple reminds me that 'grooming creates deep patterns of submission' and 'perpetrators make their victims believe they "wanted it".' She senses my landmines. Her warm eyes do not judge as we breathe through rough patches.

'Holding this in for forty years might mean that therapy takes a while, and that's OK,' she reassures as I unburden a bath-load of tears. She helps me realise that I trust too much or not at all and I'm wondering if she can get the awful out of me when something clamps my throat. Apple sees my hand, holding neck.

We see Apple sneak towards the frightening.

'What's your earliest memory?' she detours gently away.

Pause. Think. 'I was nearly two, Dad was home in the daytime. Our loungeroom was full of neighbourhood kids watching TV because … "something happened to the moon".'

Apple smiles. 'Do you have other happy early memories?'

'I got a red tractor for my third Christmas,' I say. 'I'd ride from the top driveway all the way down to the mailbox. Fast-beautiful!' Apple smile-nods me on.

'Up on the kitchen bench, I'm four … The glass mixing bowl rainbows light along the sink. I lick chocolate cake-mix off eggbeaters. It's just me, Mum and 2LM Radio.' Fifty-Four spies wet-the-bed sheets on the memory clothesline. 'That was before I became her crucible of trouble.'

'It's OK to talk about other things,' Apple says, opening doors.

Body *phoopthhs* a stale breath. Chest lurches. 'I'm exhausted by nausea.'

Apple is not afraid. 'What triggers it?'

I don't mention flashes of Perp's face, the salmon shirt … the Beast … the evil horrors.

'Why won't my mother help me?' I ask.

'Perception of no support *now* ignites a sense of abandonment *back then*,' she explains.

'Maybe,' I concede, 'but words said now are *in the now*.'

'Stay open to learning new things,' Apple gurus.

I make another appointment, wondering how I'll pay.

~

As I drive home, memories strobe as I contemplate karma. I locked my best friend in a broom cupboard in Grade 1. I faked bronchitis in Grade 2, to avoid the maths class knuckle-whack from Sister Columbus. In fourth grade, I scrawled wax crayon on cement and, fearing punishment, refused responsibility. I lied.

In Grade 5, I was invited to a large girl's birthday sleepover. I had to lay plastic sheeting in my bed because I was a 'widdler'. My mother had often been snide about people's body-weight; that modelling ensured I got in first with the name-calling. After that, 'Cathy the playground bully' became part of our family narrative.

I'm a lying bully.

Becoming Thirteen

Late October

Apple reminds me that abuse at a young age can fragment our identity map; our ideas of who we think we are. She asks what brings me joy. Answers tumble out: 'Surfing scrubs me clean … My child and grandchild … stop me from jumping.' Change tack. 'I didn't do this to hurt my mother or siblings.'

'Is it your job to keep the family together?'

Her question snake-squeezes my throat. *Phoopthhh.* A cat-furball arches my back, shoves chest up out of chair. I apologise for the air-vomit. *I'm rotten inside.*

'No problem,' Apple says. 'You have compassion for others.'

Broken-bully does not believe her. I tell her about the turret-rescue meditation from my twenties; 'I learned that I need to show compassion for myself.'

'How's that going?' Apple asks. Upside-down mouth doesn't answer.

We try using 'Family Parts Therapy' to identify my younger selves, who might have 'different beliefs, mannerisms, voices.' Apple says it's not the same as Multiple Personality Disorder. 'Some parts might seem disconnected, need to feel safe, be heard.' Apple tells me she can 'handle anything'.

Good. I don't want my monsters overwhelming her.

As I acknowledge Thirteen's presence, her unmistakable energy steps forward. Body recognises the strangeness of being both adult and child. Skin feels tight with both of us in it.

'Sometimes your parts want to re-unite, sometimes you'll retreat into them,' Apple says, without judgement or disbelief. 'Shall we talk about what happened to her?'

Thirteen's electric walls switch on as fear squeezes torso. Hostages are *not* allowed out.

Apple talks. 'Sometimes you don't realise how afraid you were.' *Are.* 'People who've suffered abuse can have parts that still feel it's dangerous to speak.' *Yes.* 'Therapy can help you become familiar with parts that have been cut-off.' *Abandoned.* 'Over the years, you've used a lot of energy keeping your parts apart,' says Apple. 'Some parts romanticise the abuser, because you didn't know what else to do.'

Thirteen intently observes. *A real rescue?* We both wonder if I'm up to the task. I don't understand what keeps Thirteen trapped. He's dead.

Something guards the open cage.

'How's Thirteen feeling?' asks Apple. Body shudders.

'Can we speak with her?'

'Yes.' The clear answer surprises me.

Throat knows Thirteen's voice. Snake squeezes.

'What would you like to tell Thirteen?' Apple asks, and Fifty-Four howls:

'I'm sorry you had to deal with all that by yourself. So sorry I left you in the frozen place and never came back. I want to help you now.'

My words reach into Thirteen and I soak all the tissues.

'Being sexually abused by someone you trust creates a particular kind of horror,' Apple says. 'It can split a person into pieces. Dissociation is a protective mechanism, a safety valve.'

The fracture. The floating off. The brain pockets. Apple understands!

My exiles are with me: Thirteen the afraid, Fifteen the blamed, Eighteen the escapee, Twenty-Two the ashamed.

I feel them here, now.

Apple talks about 'manager-meta-parts' that prioritise efficiency, to keep a person going. When you're stressed, you might become bossy and controlling, because you're desperately isolating. Some survivors must constantly 'achieve', running their engine without fuel; burning themselves up just surviving.

Hello, my straight-A-student, Miss-Bossy-Excellent-Project-Manager, Protector-Warrior-Mummy, 'Be productive' façades.

'Compartmentalising is useful during danger,' Apple informs me, 'but it creates a burdensome perfectionism.' Thirteen bites my bottom lip in recognition. 'It's difficult to switch off if you're always seeking safety, for your family of parts, or your real family.'

Apple talks directly through me, to Thirteen's electro-chemical memory-body.

Becoming Thirteen shrinks me into a past version of self, a small but complete being. She's not a passing emotion, but a complex, distinct character with her own stunted history. Blamed, misjudged, trapped, still waiting.

Hers is the voice that enters my throat; the TiddlyBom flutter-bird that fear chokes.

I sip water as we listen to Apple. 'Some parts disconnect entirely, afraid what might happen if truth finds a voice. Some parts take risks, replaying hurt in more extreme abuse, trying to learn where you went wrong. Some parts internalise blame, becoming severely self-critical.'

I snort out dragon breath, adjust Body.

'You might judge yourself harshly,' Apple explains. 'Inner conflict between parts can feel like seething in your skin.'

Hello ants.

'Shame turned inwards can make you believe you're a bad person,' says Apple.

Gut spasms. I dry-retch-swallow ugly visions but *do* tell Apple about flashes of Perp's face and the post-Ruin blank. 'Where did I go?' I cry through shards of mirror.

'You were a child, forced to submit,' says Apple. 'When an abused person fractures, fear keeps their parts separate, to stop them disintegrating. This can create missing memories.'

Apple says we can deal with my missing pieces later. First, I need to reconnect with Thirteen. I *phoopthhh*, feeling incapable. Apple gets me more water, offers mints. Suggests I watch my body and mind closely, for where I feel resistance, especially to disclosure. This can flag something important. *Unspeakable thoughts.*

'It will take time to dig inwards,' warns Apple, 'but I see you're a kind, caring person.'

I retreat from the compliment, rush backwards through hallways. Hear Ghost-Mother mocking: 'A therapist can't know you like I do. Too clever for your own good.'

I am the selfish liar, slut ... irreparably broken, the one to blame.

'I don't know how to fix it,' I sob. 'To fix *me!*'

Apple does not rescue me with empty words. She lets me realise.

I cannot change the past.

Finding Voice

I email Amanda Steel, requesting a court date. She does not respond.

Lianne phones to ask why I don't want Ghost-Mother visiting. Mind races to clifftops. 'More hurt is dangerous.'

We sit in the stretched-out minute. Lianne wants to help me but can't help herself:

'Who cares if someone knew back then? What about *Mum*?'

'What about truth?' My legs fill with cement.

'Everyone has their own truth,' Lianne volumes. 'Move on, Cathy.'

I hang up as chest pounds. Behind closed eyes; a horror of blood and babies.

Oh! I'm really messed up.

How long before she cuts her way out and really does some damage?

~

Ghost-Mother texts: Getting ready to die. She wants me to take some things, to 'empty her house'. I shove ginger bears into gob, Vicks up the nose, determined to stay calm. By step 220, there's a swamp in my lungs but Ghost-Mother's gravity hauls avoidance from my bones. I stand at her mailbox, contemplate turning back.

'Are you still doing therapy?' She steps out to collect her mail.

'Mmm-hmm.' I swallow her derision.

'It's not working,' she mocks. 'You look down.'

As we climb her crumbling steps, body-memory carefully steps over the grassy section where snakes used to sunbake, where, as a 4-year-old, I'd stop. Check. Sprint to the mailbox. I remember one summer, a king brown slid up the full length of the lower glass door, 'a danger to the children'. The frenzied four-man bloody shovel-kill was shocking. Gruesome.

'What did you need?' I refocus.

'It's mumbo-jumbo, you know,' she says, confusingly. 'Therapy,' she clarifies. 'They'll keep you wallowing.' She fusses over little piles, offers an old towel, a photo of Kal, a plate I gave her. I grab her unwanteds and head for the patio, but careful long-breathing stalls me at the dining table. Then words come: 'Yes, I *am* down.' I scan for angry. 'I'm tired of fighting: to be heard, to be believed. Fighting for my life, actually.'

She rolls 'don't-exaggerate' eyes. Voice keeps coming.

'I'm disappointed that my own mother won't stand with me.'

Throat spasms. *Ghost-Mother is quiet!*

'You've denied knowing anything. Yet you knew *something*.'

She does not interrupt! Voice continues.

'Instead of being "on my team", you've blocked, dismissed, and undermined my words. Your actions, then *and* now, protect a criminal culture, of man-gods and child concubines.'

'Don't go back into that,' she directs. 'What do you need … to move on?'

Moving on feels like betrayal.

'Healing requires an acknowledgement,' says Voice, 'that you should've done something about the criminal. I can't "move on" if you keep side-stepping.' She saddens. I soften, towards compassion. But Voice will not concede. Not this time.

'First you refused to make a police statement,' I say calmly, 'then you delayed writing one for my lawyer. You keep blaming the "confident, clever one". You said you'd only ask other teachers if I wasn't in the room, and you haven't even done that. Hiding your shame is more important to you than my healing.' I leave her detritus and stagger seawards.

Why can't I move on without their help?

All I can do is move the body. So I run. I run into rain; along beach trails and overgrown tracks. I run and run until dizzy-nausea makes me vomit. It doesn't look like anything I've ever eaten. None of this mess is mine!

Then I'm standing at a Coastcare planting site where I hauled mulch and argued against poisons. The seedlings are now higher than the weeds. Canopy is forming. Ground cover is flowering. There is beauty in this struggle.

'I am a good person!' I scream into the stinking wind, and hear the younger-wiser: *Other people's fears are not my burden.*

Thirteen, stronger than all of them, does not need their help.

~

Stepping through my door, I get a text from Lianne:

> I'm sorry we didn't do anything for you then and we've not done enough now. I can't imagine your pain. I love you, little sister. Xx

'Progress!' I say aloud.

Then I email Ms Lawyer, asking for a court date. She replies:

As previously advised, the Department is not responding. We've arranged an independent medical in December.

No progress.

Hunting for my angry

November 5

Vince is cooking pork sausages. He sees my puke-face, trying to not-breathe.

'It's just a smell,' slurs his already-drunk-a-bottle voice.

The gas burner is on high, spitting fat. Exasperated, I slip on greasy floor blobs as I wade through miasma to turn it down. I take a bottle of soda fizz outside and watch the sun slide behind the papayas. *The numb have no fuse for anger.*

Now he's banging pans in the kitchen, storming about like an insult. He stomps past me, upends his panfry into the garbage. 'Gone. All fucking gone!' he yells, retreating to the TV room, slamming the door.

'Thanks!' I shout through the window, '… for being so accommodating, after my twenty years of patience!'

'What the fuck do you expect me to do?' yells Mr Shiraz.

Suddenly, my Almost-Angry is at the TV room door: 'How about you stop denying my reality and acknowledge my nausea?' He doesn't look at me. 'How about you remember last Christmas when you promised not to cook pork, but I had to leave the glazed-ham-house for hours, and you got shitty because I didn't want to sit inside to eat? The not-just-a-smell makes me horribly sick.' He changes the channel. 'How about you just don't cook pork?'

I deserve to breathe.

When I go back in, Vince has opened all the windows, but he still seethes.

'How is any of this my fault?' I try to reason with a drunk.

'I'm sick of looking after you,' he says, finishing a beer.

I cry in the bath, close our bedroom door and grind my teeth through the night shallows, worried Vince and I won't make it. Sober, Vince is gentle and caring. He feels the weight of my turmoil. It doesn't help that I'm avoiding sex. Or that he's stewing in alcohol.

We get Covid border passes and head to Brisbane for baby hugs.

November 10

Driving back to Tacking Point, radio news discusses an Independent Inquiry into the Tasmanian Department of Education's Responses to Child Sexual Abuse. For decades, that Department ignored and disbelieved students, shielded and moved pedophiles, protected itself against financial and reputational risk. 'Past crimes can't be dismissed because "that's the way things were",' says the reporter.

Hello New South Wales!

The inquiry report says that although policies have changed, problems continue. 'Refusing to examine their inaction, institutions extend the culture of silence into the present.'

Hello Tacking Point High!

'Teachers fear being implicated during court proceedings.'

Hello Schiller, Donnelly, Marsh, Rolfe, Richards, Beaver. And you, Mr Leary. We know about you! Gutless, all. Skin is alive with ants.

Mid-November

I can't sleep. My 3 am ear-siren directs me to the New South Wales Department of Education's current child abuse 'Failure to Report' policy. The website says: 'For the offence to apply, the risk will need to exist at the time that it is apparent to the person'. *What does that mean?* It says the offence 'targets those in positions of authority' and the 'Failure to Report' offender will need the power to 'reduce or remove the risk, by virtue of their position'. *What?* Ghost-Mother was a powerless casual teacher. Could this policy be misinterpreted by those afraid to speak?

You are tired, I tell myself, watching stars dim into dawn.

Over coffee, Vince shares what he's learned in his own (paid, medically coordinated) therapy about 'the lizard brain' and its 'amygdala adrenaline surge'.

'I know,' I say, holding the back of my skull. 'I've been protecting you from *my* therapy.' I boil over. We get crotchety. *We're all we've got.*

November 22

In morning news, Australia's cricket captain sent a young female an unsolicited dick pic. Cricket Australia's integrity unit says he's an 'exceptional leader, with distinguished service'. Tongue slides along slime-teeth.

Amanda Steel calls, wanting photos I gave the police months ago.

'Didn't the police pass them on?'

'That will take longer,' she says.

Life is nothing else. I dig into my computer, re-find and email the images, then vomit.

Steel responds with a request from the Department's insurance firm's lawyers. The documents are designed to confuse and exhaust me. Steel attempts to decipher their pretence at investigating: they want to know 'how long each of the penetrative incidents lasted', 'what was I doing immediately before each incident?' and 'what was I wearing?'

Wait. *What?* Head ignites. Nausea churns guts. Steel tries to convince me these questions are a good sign. 'After ignoring us for five months, at least they're responding!'

Delay. Frustrate. Re-traumatise. *These are tactics.*

They still won't release the maths master's report or Perp's employment file; still hide behind a dead perp's privacy. His suicide robbed me of more than my day in court. This legal process could take years, of time-wasting, victim-blaming.

I don't have energy for Angry. Why continue?

Then Steel tells me I'll have to pay for the medical upfront, or be charged interest, 'up to $5,000,' she kindly advises.

She reminds me that Perp had 'no assets of significant value'.

'I'm not after his assets,' I hiss.

'Yes but—'

'No "but",' I interrupt. 'I don't want to make things worse for his children. It's horrible enough, the truth of their father.' *Protecting everybody else.* 'My case is against the Department.'

She explains: 'The Department will aim to cover their expenses. If he has no assets, they might not …' her words dissolve.

I hang up, see an email from Victim Services. *No.* They will not reimburse my $550 medical expenses. Ears flush with heat as I taste furry metal.

I want to hurt something. Is this Angry?

Meeting Fearless

November 23

Ghost-Mother wants coffee. Afraid to be alone with her, I agree to the beach café and plug my ear to dampen her barbs. She jokes about her friend's 'faulty filter … a mouth that says inappropriate things'. She reprimands a young woman for putting a tiny dog on the next table. 'On the table! *Really?*' the Ghost hollers. 'That's against the law!'

Ghost-Mother mutters vitriol. Then whispers: 'I *do* care about you.'

I play-pretend in the thick air as she discusses ill relatives. A mudlark screeches outside. *Everything seems surreal.* Luckily, I have a reason to leave.

'An appointment,' I say, and quick-march home to write my 'best and worst' memories for Apple, feeling feverish as they flood in: *Perp's clothes. His face. The Beast's demeaning. My shameful acquiescence. His kill threats.* Other not-memories I push away.

'Far out!' I hold sad-heavy head. Vince hugs my tears away.

'I'm so sorry,' I blub.

'You don't have to apologise.' He holds tight. 'I'm here for you.'

The broken ones snot all over his not-salmon shirt.

~

In Apple's cocoon-room, I read my memory lists.

'Anything you didn't include?'

'No,' I quick-deny the glistening visions.

Apple asks if I can share something off my 'worst memories' list. I take a deep breath and feel my lips pout like a 5-year-old's.

'In kindergarten, Daryl Chandler chased me through a puddle.' *I see it clearly.* 'He grabbed my hand, and we slid through black mud. The nuns stripped me of my soddens and stood me in the street, in my home-made flannelette undies.'

'That sounds difficult,' Apple says. 'How does that little five-year-old feel?'

Mouth scrunches and I waggle my foot. *Dirty-Naughty waits with her school bag until the cruel God delivers Mum in the white Ford Falcon. I know the trouble I'm in.*

'I'm naughty,' says a tiny voice, as electricity surges into fingers. Then I burst into sobs.

Apple talks about how fear, shame, and a sense of injustice, can be held in the body. The *I'm naughty* idea is finding its way out.

Apple asks grown-up me what I think of that memory now.

'Those nuns were mean.'

'Yes,' Apple affirms.

'It was unfair,' says another voice, incensed. 'Daryl got given dry clothes and went back to class.' I tell Apple that voice belongs to Fearless, who is 7, who knows this was not my fault. 'I hid those undies in the back of my drawer and never wore them again.'

For the adult, therapy feels like shovelling mud. Apple asks what grown-up me wants to say to the 5-year-old.

'You're a brave little hero,' I manage.

Apple asks me to hold two pebble-sized vibrators which activate bilateral nerves.

Body feels strangely calm, distant, like I'm meditating in the next room. We revisit the child-memory, with adult perspective. I squeeze the pebbles. Heat flares behind my skull. Apple asks me to tap my feet with the vibrations and imagine helping my 5-year-old self.

'I'd give her a blanket, tell her she's not in trouble,' I blurt. *Buzz-buzz. Tap-tap.*

'She shouldn't have been left half-naked outside,' adds Fearless.

'What would Fearless like to dress her in?' asks Apple.

'Her red cape and silver-sparkle boots.' *Seven is proud of Five.*

We buzz-tap into this memory a few times. The colours dull to monotones and I feel easier about it. De-charging memory is part of EMDR.

Apple stops the pebbles, asks if I have 'other memories with electric charge'; might we 'try EMDR with Thirteen?'

Immediately, sharp nails claw my insides. Hand clamps over mouth. My back arches as I *phoopthh* nausea bubbles. *Thirteen is best left alone.* In her vortex, an entirely separate imprint. I sense the chasm, the black-hole edge I'll have to cross.

Apple is patient, waiting, wanting me to reach for the exiled.

Brain is tempted. Body is terrorised. Thirteen has established surveillance. Electric fences prevent entry. Ice grips my gut. Skin feels too big. Eyes dive away. Then I slump.

'How old are you right now?' Apple asks, but I don't reply. 'Where's Thirteen?'

A sharp pain in my sternum forces hand over heart.

'What year is it?'

Brain knows I am 54 and it's 2021, but I cannot vocalise this. Thirteen has my mouth. I am a fish on a hook, awash with old hurts.

I don't like this feeling. Not at all.

'How old are you?' Apple repeats, trying to buzz-anchor Thirteen into the present.

Stubborn, Thirteen bites on the lure. Hands squeeze the pebbles.

'What year is it, Cathy? Tap your feet,' Apple persists.

Phoopthh, I cat-furball and see Thirteen in bandages, slumped in the tower of rubble. I burp. Taste metal. Stop tapping. Shake my head. *Not yet.*

Apple turns off the pebbles.

'Focus on breathing,' she says. 'Touch fingertips to thumbs. Slower.'

'Sorry,' I say, squelching my face, burping.

'No problem,' says Apple. 'Can you take me through what happened?'

Exhausted, I shake my head. 'No.'

Apple gets a soft ball and we throw it back and forth, to be in the unthink. Sounds from the street muffle me back. We talk about my cat-furballs, ear-sirens, skin-ants, the arm-flick-knuckle-crack. Then jaw-stretching and mumbling nonsense *zhurr-zhee*s.

We discuss therapy goals. I hope to cure insomnia and constant nausea. Apple says we'll work towards that.

Late November

The constant brown smear of ocean makes compassion difficult. Not surfing, I don't feel whole. Another drizzling day nestles me into Apple's safe-room.

We buzz-tap our way through pre-Ruin memories, fighting sweet metal and skin-ants. Memory colours change and feel more authentically dated. Afterwards, I cry with relief. Apple explains that re-coding can open channels into my subconscious. Deeper hurts might emerge.

'I must be bad for all this to happen.' The words jump out.

'No child can ever be blamed for sexual abuse,' she states gently.

I struggle to believe.

Apple detours, asks how I cope without sleep.

'I have to physically exhaust myself.'

'That will help metabolise your stress hormones.' She writes 'ATP' on her notes, tells me that body-sugar dysregulation is common in abused children.

Later I research Adenosine Triphosphate; a bio-chemical energy transfer involving enzymes and oxidising glucose. I don't grasp the science. All I know is that when stressed, I taste an awful sweetness. During EMDR, I feel something happening inside my head. It's itchy. Maybe I'm 'hydrolising'. Maybe ants are feasting.

Medical exam

Early December

Independent medical exams are an ugly side hustle. I navigate emergency Covid tests, border pass rule changes and a long drive. I arrive on time, then wait ninety minutes. Already dehydrated, I'm finally invited into a large, messy office. A thin-haired, sweaty man, whom I've never met and will never see again, wears his lunchtime running shorts. My case relies on his assessment.

Every muscle stitches into bone. I try to breathe as bowling balls thump through my chest. Sweaty-man speaks into a microphone, says his voice recognition software is 'a bit off' but he'll 'fix details later'.

It's a three-hour grilling, through unremarkable early family life, then grooming, rape, dissociation. We discuss my overloaded education and erratic work history. By the time we get to 'relationship history', head is boiling, neck is swarming. By 5:30 pm I'm exhausted. I forgo several mid-twenties sexual disasters because I need this to be over.

He asks how I felt about turning to women. *Safe.*

'You were heterosexual. Now you're with a man. Was it strange?'

Not all lesbians are escaping arseholes! I want to shout. Sexualities are not boxes.

We skirt flashbacks and marriage nightmares. I block details, scrunching my awfuls into my allotted time to render a life. Everything feels too packed in and skipped over. I'm astounded by the inadequacy of this process.

I'm thirsty and my ear is screaming.

He asks if Perp's suicide made it better or worse.

'Better for everyone else,' says Voice. 'No public accountability, no document release, not even his police-recorded confession can be shared with my family. Definitely worse for me,' I say. 'He lived his life as if he'd never done anything wrong. He never had to lie to *his* family. No-one asked what *he* was up to.' I vent injustice, burp metal-mouth. Sweaty-man makes notes.

'He was brazen! He sang a song to me in front of a crowd of parents and teachers. No-one did a thing.' I feel outrage. *Good-Angry.*

'Yes, a narcissist,' nods the psychiatrist. 'How many times did you have sex with him?'

'Before and after school … four times a week, more? … for five years?' Brain tries the maths. *More than a thousand?* 'He didn't think twice about hurting me.' I cry, as pain shunts hands to skull.

'Why didn't your mother want to give a statement?' he asks.

'Great question. You're the psych. What's going on there?'

Despite his hefty price tag, he doesn't offer an opinion.

Psychiatry-man asks about the Beast. 'Was that a criminal relationship?'

I relay the Darwin rape, the Sydney knife at my throat. 'I was twenty-one, but not a functioning adult,' I manage. 'I didn't understand boundaries. He was my boss; made me rent an apartment, sleep in his bed. He force-fed me oysters … refused to take me to hospital when I was severely ill. Threatened to kill me if I left. Is that criminal?' *Did I say all that?*

'How might your life be if this didn't happen?' Psychiatry-man goes crystal-balling.

It did happen.

The question reminds me that a court case will focus on 'damages': how much my never-to-be-lived life might have been worth, in dollars. There's no hope of justice or truth. This is mercantile and quantitative, but feels pointless. Immeasurable. Too risky. Vince and I could lose everything. I cry-snot on my own shirt. He doesn't offer tissues.

'Many child abuse victims struggle with trust and obligation,' he says.

'Oh.'

'Female victims can suffer long-term, damaging hormone surges and are susceptible to hypercortisolism.'

'Oh.'

'Cortisol regulates blood pressure, blood sugar, inflammation and digestion.'

I'm trying to comprehend and wonder if he always meets clients in smelly shorts.

Finally, at 6 pm: 'What are your plans for the future?'

I shake my head in disbelief, unable to glimpse tomorrow.

'Good luck,' he says, walking me towards the lift. In the now-deserted building, I feel a tad unsafe with Mr Short Shorts.

Later, at Kal's, I try not to beat myself up with everything I forgot to say.

Child-closeness is comforting. Kal knows my love. We chat, surrounded by books and Lego and artwork and fluffy toys.

Watching a trippy *Star Trek* movie, I'm falling asleep when I full-body shudder, arch my back and *phoopth* out a breath.

'What happened?' Kal is shocked.

'It's OK,' I murmur, pulling up the blanket. Kal pats me to sleep.

Dialogue

Garry, the boy who cared, comes to see me. Despite years without contact, it's easy between us. Affirming. We talk of Scott's bravery, confronting my father at school. Then Garry's lingering resentment seeps through.

'Perp was my senior music teacher,' he says, shaking his head. 'I told him it was disgusting, what he was doing. When no-one did anything, I had to leave.'

I tell Garry about Donnelly being afraid to help, even now.

'Pathetic,' says Garry, stunned. 'Perp killed to keep his secrets, but Tacky's teachers still protect each other.'

I'm relieved when Garry offers to speak with my lawyer.

'Be fearless,' he says. 'Keep going.'

~

Cloud-clots gloom over Tacky as time waits for a shard of light.

I need to leave this place.

I tell Apple about my trouble with intimacy. 'I want sex to finish quickly. I count to ten over and over. That's normal, right?'

Apple offers strategies: keep my eyes open; tell myself how old I am; remind myself Vince is a good man who I love and trust.

Apple says that trauma-coping behaviours create long-term patterns. 'We need to unpick the memories, reintegrate those experiences with adult understanding.'

We can change how we create meaning. We can rescue our trapped selves.

Apple asks how I feel about Perp's suicide.

'Blame,' I dry-retch, 'and confusion ... about his wife. On his arrest he'd said 'It's happened.' They were ready. He shouldn't have gotten bail. I'll never get to tell my story,' I rant.

'Is that what you want? To tell people?' Apple sees me pout-slump into my shoes. She loops back. 'How do you feel about it now?'

'Ripped off,' rages Thirteen.

Apple waits until grown-up me unslumps back into the room.

She's concerned about continuing with EMDR while my legals are uncertain – 'EMDR is invalid in the courts, it's misrepresented as inserting false memories, like hypnosis.'

'Rubbish,' I protest. 'EMDR is working. I can't wait for my legals before I start healing.' But a ruthless barrister will discredit me. For the rest of the session, we use other therapies.

~

Ghost-Mother texts: I have marmalade for you. Come up.

Nausea balloons. Safety steps out of my skin. I tap my chest, letting Thirteen know we don't have to. We push obligation away, resist the urge to reply.

Doomscrolling, I see that bell hooks died. She argued we should 'choose beyond simply surviving adversity; we must dare to create lives of sustained optimal wellbeing and joy.'

I like her but … high bars can be dangerous. Occasional joy is quite an achievement.

December 20

I fidget in Apple's comfy chair, trying not to unzip. 'I read a horrible book once …'

Don't tell her that!

'Something revolting happened to a woman, during war,' I swallow bile. 'But …'

Tears river my cheeks as I puff-breathe. '… I responded like I was on the wrong side.' I shake my head in bewildered horror. *Who spoke?*

'Do you mean that your body responded positively to something you feel is terrible?'

'Yes.' I retch.

Apple says that abused children can have confusing body responses. 'It doesn't mean you're a bad person.'

Too late. Axe-chopped body parts are inside my eyes. I cry and cry. Apple has no idea how evil I am. Grown-up me wonders how long the search and rescue will take.

When will Thirteen stop swallowing blame? When will I show her love?

We invite Thirteen to sit with us. It takes time. Her distinct otherness enters skin. Guts twitch. Sternum aches. Right arm shoots the knuckle-crack. 'She's grumpy.'

'Does Thirteen know you are fifty-four now, and have a loving husband?'

Face responds with a teenage *eww*.

'Can you tell Thirteen you're grown up, and the perpetrator can't hurt her?'

Thirteen takes over, addresses me: 'You still do things you don't want to do.'

Apple knows who spoke. *Direct dialogue.*

'Is it different to before?' Apple asks.

'Yes.'

'Why?'

'She has a choice. She's not afraid.' Thirteen's honesty is luminous.

'I still have sex, just to … get it done,' I admit. 'Isn't that normal?'

'What's important,' Apple addresses my adult, 'is that Thirteen knows you're here and you can have a conversation.'

Apple asks if Thirteen is ready for a difficult memory. Electric barriers instantly sever my torso. Below navel is out of bounds. Thirteen watches as Apple and Top-half talk. We see Perp in a salmon-coloured linen shirt. I dry-retch in horror. 'Vince has that shirt!'

'Hold that image,' says Apple, turning on the pebbles. She asks me to watch her fingers, moving left-right-left in front of my face. 'Hold the shirt image, lift your feet, left and right, in time with the pebbles.'

Body spasms and shudders. I burp. Cry. We try to articulate what I'm sensing, try to allow, without judgement.

'Just speak what you see or feel,' encourages Apple.

I describe images of Perp's face, as Body twitches. Seeing the shirt, I keep trying to separate his face from Vince. *My Vince.* As I buzz-tap, spasms travel up my torso. The smell-taste in my mouth is disgusting. Shit. A total upside-down enema. I'm relieved when the pebble-buzz stops.

'None of this was your fault,' says Apple as I sniff Vicks to remove the stench. 'Does Thirteen know that?'

The self-blamer pulls back. Cries. Apple gets more tissues.

When I resurface, I tell Apple I want Ghost-Mother to apologise for things she's said. 'But she'll blame me again and dissolve my courage to continue.'

'With the legal stuff?' asks Apple.

'With *everything*.'

Apple sits back. 'Some things you feel you need from your mother, she might not be able to give,' she warns.

'I know,' I sigh. Mother's fears stop her from learning. Curiosity is my battery. *We clash.*

'How would it feel to not ask for an apology?' Apple looks into me.

'I'd feel … already dead.'

Driving home, I tap my chest, and promise: 'You were frightened, raped, controlled for years. I'm not afraid of that truth. He relied on silence, but he's gone now. People should have helped you. But I'm the grown-up now, and I will not shy away from the work to be done.'

Christmas cheer

December 22

What I didn't want my life to become has infested me. I *am* the awfuls: coping and waiting. Vince and I hang by threads. Kal's gone back to the city. I've stopped teaching, stopped volunteering, stopped laughing.

I want the Ghost's apology for words said in the now.

The blazing sun squats on the scrub, refusing to drop. The air is storm-sticky. Lianne and Ghost-Mother have agreed to hear me out. Maggie has promised to come straight from work, she'll 'be there'. At five-thirty I wade towards the old house.

Ghost-Mother steps out. 'I'm very afraid …' she says theatrically.

Of what I have to say? '... of the giant grasshoppers.' She points to one on the railing. 'Maggie won't be here till six.'

Heart spasms. Tapping chest, I tell Thirteen: '*You're OK. We're OK.*'

Ghost-Mother warns: 'A wicked storm is coming from the west, so we'll eat inside. I'm making fritter batter,' she chortles; recites the menu: 'Hummus, chicken, salad, cherries, and both your grandmothers' fruitcakes – for after our ... little chat.'

I escape to the patio.

'I'm here for you,' whispers Maggie, arriving at six-thirty with Lianne's favourite champagne. They chat over bubbles. I dissolve into garden shadow.

'What are you expecting?' Maggie offers me a glass. I decline.

'To be believed,' I answer, loud enough for Lianne to hear.

Speaking risks everything. Do I need an apology?

Ghost-Mother offers olives, asks: 'How aaare you?'

I don't respond.

Lianne calls time: 'Mum, take a seat.'

We gather around the metre-square dining table.

They speak of ordinary nothings. Speak over me. I fidget, wait, want them to understand.

Maggie helps: 'Talk to us.'

I suck hot air, blink away horrors. *Breathe.*

Already, I'm sweat-stuck to the vinyl chair, in tears.

'It's good to see you cry,' says Mum as we hear thunder.

Speak now. Reveal the stench that lingers.

I tell them again about my head explosion, beach dissociation. I hold off a flashback, show my stiff-as-a-board sex position. I describe his angry-'slut'-voice, how trauma shuts down the brain, how abused children lie. Maggie listens. Lianne seems frustrated. Ghost-Mother bites her tongue. *I ruin Christmas.* Again.

They only know the version of me that powered through the world like a freight train, delivering stories of achievement and adventure. Not this broken thing emerging from rubble.

I mention that old classmates have contacted me. New sinkholes appear that I can't quite leap over. I start to numb. Can't raise wet eyes to seek apologies. Ghost-Mother asks why I'm not 'moving on'. I tap my heart, for Thirteen.

Maggie apologises; wishes she'd done things differently. Lianne objects to the inference that 'Dad knew'.

'*Evidence*, not inference,' I say.

'I don't know about that.' Lianne raises her volume.

I exhale, dragon-slow. 'OK, so again … Dad was told: "Cunning is screwing your daughter." Perp phoned here and spoke to one of you. Mum and Dad went to see his parents. The maths master reported, and Dad was called to the principal's office.' I seethe. 'It's not as simple as "they knew nothing".'

Lianne pales. 'I don't know *anything* about that.'

Thunder rolls from the west. 'You *do* know,' I insist, 'because I just told you, *again*.' I sigh. 'Why aren't my words enough?'

'Seems your words are the only ones allowed!' spits Lianne. 'Well, I'm *sooo* sorry,' she shouts sarcastically.

The distant crack and boom quivers ants under the house. Sand, the only thing holding us together.

Ghost-Mother tells Lianne to 'lower the volume'. I'm astounded when she adds: 'I suppose we have to accept that it happened.'

Is she finally standing with me?

She corrects herself: 'Your father didn't tell *me* about it.'

I rip my sticky legs off the chair. Outside, a mudlark screams.

'For God's sake, Mum, you minimised what Perp did by saying the Queen got married at thirteen!'

'I said no such thing,' she squirms.

I push on. 'He was the criminal, but you still see me as the manipulator, apparently "controlling you since I was four".'

She scoffs. 'I don't remember saying *that*.'

Lightning pulses the dune. We all jump as thunder punches the walls.

'It doesn't matter what you *remember* saying,' Voice is clear, careful.

'I know how trauma hides truth.' I breathe down my volume, try to let Buddha in to cool us off. But Lianne is blooming red, stewing.

'That's *your* truth!' She slams down her glass, then hurls the axe: '*If* Dad knew, I feel sorry for him!'

I'm shocked by the sharp pain, from clavicle to sternum.

'I've already said sorry,' Lianne screams as thunder booms us all into smallness.

'You were a child,' I say, resigned, massaging my chest. 'You're not responsible.'

Maggie sees I'm about to leave. 'Lianne, Cathy knows you're sorry. She needs you to include the stuff about Dad in your understanding of the story.'

Hallelujah Maggie!

'But that's *her* story,' Lianne insists. 'I don't know about that.'

'But you know about it now,' says Maggie calmly.

'So, we have to accept what Cathy says as true!?' yells Lianne, disgusted.

I bite my lips. Then Maggie becomes magical.

'Let's try this,' she says. 'Don't turn around, Lianne, but it's raining outside.'

Lianne stares blankly.

'So,' continues Maggie 'is it raining? Do you believe what I've just told you?'

Lianne-the-scientist reddens, huffs, wants to see for herself.

'That's Cathy's story,' Lianne repeats. 'It's Cathy that needs to—'

'No,' says Maggie firmly, 'it's *you*. You doubt her word. And words of others.'

Maggie for Team Cathy!

Outside, the low sun casts a pale glow on rain-shined leaves. The temperature drops.

'Was this helpful?' asks Ghost-Mother, bustling off to warm the fritters.

I shovel fruitcake into my gob and pour myself a triple whiskey. It stokes my throat. Then Voice speaks: 'I *will* fight this social sickness. I'll be proceeding with my case.'

I don't need you to believe me, I don't need your apology. I drag cement legs home and send a drunken email to Amanda Steel: *When will we get a court date?*

~

Vince drives us to Brisbane as I text:

> Merry Christmas, Mum. I forgive you. For not standing with me. For not rearranging your social calendar to make a statement. For making me promise to not contact your friends. For your anti-fem rants and weird silences. For assuming I was controlling the game. You are absolutely forgiven.

The Ghost does not respond.

11 La Niña

I don't want to hear you

New Year, 2022

It doesn't feel like summer. Cyclone Seth pisses down the coast. Black Lake is the only safe swim. I carve long strokes through goose-bumpy coolness, quenching the fire at the back of my head. Deep-dive-exhaling for as long as I can, I wait in bubbling stasis, eyes shut against intruders. But the will to continue inflates me. I surface as an inky squall curtains the lake. Needles of rain *ting-ting*, smashing air and water into a sparkling opera. White-trunked melaleuca stand reverently, applauding. *This* moment is healing.

And too soon forgotten.

Back home, I drip through my waterlogged garden, smothered in buffalo grass. Stubborn oxalis keeps coming up, invading every pathway. *Fighting is pointless.*

Vince, avoiding his own triggers, watches TV, eats chips. Still in my wetsuit, I notice the creep of mould on skirting boards. A furry grey scum slinks behind blinds, inside cupboards. Everything smells sour.

We'll have to sell anyway.

Lianne text-invites: Come up for tea. This surprises me, since

Ghost-Mother's not been responding to *my* texts. I gobble fruitcake as the Ghost belabours relatives' health issues.

Why did I come?

Then she puts her 'caring' face into mine. 'How aaare you?'

I sniff Vicks to ward off the surge.

'What's that for?' she pries.

'My nausea.' *You make me sick.*

'When can I visit *your* house?' Ghost-Mother pouts. 'It's sad to not feel welcome.'

Gut clenches. Thirteen, wanting honesty, sternum-stabs me to respond.

'It's not …' sigh. *Safe*, I don't say, patting my chest.

Lianne pounces. 'It's not *right*, ignoring Mum's texts!'

Wait … *What? I sent grandchild Christmas snaps, Kal's birthday pics. I texted 'Happy New Year'.* Got no response.

'You not replying makes it tough,' Ghost-Mother adds.

I empty lungs, dampen my fuse, whisper: 'You denying your words makes it tough.'

'I never told you not to contact Meg Morrell,' she bellows.

'DENIAL!' I shout, almost angry but wanting to run.

Lianne howls: 'I don't want to hear you …'

She reddens. Swallows. Her words stop the world. Dead still.

My eyebrows rise on a disbelieving breath. Jaw drops.

'I mean …' She backtracks, then yells: 'I don't want to be told it's *dangerous* to call because *you* might suicide.'

Part of me knows that Lianne poorly expresses herself, that she fears for me. But Thirteen's hand catches my slack jaw. *Lianne's angry because I'm suicidal? She doesn't want to hear?*

'Imagine how awful it is for me,' Lianne cries. 'And Mum!'

Walls bend and droop. Cicadas shriek in furious symphony. I separate into shards.

'How caaan we help?' the Ghost steps through dishonesty.

'I asked for your help *three times*, and you refused!' I clutch my throat.

'The poop is back on the table!' Thirteen yells with comic flair.

I storm my broken pieces home. If Ghost apologised, maybe I'd drop the legal fight. If I continue, I sacrifice what's left: old family; our house; Vince. *I should just stop.*

Little bird

January 10

Teeth grind through dreaming. *Perp is across the road. I scream-warn Ghost-Mother. She gawps at me, as if he's no threat.* BomTiddlyBom bird is jazzy-wild. *Can he still get me?*

Vince hugs me as I whimper awake. 'He's dead, right?' I ask over the blast of Cyclone Seth. Day after day, more rain, more nightmares. Axe-chopped little bodies. I hurl them. Eat the pieces. I wake disgusted, knowing. *I was always a danger.* Nausea prowls.

Clouds deluge and I don't step outside for a week. Even Black Lake is a no-go zone of poisonous algae. La Niña weeps in the bath over haunting snippets.

It's what you wanted.

My grip tight on the whiskey neck, I swig, and wallow in the evil my mother knows.

Move the body!

When I tell Vince I'm going walking, he worries. 'Stay home.'

'I'm numb.' I snot on his chest.

'Let's look for a campervan.'

This pulls me out of doldrum. 'Can it be electric?' I ask. He frowns.

'With surfboard racks?'

'Absolutely.' He smiles.

Mid-January

Post-cyclonic swells scrape un-swimmable beaches. The air is a glaring salt haze and thrash-metal cicadas pierce the world. A volcano erupts in Tonga.

I meet two old friends who share their experiences of reporting childhood sexual abuse. Rani's mother urged her to 'get over it'. Maree's mother found the police process 'rattling'. Perhaps mothers feel they've already given everything. They've run out of child-caring. Perhaps they're afraid they created us.

January 22

Kaleido calls: 'Nan says you don't reply to her texts.' *This has to stop.* Little bird chest-flaps up to the big house. Ghost is in her garage, with fresh groceries.

'Why are you telling people I'm not responding?'

'I haven't had any messages from you, for weeks,' she says, seems confused.

'I sent you Christmas photos,' I huff, watching for gaslights in her impish eyes. Then I realise …

'Show me your phone.' Gut spasms as I check her settings. 'You blocked my number?!'

'I didn't,' she looks away. 'Maybe accidentally, with my old, fumbly fingers.'

Body, choking on disbelief, carries her groceries upstairs.

'What about my note asking for an apology that I left in your mailbox?'

'*My response* is in *your* mailbox,' she huffs.

So tired, I trudge home to read her apology:

> *Cathy, I'm sorry for the suffering that the criminal abuse had on your body, your mind and your life. You were a child and should have been protected. I am so sorry for everything I've not done, and done, that has negatively impacted your life. Forgive me. Love Mum.*

Finally, no excuses. Perhaps-Mother is forgiven.

Not OK

February 1

I wall-push, following Apple's instructions, ignoring the RSL Club, watching the brown river. Gutless Donnelly lives across that raging water, in South Tacky. The next rain bomb might haul him under.

'How would Thirteen feel about working towards the rape memory?' Apple asks.

Thirteen Tarzan-drums my chest. I *phoopth* sawdust.

Fifteen detours: 'Donnelly was a great teacher. Once, over a crowd of students, he jumped down two flights of stairs, to whip-crack a huge brown snake.' Apple waits. 'Why won't he help me?'

'Let's check in with Thirteen,' she redirects.

Fear squeezes my throat as we dive into frightening empty.

'Your nervous system focused on escaping danger. The missing bits are not your fault.'

Sharp fingers dig into chest, clawing at the dark hollow, more frightening than white-hot eruptions or foggy float-aways.

'But ...' I start-stop, 'how can I know what's inside a black hole?'

'Black holes don't necessarily hide anything, but frightened children often fill gaps with horrors,' Apple says, starting the pebbles. *Buzz-buzz.*

We go post-rape, to the beach carpark. *Buzz-tap.* And suddenly I'm reaching for Thirteen's silver thread. I snort-breathe, crying in Apple's chair.

'What do you feel?' she asks, watching me shrink-slump into ...

'Terror,' I whisper, 'and the back-of-head furnace.' Brain starts to rip.

'I'm here,' she assures, 'you're safe. What year is it?'

'Twenty ... twenty-two?'

'What do you feel?'

'Did I die?' Smothering *phoopth*-panic. 'God, did I?'

'Where are you?' Apple's voice is clear, but I'm no longer in the room. 'Cathy?'

'Mmm mmm …' I shake head as torso spasms into abdomen, squeezing bloated gut. I burp stale sawdust and close my eyes.

'Open your eyes, Cathy. Feel the pebbles. Tap your feet. Tell me where you are.'

Phoopth comes a sudden gust. 'I'm re-feeling old …' *Where are my feet?* 'I'm … in Richman Street with … Apple,' I force the words. Dual awareness is exhausting.

'Count backwards in fives,' she instructs. 'Fifty … forty-five …'

'Forty …' I flux in and out of now and then. 'thirty-five …'

'How old are you?'

When I don't answer, she leans over, turns off the buzz-pebbles, hauls me back, dry-retching. She passes her bin. I cry through all her double-ply, unscented tissues. We work through it again, using eye movements, buzzing, deep breathing.

Thirteen needs to see if I have what it takes.

On the third go, I dragon-snort as a sharp pain in my coccyx forces my lower back to arch. The purge swells through torso, shoving chest forward, shoulders back, chin up. I cat-furball, drop the pebbles. Body is re-cataloguing. Both arms flick-click out horizontally.

Afterwards, my chest aches but the beach memory becomes less electric.

Apple wants to speak with Fifty-Four, who's already refocusing on legal realities.

'Going to court will throw Mum under a bus,' I worry-excuse. 'She tried.'

Apple sits back, checks her notes, waits.

'If my case fails, I might lose my family, my house, my husband. I should be *angry*, but I'm just numb.'

'Try not to confuse legal work with therapy,' says Apple. 'Legal resolution is *not* required for healing.'

Now, Thirteen *is* angry. *Apple doesn't get it!*

I stretch-click my jaw, to swallow Thirteen's protest. Pacing Apple's office, right arm flicks out, knuckle-Glock ready. *Some justice is required.*

I try to breathe back into trusting. Apple is kind to my resistance, but therapy is not justice.

I drive home in a daze and gobble half of Vince's fresh-baked jam drops. Everything feels wrong. Body writhes. Skin feels sewn-on, inside out.

February 8

I wake to a lump of rock for a neck. We go to town for fancy eggs, but when a schoolboy glares at me in the café, we leave my nausea on untouched chilli-scram.

Back home, I rub my neck with lavender oil. Tiger balm. Nothing works. I drink Mary J tea and slide into her refuge. When I visit Apple, Thirteen is cross at both of us.

'I can't escape images of Perp's face.' I shake in disappointment.

To encourage patience, Apple asks about progress.

I focus on legals. It's not what she meant.

'I'm *still* waiting on the medical report.' Grumpy Fifty-Four feels ignored. 'No-one gives a damn how long this marathon takes. *They* all get paid. I can't even function.'

Apple lets me grizzle. We try sensorimotor activities. I push against walls, against blame and shame. Soon I'm breathing more deeply, ready for Thirteen's memory blanks.

We work backwards to '*... wiping blood from inside of me.*'

I splinter into multiple viewpoints. 'They keep switching: Thirteen, Eighteen, Twenty-Two. It's noisy,' I complain. *I'm not OK.*

'Let's ask the others to wait,' Apple says. 'How's Thirteen feeling?'

'Can't find angry ... only hurt,' we vent.

Apple helps: 'Tap your feet in time with the pebbles.'

I drop back into Thirteen, isolated. Not trusting *anyone.*

Nausea punches slick visions through me. I swallow the not-OK away.

Apple sees we're not ready, brings us back. 'What do you and Vince enjoy together?'

'We play Scrabble, and Bananagrams and eat ice-cream. We're looking for a campervan.'

I don't want to leave Apple's warm glow, but I carry flaming ant-skin to my car. I cannot swim because the ocean is brown scum and Black Lake is closed. I shower outside and scarf handfuls of dried apricots.

I avoid the mirror, afraid of who – what – I might glimpse.

Mid-February

Amanda Steel emails, wanting tax-and-income details from thirty-two years ago. *More victim-work!*

Any response from the Department? I reply.

She phones: 'The Department's only response, in August 2021, was that they won't release the perpetrator's employment file because he has a right to privacy for thirty years.'

Convenient. Chem-flush pours molten metal into veins. 'How long can they ignore me?' I demand. *Oooh, that feels angry!*

Steel talks me down from indignation. 'If you wish to proceed to litigation, it's *your* choice.' She is professionally curt. 'But *we* advise waiting for the medical report.'

I explode in frustration. 'You *say* it's my choice, but …' Body knots with implications. 'My whole life has collapsed. I can't work, can't sleep. I just cope, and try not to break. It's all *my* risk!' I shout. 'I wanted *justice*. They won't even give me truth. It's been nearly a year. They can't keep stalling … can they?'

~

I take a dump-load of stress to Dr J.

'My ears are getting more sensitive,' I tell her. 'It's *painful.* I grind my teeth and bite my tongue until my jaw aches and all I can do is vocalise *zhee-zherr-xiao* nonsense.'

Wide-eyed, Dr J takes a breath. 'There's a link between trauma and auditory distortion. It's called "hyperacusis",' she explains. 'PTSD activates the part of the brain that codes sound.'

The doors locking.

Doc rouses on me for not visiting the hearing clinic. She updates her referral and suggests a blood test. Sigh. The $140 audiogram consists of excruciating headphone sounds until I launch from the chair in tears.

Perhaps-Mother texts, wanting to 'make things better'.

Do not mistake my silence for anger, I don't-reply.

Maggie calls. 'When will you stop digging?'

When I'm ready.

So tired. Depleted. Not-OK.

Swallow or drown

Late February

I wake, choking on half a tooth. I haven't seen a dentist in two years. I explain my powerful gag reflex to the blue-gowned Indian man.

'I'll stop if you raise your hand,' he promises, against the great white of fear in my eyes.

I focus on a TV screen above, where a green sea turtle swims. *You're OK. You're OK.* I breathe turtle-calm against the high-pitched drill squeal, the pressure to swallow, the drowning thing in my mouth. Tension builds in cramping toes.

I want him to hurry up but slow down. I'm trying to look up, to pull my head away. Body is about to flee the blue-balls flashback. Swallow or drown. *Can't breathe!* I wrench my jaw backwards. Raise hand.

Dentist keeps his promise. After, my swollen face cries in the car but I've agreed to collect Perhaps-Mother from her mechanic. She suggests a while-we-wait coffee.

I point to jaw. 'Can thalk. Denthist. Don wan thoffee.'

She fills my silence on the drive home with inane chatter about traffic, other people's illnesses, the bat smell at the end of Bay Street.

I pull in close to her mailbox so she doesn't have far to dash in the rain.

Thirteen pokes me: 'Mum, today ith firth day for munmpths, I'th not fell nauthus in your prethence. Thath why you carn vithit my houth. Thath why I doan do yoga. I'm not doing thith tho hurr you. I'm protet-ting me.'

'I'm sorry,' she says. 'You're so strong. It's amazing you're still standing.'

I am broken. Not strong. Barely standing.

Sky-tears envelop her as she walks the ant-sand path into her empty house. Windscreen wipers struggle under the weight of water.

~

As I drive back into town, to Apple, Thirteen feels cut off by guilt. Apple asks what I might say to a friend in my position.

'Be kine to yoursthelf.' *I am hard on me.*

We revisit the beach dissociation and I'm less frightened. EMDR takes me closer. Other post-rape moments also feel less charged. I can watch now, without being seized. We edge inwards, slice by tiny slice, re-coding. Flashbacks re-file as 'memories', not 'triggers'.

Apple suggests we approach the rape. Thirteen wants to run. Just beyond her tower lies a swamp of self-loathing. I remind Thirteen it's not her fault. 'She had no power, no voice.'

Nausea cat-furballs up through torso as we lower the drawbridge.

I am with you. Grown up now. You are safe.

I shrink-slump into Thirteen. Body. Mind. Persona. We see through her eyes, and step into his parents' house. I hear the weaponised *click* of locks, the sound that tuned me for submission. Thirteen is confused, terrified. She howls. *'I don't know what to do.'*

I puff-burp. Guts constrict.

'How old are you?' I follow Apple's voice, struggle … but grab the right number: *Fifty-four*. 'What year is it?' *Twenty-twenty … two?*

'Count up in threes from twenty-nine ...'

I tap my feet. The pebbles are under my knees so I can fling arms, fire my finger-gun. Voice feels faraway-garbled, underwater. 'Thirty-two ... Thirty-ffffive?'

She brings me back into now. 'What do you recall just after?'

'Blood ... on the towels.' I *phoopth* as chest shudders, but the charge has dulled. I buzz-tap as we rock back and forth in time. Then to now, me to her. I'm straw-breathing through a time-warp as colours shift, away from saturated terror.

We are safe.

Thirteen has trouble believing I'm grown up. Apple asks what's happening in my body.

'Hot feet tingles, phantom arrows through the ... spleen?'

We switch from eye movements to buzzing pebbles. Apple gets me to stomp my feet when I dissociate. I'm biting my tongue so hard my jaw seizes. Suddenly, a river of tears. Apple passes me Kevin Koala.

'What are you feeling right now?'

'Surprised.' I hug. 'Thirteen feels ... grateful.'

Apple smiles. 'Why wouldn't someone feel grateful for your help? You're a kind, mindful person.'

No. Parts retreat behind mirrors. *Compliments do not belong to me.*

I cry until I'm empty.

Apple tells Thirteen: we might approach 'the awful' next session.

Something thumps my chest. The rescue will not be easy.

I grip the steering wheel home through float-away squalls. *Should I be allowed to drive?* Hiding inside the snug of children's TV, sipping hot Milo, I clutch my ear at the metal-scrape sound of the barn door in *Shaun the Sheep*.

My next Apple session already squeezes my throat. *Will Thirteen trust I'll keep fighting? Will I be able?* Overloaded, overwhelmed, completely over the incessant bloody rain, I run to find Vince in the garage.

'I can't do it anymore! Even Apple says to stop focusing on go-nowhere legals.'

Vince hugs me into his warmth as another squall scrapes a ditch across our driveway.

'It's hopeless! We might not even get to court. We should stop, before I lose it ... before we lose *everything*.'

'Let's look at campervans,' he hushes.

Escape is not justice. But there's nothing left for us here.

Loggerville shit

Late February

Radio news is a flood of warnings: A monstrous low-pressure system whips the Coral Sea into the sky over eastern Australia. Then, a cyclone off Madagascar, a high-pressure system off New Zealand, and a polar vortex off Antarctica join La Niña's 'Drown 'em out' party. The crying girl is completely unplugged. Tsunamis slap windows in furious release.

Ants panic in a storm. They climb the walls.

Early March

Already soaked, the River Region gets another 700 millimetres overnight and Loggerville's sewage system collapses. Sludge-brown horror oozes through the Island of Lies.

Vince and I wake to thick fog and eerie quiet. No birds. No dogs. No wind. No tradie trucks. Nothing but the heavy hush of gone. The ocean bloats with yellowy poison. Air feels greasy; the stench so foul we close every window. Nausea slinks in the silence.

Loggerville and South Tacky escapees drape wet desperation from the lighthouse to the cemetery, the only high ground. On the break wall, doomscrollers come to see for themselves, dumbstruck by sheer power. Waves scatter water tanks, tractor tyres, fridges, and enormous trees. Pieces of boat nudge eyeless cows and plastic-wrapped stockfeed.

Diesel drums leak oil-slick over weirdly bent limbs. Pigs? Wafts of revulsion churn the abluted flood-mess. A weighted buoy dances in the surge.

'Hooray for La Niña!' I shout, glad I'm not the only one ruined by Loggerville scum. Embarrassed, Vince tries to shush me. *They can all go to hell.*

I think about Donnelly, across the river. Wonder how his kids are coping. Sympathy rises, but my kindness drowns in the undertow. Donnelly would have entered floodwater to rescue a dog, but he refused to help me. *Detritus.*

I watch a cormorant dive under gastro-sludge and disappear, like I want to. People die in this flood, like I want to. *I hope the turtles got out.*

The path home tastes phlegmy. I gag on heavy air that compresses me into bog with each squelching step.

~

Apple's office is under a foot of filth. She cancels my appointment. No matter. I'm not worth anyone's botherings. There are people with 'real trauma' now.

Maggie calls. The Flood Recovery Centre needs volunteers. But I don't go to hand out food, or wash houses with vinegar, or coordinate assistance. *How could I?* The uber–project manager is gone. Vileness surges. Now, everyone can know how true the narrative …

I'm horrid.

I wallow on the guest futon, aiming to saddy myself to death. Then I notice black lines on the walls. Leaking roof? Mould? *Moving?*

Swarms of ants cling in a writhing mass, dripping down damp plaster, onto my not-screaming, not-running body. I hope the marauders leave nothing but cold bones and bandages.

I let him climb onto me.

Toxic overload

I don't celebrate March 4th. Instead, I spend days in bitter torpor, nausea-migraines and Panadol, a kind-of food. Loggerville releases four megalitres of blackwater every day.

My skin is see-through now and always wet.

Vince helps remove the ants, but remembering the writhing shroud becomes my excuse for not helping the town that abandoned me. *Twice.*

My hands still shake. I still cat-furball, flinch at sounds. I still see things.

Perp waits, in a waft of bacon, a screech of brakes, the shrill of a mudlark.

'Everything is attacking me,' I whinge at Dr J, who reminds me that 'cumulative chronic stress overwhelms our coping mechanisms.' She tells me I've lost my buffer. That now, a hiccup can make me overflow, like a blocked sewer.

Vince and I get out of bed later and later. We watch daytime TV. My hair needs a cut. I eat gobs of peanut butter on cheese. I bloat and fart, like the river. *Who cares?*

I phone the Flood Coordination number and offer our guest room. I'm a good person.

Liar!

Decomposing beasts and clumps of turtle-killing plastic drag sorry-stink onto my beach. The 'Shit-from-Loggerville' makes life hell.

As he always did. *Does.*

Commitment 12

The golden gift

We spend a fortnight cleaning our own house. Donating, clearing, weeding. Sometime mid-March I wake feeling disoriented. Good-different. Fingers tap slowly across chest, strumming commitment to Thirteen. 'You're safe now.'

Sunshine spills onto my bed and I realise I'm not nauseous! I grab hold of gratitude, jump out of bed, do yoga. Glimpses of garden-beauty surprise me. *It's time.*

Parked outside Apple's office, I sit with Thirteen, deep listening. Warm, calm energy fills my chest. I close my eyes and see a vision of a beautifully wrapped box, glowing in gold paper, gold ribbon. A gift.

I carry the precious gleam of it up to Apple's comfy chairs.

'I'm relieved,' I explain, 'at feeling good again. But … Thirteen's gift carries obligation. She's not sure if I'll stay strong … I don't know if I'm up to it.'

Apple tells me how brave Thirteen and I have been. *We'll stick together.*

We edge towards the Ruin, buzz-tapping through the before. When I start to shudder, Apple eases off, we try the after.

'Where are you? What year is it?'

Thirteen slumps into panic. 'I'm … It's …' Brain struggles. *When?* Then Eighteen, the escapee, shows up.

'It's 1985. Why didn't you help *me*?'

Apple helps fractured Fifty-Four to say 'I'll help now, I have strategies, but Thirteen needs us all.'

We nudge closer from each time-side. Thirteen is avoiding, not ready. Disappointed in myself, I try to believe in us. *I want this to be over.*

Apple encourages patience, but I've run out of Medicare-rebated sessions. She says I'll have to take a break from therapy.

Thirteen's gift remains unopened.

~

Ms Lawyer emails the medical exam invoice, calls to remind me; I can't see the report until it's paid. 'I already paid,' I protest-bark, 'with my childhood, my down-spiralling career, my uncertain future …' I haven't worked for months, so I ask to use her firm's trust fund. She warns that I'll pay interest. If I lose, or walk away, all costs are mine.

Still paying.

Perp's suicide ensured that my family and community will never consider how they might have acted differently. In law, I am powerless and irrelevant. Only the process exists.

I doomscroll: a prominent church minister conceals child abuse; the 2021 National Student Safety Survey finds one in twenty university students are sexually assaulted on campus, often by staff. Most victims are unsure how to report. *Society does not value justice.*

Vince and I rent a campervan and head for the Bunya Mountains. On the way back, we get grandchild sleepover hugs. Brisbane's own flood-ravaged water supply gives me the worst gastro of my life, reigniting nausea.

Mr Loggerville still swirls nearby.

March 26

Red-smeared, eating hacked off chunks of baby. I'm shimmering, not screaming.

I wake revolted, confused by my inner protest: *I am a good mother.*

'Nightmare?' asks Vince, bringing tea. We attempt intimacy, but I sense someone else.

'Sorry.' I push him away. When he reaches for his salmon shirt, I scrunch my eyes against intrusion.

~

Loggerville floods again, coating Tacky's blackened river with slimy fish-kill. Toxic scum oozes across beaches. Even Cressie chokes in excrement.

'Stay out of the water,' Maggie cautions. 'There's pinkeye, skin rashes and vaginal infections.'

I tell Dr J that 467 days of nausea is too much. 'I need to scour myself.'

So melodramatic, eye-rolls Eighteen.

'We have to leave,' I urge Vince.

'Yes,' he says, distracted. 'Check out this pop-top van …'

Apple phones to tell me that because my primary self-care is surfing, I can apply for 'flood recovery funding' to continue therapy. *Bizarre.*

To obtain this state-funded miracle, I must answer gatekeeper questions about 'suicidal ideation'. *What is that? Vague plans? Clifftop walks?* My lower back spasms through the call. 'Someone' will 'let me know'. I swallow Panadol, sit with Thirteen's still-wrapped gift.

I am not small. I will reach through black-ice fear and haul you into light. I promise.

Exorcism

April 6

Waiting for funding, I tell Apple that I need to keep going; 'I'll pay.'

'How's Thirteen?' Apple checks in.

I become tentative; teary and cat-furballing. *I thought I was ready.*

'Any more issues with Vince's shirt?'

'I understand it's a trigger, not a danger,' I boast, then exhale a sudden *phoopth*.

We buzz-tap through Perp-shirt flashes until the charge lessens.

Apple asks about my relationship with food.

'Just fuel. I forget to eat. Then crash. Then sugar up.'

Apple tells me that sexual-abuse survivors often have difficulties with hunger and sexual sensation. 'You had to cut off certain body signals. Rewiring takes time,' she assures. I feel gut-brain synapses shift.

We re-approach the Ruin. Apple notices my slump. 'What does your body feel?'

'Fear,' says Thirteen, as calves cramp.

Apple moves her fingers back and forth in front of my eyes, asks Thirteen to recall.

My whole body sways as we remember ourselves back into the yellow house. Little bird frantically flaps. *This is dangerous!* someone yells as a dozen fishhooks dig into my chest and fling-haul Body backwards.

'What just happened?' Apple gasps.

'I d-don't know if I can … keep her safe,' I howl. 'The door is open, but …' Thirteen's eyes bulge-scream: 'We can't wake it!!'

Apple sees my coil of fear but stays calm, ready to take us there. She pushes the pebbles into my hands. *It's time.*

Her fingers move in front of my eyes. We talk through the motorbike ride. The sunbaking. His angry. My uncertainty. We ride off. *No-one knows where I am.*

'Keep tapping your feet, Cathy.' We enter the house. Locks *Click.*

There's a white, lacy bedspread. Photos on the dresser. He lays out towels.

In Apple's chair, I shrink into powerlessness. He removes my bikini. '*Don't move!*' a child-voice whispers. Horror spawns from the abyss. Soul-chill rises.

'Breathe,' says Apple.

Thirteen claws into the frozen hollow. Fifty-Four trips on charged wires.

'I want him to stop.' *I don't want to see …*

'Open your eyes Cathy …' I hear her words, almost too late. Flailing, I anchor in Apple's kind eyes as she switches me back and forth through memory-slices: his slurping, sweaty growl; my ice-stiff body; his in-out shoving. Fear writhes upwards, squeezes. Dry scales scratch my throat as Thirteen burrows deeper. 'I' am about to exit.

'Keep tapping your feet, Cathy,' chants Apple. 'We can handle whatever comes.' *Perp's face.* Then reassurance is lost as the black-eyed python explodes up my throat, blocking my airway. FEAR. Neck spasms, then locks. Pure terror unhinges its jaws to devour me whole.

Can't breathe! In deep black, I surrender to choking panic, until a burst of adrenaline defibrillates me and I slow-motion vomit the taste of sawdust.

'Where is it?' Wide eyes scan the room.

Apple eases pebbles from my scrunched hands: 'Touch your ring finger to thumb on your right hand, and your middle finger to thumb on your left …'

Confused, I follow her instructions. *Was that snake real?*

'Now touch each finger to thumb.' I breathe more deeply. 'Slower. That's it, now tap your feet.' Apple helps me back into Body. 'How old are you?'

'I'm … fifty-four? It's … 2022.' Am I safe?

What was that soulless snake? Brain has no concept. No logic will explain.

Apple tries: 'When the subconscious takes centre stage, our deepest fears manifest.' She reminds me that dissociation helped Thirteen cope but also trapped her in fear. My inner rationalist knows something very strange just happened. It felt like exorcism.

'Don't try to make meaning,' Apple suggests. 'Let it be and let it go.'

Whatever *that* was, I never want to meet it again. Somehow I feel calmer, emptier. I rub my jaw, splay my fingers, surprised at how old my hands look.

'How's Thirteen?' Apple asks.

'Thirteen protected everybody.'

'Yes.' Apple reminds me: 'She shouldn't have had to.'

It was never my fault.

'You need to take care now,' Apple warns, 'When EMDR removes blockages, it can release deep emotions.'

Later, gobbling apricots, I search 'EMDR' again. The process accesses the 'back door' of the brain, slows the amygdala and synchronises brainwaves. Traumatic memories are re-lived, then re-encoded by the frontal cortex. The bilateral foot-tapping, eye movement and counting releases trapped energy and patterns of fear from the nervous system.

I cannot comprehend the science. But fear feels smaller now, and I feel lighter.

Grief drives

For a few days, I'm less nauseous, less anxious, strangely hungry. I wake at dawn, not midnight. Brain-Body feels odd. Odd-better.

April 15

It's a sparkling autumn day and I'm driving from grandchild hugs to collect Kal. We'll have brunch, visit the gallery. I slot into the freeway fast lane. Steel calls to let me know the Department is 'not investigating'.

None of the witnesses have been contacted.

'Surprise!' I say, not-caring.

I listen to news about flood damage and the slow response by state agencies.

'Surprise!' says my cynic. I switch to CD and zone out to the Indigo Girls' 'Galileo', a song I remember them playing live in New Orleans, when at 24, I'd escaped my life.

I float-drive towards a glistening city, cross the Story Bridge singing loudly, wondering if my soul will ever 'get it right'. In the swell of music, my thorax expands. Then, a sense of enormous loss wells up, clogging my throat. An oversized chunk of too-sweet, starting-to-rot oyster. I need to getout of thistraffic. But Ican'tsee because I'm behindthewaterfall.

I'm separating!

But I'mAlready on theFreewayRiverRamp. Neck muscles bulge Andtwitch. I'm *phoophing* air as I near theMistingEdge, sense the-Dropbelow, griptheWheel, peer over the bloatedBrisbaneRiver, at Otherboats. *Cars!* There'sNowhereToPullOff.

I drive one-handed, slapping my thighs. As I crest the waterfall, a guttural moan spills grief across the dashboard like gushing water.

I'm going over!

My jaw opens wide enough to push the enormity out. From deep in the turret, a wolf wails; mourning for Thirteen. Then, my back arches and I cat-furball a glob of something onto the windscreen. Shudder-shocks pulse as I furiously blink tears, mop snot into sleeves, still slapping my thighs, still driving.

Grief is dangerous.

Patience

April 26

In Apple's office, I noisily pop hips into warrior pose, then tuck bare feet up into her blue chair. Apple looks sternly over her glasses at the rebel teen, asks grown-me what I've learned lately.

Fifteen and Eighteen grab the microphone: 'Forgiveness without remorse is false … Remorse without action is nothing … Justice without accountability is impossible … Truth without justice is empty,' we orate. 'Perhaps-Mother brought "sorry" flowers,' pouts Thirteen.

Apple will have to play the child's game.

'Could *you* have done anything differently?' she asks gently.

'Yes! Thirteen shouts for help at the petrol station! Meets him in the beach carpark with the police, his semen in a bloody tissue! Thirteen shows the sexy photos to the PE mistress, who raises a posse! She steps onto the RSL stage to read a poem about what he made her do in her school uniform!'

Apple watches Thirteen relish her story re-told.

'If I'd stepped up to Teacher-Perp, the Beast wouldn't have stood a chance,' I droop into sadness.

'You have another chance now,' says Apple.

Thirteen feels our determination curing. Apple asks grown-me what I'd say to those who've refused to help me as an adult.

'Make your guilt useful.'

'And what would you like to tell Thirteen?'

'I will not abandon you.'

Thirteen wonders.

May 5

Apple tries to convince me that Thirteen and I are the same person.

'What do you like about her?' asks Apple.

'She's copper-tanned and wins surf contests against boys. She has skateboard-stunt knee scars and she cleans her lime-striped soccer boots every week.'

After a pause, I say: 'Thirteen is sad we can't change history.'

Apple asks what Thirteen would like to do now.

'Swim in the sea.' We pull a sad face.

'What else?' Apple knows we can't.

I float into silence, thinking of ice-cream. Later, I find myself inside our steam-fogged bathroom mirror.

'Rise up, little warrior. Grab hold of your shallow-trapped breaths and rope them together. I will help you climb.'

Grown-me dragon-breathes, draws her name in the steam-mist: Thirteen.

'Let's amplify our stolen-silent life into some heard thing,' I encourage. 'Let's beat our warrior drums.' I put on music, begin to stomp; to 'Reel Around the Sun'. 'Let's catch that shimmer of truth for show and tell!'

May 10

I email Steel: *Please follow up again with the Department. It's unfair they simply ignore us.*

With Apple, I huff-n-puff, waiting for guts to stop twitching, moaning about Perhaps-Mother's continuing heartless comments. Apple redirects, asks what I like about Fearless. 'Resilience, resolve … a cape-and-boots costume.'

At home, I inhale Vince's lemon cake. We dream-scroll escape campers but can't afford anything. Now that state borders are open, we visit caravan yards from Kempsey to Noosa. None have stock. *Will we ever get out?*

Only six days in May are without rain. I get snotty and crabby. We wash mould off windows and walls, discover scum in cupboards, in clothes. We scrub and sort flood donations.

Amanda Steel calls; she's frustrated at the Department's 'lack of progress'. Tells me their insurance company has switched lawyers. She'll have to re-brief. Start over. *No!*

She asks for patience. *Deterrence is a tactic.*

I hear on the news that Australia's sexual assault services are 'struggling with record demand … wait times have blown out to more than a year.'

Vince and I stress over money. Tacking Point festers in black mould.

Hunting freedom

May 24

Amanda Steel reminds me: 'Mediation is a compulsory pre-court step in Queensland.' She's asked the Department to commit to a date. They ignore her.

I ask Maggie to re-approach Gutless Donnelly, hoping to avoid court. She doesn't hesitate.

'I told him you're struggling,' Maggie says. 'He insists it was reported to the principal, who met with Dad, but he won't write anything. He said if he was subpoenaed, it would be his word against somebody else; that he got nowhere then and it would be the same now.' He tells another concerned ex-student friend, who approaches him on my behalf, that he 'doesn't want his actions judged by today's standards'.

His actions are taken today. Which 'somebody' won't he speak against? The myth of my father? A dead principal? Retired teachers afraid of their pasts?

I send the conversation to Steel, pull up my nausea blanket and stew in saddy-juice.

June 6

'The cowards are afraid,' I rant at Apple. She tells me that other people's reluctance to help is no reflection of my value, that I am a good person.

Slam! … the screen door at the back of my head.

Apple repeats her message, trying to find a way in. Slowly, I respond from an earlier self. Fearless knows it was never our fault. She stomps her silver-sparkle boots as we ready to enter the missing memories. Strangely, there's little resistance.

As if circumnavigating a black hole until the pull no longer scares you, allows …… you ….. to ….. enter ……….. slowly ……… enough …. to… see ……. that ……… Fear …………. has already left.

'Is that it? Am I better now?' I ask, as a sharp punch crunches my sternum.

Horrified, I look at Apple. Nausea flushes my shoes.

'It's OK,' she says. 'Let's take a break.'

When I get home, I eat all the berries in Vince's pastry. He shows me a green campervan, out of our price range.

From our balcony I see the ocean is still revolting. The joy-stealing shit from Loggerville seeps into another day.

I mantra-walk alone, well back from the cliff edge. At home, I do a full-body TRE shakedown. Light flickers behind my eyes as torso shudders. I plug into deep breathing, non-judgemental allowing. My solar plexus shimmies, releasing cat-furballs … into tired calm.

Body knows what to do.

I wander barefoot in the garden, go to bed early, and wake with a sense of togetherness.

'Let's put a deposit on that van.'

'Yes!' Vince shout-jumps out of bed, too-quickly pulling his jeans on and tripping through the door. 'I'll make tea!'

In a desperate attempt to manifest freedom, we order the sea-green pop-top Kombi we can't afford.

'It's not the getaway van,' I tell Thirteen. 'It's the prize for committing to the fight.'

June 9

I email Steel, expressing frustration at her lack of communication. My skin tingles, on fire.

Good-Angry?

She informs me that several Tacking Point High teachers refuse to take her calls. 'Others admit the perpetrator's involvement with you was widely known but refuse to comment. Sadly, it's not uncommon.'

Regret is defaced by selfish fear.

Steel gripes that, despite the Royal Commission's findings, people remain 'gagged'.

On the radio, I hear the New South Wales Premier acknowledge that 'workplaces fail to deal with sexual abuse', that he 'regrets the distress survivors go through.'

Vince suggests challenging those empty words.

Righteous ants surge as Miss Sparkle-boots hammers out a letter to the Premier, thanking him for his comments and highlighting the moral vacuum of his Department of Education. I ask him to prompt the Department to act, copy the Minister for Education and Amanda Steel, who advises me to not send it, then instructs me to remove her legal firm's name.

I check my motives: *to seek and speak truth. Listen to instinct.*

I send the letter from me, just me, all of me. For Thirteen. For other survivors. Go with Good-Angry.

Mid-June

Cressie is mesmerising. Ribbons of light melt through obsidian green. Not a breath of breeze, only gentle sunshine. I paddle through healing, cooling silk. Me and Thirteen.

Out beyond Cressie Bay, brown scum snakes south to Tacking Point. I stay bayside, smiling into blue sky, breathing hope.

Civil Justice

13

Meeting in chambers

June 17

Vince has his fancy blazer on. I'm in comfy, threadbare jeans and hiking boots. *Did I brush my hair?* In Brisbane to meet a barrister, we're ten storeys up, in a wood-panelled reception, with a marble bust of some white man.

I ask Vince to make sure we cover my bullet points – *Costs? Contacts? Next steps?* – because 'I might get wobbly'.

'Good to see you,' says Amanda Steel, entering in dark blue and heels.

Fearless is cross at her for not endorsing my Premier Letter, but I politely introduce Vince, then we're invited in. Mr Barrister steps out from behind his imposing cedar desk, shakes our hands. Not pretentious, Jason Harbour, in short sleeves and chinos, seems sincere.

Was I expecting a wig-and-gowned snob? Someone thinks: *Please don't close the door.*

He closes the door and sits facing his large picture-frame window. I survey the old books behind him. Harbour begins by saying the Department will claim non-liability for crimes committed by off-duty staff. 'Liability is not straightforward where the abuse occurred off school grounds, as yours did.'

School musicals. School camps. School music room. School bus trip.

'With a civil claim,' warns Harbour, 'you risk legal costs.'

I know this already. Am confused why we're starting here, in defeat.

'If your case is unsuccessful, you'll be ordered to pay.'

Disbelieving ears shove his warning into cement gut. Vince shifts in his chair.

We had such a lovely shack.

Mr Barrister 'rest-assureds' me that he and Ms Steel are 'doing everything they can' to progress to mediation. Little Brave is wary. No progress has been made. *He wants trust.*

I listen as a small voice apologises for my frenzied letter to the Premier. Mr Harbour Barrister pounces on the conciliatory opportunity.

'Cathy, you never need to apologise. You have every right to feel aggrieved.'

Empathy flushes my bog-dweller's fountain. Tears bubble up as Jason exits, returns with a box of remarkably cheap tissues. *Don't all his clients cry?*

Vince awkwardly changes the subject, to the Broncos' last game … finds his footing and rephrases: 'Cathy needs better communication.'

They both nod. Mr Barrister says he'll be 'as honest as possible'.

Either you are or you aren't.

He reminds me that 'all risk is mine' but 'thinks' I have a case.

Either I do or I don't.

If 'they' lose, 'they' risk nothing. Only Vince and I will pay.

'Of course, if we win,' Jason says, 'we're entitled to half of any settlement.'

Head breathes hot-fizz. This is gambling. If 'they' lose, *I* have to pay for the Shit-from-Loggerville's crimes. *I'll* lose a house, a family, a husband. Maybe I'll lose myself off a cliff. *I've already lost and paid and still will yet.*

I stand and shift from one foot to the other, staring out the window. I float towards an imagined grave I want to deface: *Cunning Pedo!*

Mr Barrister's voice returns me to '… the Department's duty of care, their responsibility to act.' Grown-up Brain asks questions as Mr Barrister gives examples of unsuccessful cases. He makes sure I understand that he's briefed me fully on *my* financial risk.

Vince nods his solid support.

Then, Mr Barrister tries flattery. 'You are clearly intelligent … I don't usually spend so much time explaining the finer legal points, but I see you are educated.'

You don't inform the uneducated? Don't they get this far?

Most never step into the police station; many baulk at The Phone Call. Others fall into self-medication. Some take the cliff option.

I remember my dot-point list but can't find larynx-brain connection. Voice is a half-swallowed thing. Hands shake. Victim feels irrelevant.

Vince is perturbed by my emerging panic. 'Well, we've taken enough of your time …' He readies to leave. *Are we racking up costs already?*

TiddlyBom chest-flutters as I ask Ms Lawyer: 'Did you contact Mr Quinn, the teacher who confirmed public knowledge of the relationship?' She blank-stares me.

'What about Giles Trotter, the maths master. Have you contacted him?'

Ms Lawyer doesn't speak. Did she read my document? *Did I send it?*

I become the small, polite thing. 'Will you *please* contact them?'

'I'll let you know when the Department responds,' Steel dismisses.

We forget my dot-points. Vince guides me to the car.

I don't remember driving to Rocky's. I eat three chunks of Rocky's strawberry torte and suddenly see with cake-clarity: *I cannot trust the powerful: not the Department, their insurance lawyers, their ministers, their bureaucrats, not even my lawyers.* They all feed off me.

'The Education Department's insurer wants their client to pay premiums now, and ten years from now,' I sugar-rant around Rocky's living room. 'So, they don't want cases like *mine* raising costs.' Rocky and Vince watch me pace.

'The Department will make an example of me, silence me. They've done it before, which is why we *never* hear about cases like this. They make the process so financially risky and re-traumatising that *no-one* will bother them. Their strategy of deterrence and frustration sends all victims the message: *seeking justice will destroy you.* "They" are a faceless institution who'd prefer that "I" did not exist.'

I flop onto Rocky's couch and dissolve into tears. 'It's only about money now,' I croak.

'No, Cathy, it's about *justice.*' Rocky pulls me up for a hug. 'Proud of you.'

I cry-eat more cake. Vince drives us home through rain and runs me a bath.

Dirty laundry

A few sunny days spark debate about the weather. Some say La Niña is finished, that 'the crying girl' has gone. Some speculate the worst is yet to come. The Bureau of Meteorology estimates a fifty-fifty chance that La Niña will drag her soaking skirts to the coast and re-form, which 'could be devastating'.

June 22

I spend a long night watching clocks, but the preciously sunny morning is invigorating. I take a basket of laundry out and peg Vince's salmon shirt. Suddenly I'm gasping, fingers freeze-clutching pegs. Legs fill with chem-flush and heart dysregulates into random thumps.

What?! I thought I was over this.

A choking cat-furball signals full panic. *Can't breathe.* I drop the laundry, launch inside and lock the door. Already covering myself with blankets when the nausea surges, I burp and fart and cry, massaging hands. Breathe. *Breathe. Let it pass.* I shiver and sweat – for how long?

More than a shirt's worth of panic.

Vince returns from his own therapy a bit wobbly, so we go for a talk-walk. On the breakwater, an old teacher I recognise turns away from the truth of me. The river mouth still purges yellow-slick. I reabsorb bile.

When I get home, Body wants Chinotto and vinegar. Vince hangs the laundry. I bin the salmon shirt. Hot headache trails behind me like a tetchy toddler, along with the not-right feeling that haunts my solstice. I watch clocks again.

The world turns. The skies darken.

June 27

I check emails. Silence from Amanda Steel, but there *is* a response from New South Wales Victim Services. Financial assistance is 'not approved'. Overruling my doctor, some non-medical bureaucrat refutes my need for audiology and nausea tests.

Good-Angry fizzes as I recall headlines about 'icare', the New South Wales government insurer. Despite losing a billion dollars in 2019, the agency awarded $4 million in bonuses to eight executives. In 2021, a taxpayer bail-out cost $2 billion. This year (2022), most executives received a $100,000 pay increase and the CEO was paid above $1 million.

I requested $344 for sound sensitivity treatment. But icare don't care. Now, everyday sounds overwhelm me. It's not just reduced tolerance to noise. It's painfully alarming and shoves me into an anxious sense of threat, making it difficult to cross a road.

I have ninety days to request a review. *More victim-work.* I get an appointment with Dr J, to request a letter, to re-justify the tests. It's farcical!

Steel asks if Perhaps-Mother will comment on 'your father's meeting with the principal?'

'Mum says she can't remember.' Sigh. 'Have you contacted the maths master?' I ask, 'or Mr Quinn?'

'I …' stalls Ms Lawyer, 'never received their contact details.'

I bite into self-reprimand, assure her I'll find the contacts. *Angry gets me nowhere.*

I venture back onto Facebook and Quinn graciously allows me to pass on his number. Then I post a community notice, seeking a number for 'maths master Trotter, one of the few honest, retired teachers from Tacky High'.

That evening, one responder lists 'The Great, Honest Teachers of Tacky High'; includes Perp and another teacher-perp who destroyed another girl. Another shouts: 'You can't suck up to him anymore'. Facebook is an imbecilic nest. I ignore the idiot, scroll through nausea until I find Trotter's number.

Why can't my lawyer do this?

July 5

I read about brave Tiffany Skeggs, abused from age 11 by a calculating predator who collected her from school, escorted her to weekend netball, and took sexually explicit photos. His charisma fooled her community for six years. Within weeks of being charged with multiple sex-abuse offences, he took his own life.

Tasmania's Commission of Inquiry found 'catastrophic system failures' but did not mention the failure to keep the predator in custody to prevent another denial of justice.

I'm numbed into awful-normal, dirty laundry. Nobody sees how broken we are.

Steel finally contacts the maths master, Giles Trotter. 'He wasn't helpful,' she tells me. 'Trotter referred to yourself and the perpetrator as "great kids", recalled "nothing too obvious" and described the 1980s as "the dark ages".'

Trotter once cared enough to report. I call him myself.

'Oh, yes, now you mention it, I do remember some incident with Rob Cunning and old Principal Crepit,' he says.

'Would you describe that incident for my lawyer?' I ask tentatively.

'I'd rather not.'

'You won't even try to remember?' my chin reverses into neck and I shrink a bit.

'Think I'll give it a miss,' he says. 'I've had a few calls and it's enough now.'

'Oh? Calls from who?'

'Bert Schiller …' I sip the straw air. '… it might've been Bert.' Then he pretends to not-remember who told him to keep quiet.

I drag cement legs into rain, unable to think or feel.

I am not small

July 12

Amanda Steel emails: *the Department has agreed to mediation*. Stunned, I run out, waving at Vince, who's attempting to whipper-snip chest-high buffalo grass.

'Never underestimate the fear of a premier facing an election.' He gives me a sweaty hug and fist-bumps the sky.

'They're still not releasing any documents,' I counter his enthusiasm.

'Mediation means they know you have a case.'

Fresh-cut grass whirls around us. Green glimmer expands my chest.

July 21

Intimacy is on ice. The surface cracks and I can't remember who I'm with. Vince makes tea instead. I tap fingers to thumbs, slowing my heart down from gallop.

We drive into Tacky for a Covid booster shot. Earplugs in, I hold Vince tight as he threads us through passing cars. Then I can't remember my phone number for the pharmacist. Or the 'myGov' login. Or my banking PIN. Re-wired brain can't function. Angry at my small-self-mess; for losing bits. Angry at another day of rain.

~

'I need to be strong for mediation,' I cry-tell Apple.

'Focus on repairing your nervous system.' She side-steps to check on my selves. Someone wants to revisit the laundry flashback.

'Perp wanted his washing hung in a particular way,' I tell Apple. *Pegs in armpits, NOT shoulders.* '... his T-shirts folded like new, from a shop.' *Front-down.Arms-in.Fold.Flip.Stack.*

I roll my eyes as Body slump-hunches into smallness.

'What does your body feel right now?' Apple asks.

'Prickly skin,' says a tight throat.

'How old are you?'

'Fourteen.' *Oh*, thinks Fifty-Four.

'It wasn't your job to do his laundry,' says Apple.

'I have to fold it carefully,' Fourteen tells.

'What happens if you don't do it right?'

Fourteen cannot find voice, shakes my head. Cheeks wet.

'Where are you now?'

Perp's second apartment, I don't say. *Holding the basket. He'll get angry. FoldQuickly.HurryToSchool.He'sWaiting.*

'I don't want to do this anymore,' says Fourteen, as guts suddenly lurch.

'What was that?' asks Apple.

'Rebellion,' we say.

Near the clothesline, sun is warm, but fingers freeze-curl into his laundry basket. Body stiffens into a chest-pain slice of Fourteen. I see the pegged shirts, cement path, pale fence.

'What do you feel in your body?' asks Apple.

Cold. But I can't speak. *I'm not safe.* My fingers will break if she touches me. Torso is a grenade. *Don't breathe. Stay still.*

'What does Fourteen want to do?'

Leave! I can't-scream. No sound escapes. My guts sieve gravel. Part of me knows that the sun on my young face is just memory; Fifty-Four sits in a psychologist's office, it's raining outside. But Fourteen is more real. *I'm stuck here and can never tell.*

'He's not here,' I whisper, clutch the basket. Feet numb-tingly.

Apple reaches into me. 'Where are you?' Fourteen cannot speak. Apple watches my stiff-grip hands, tries to let Fourteen know I'll help, but Fourteen doesn't know Fifty-Four.

'Where would you like to take Fourteen?'

Now grown-me cannot speak either. We're trapped together. *Don't tell.*

'You can leave now,' Apple assures. 'You won't be in trouble.'

Fourteen is suspicious – *do the laundry, rush to school.* Fifty-Four is in the ear-scream.

He's waiting.

'Your younger self feels afraid, but you can help her to safety,' Apple encourages. 'Where would Fifty-Four like to take Fourteen now?'

We push tiny breaths against sharp sound. *Phfooph. Phfooph.*

'Ice-cream,' I gasp and Fourteen drops the basket, hands spasming. *Still holding pegs? Phfooph. Phfooph. Phfooph.* Cat-furball dumpers hit the shallows. I'm tapping feet like an agitated child.

Apple helps me speak: 'He can't hurt me … It's not my job to do his laundry.'

We find our way to 2022. I am 54. *I am safe.*

We buzz-tap backwards and forwards in time. Body flicks the live-wire of my right arm, discharging static with a gun-knuckle *craaack.* Breathing slows to calm.

Apple scribbles 'intensely somatic' in her notes. 'What just happened?'

'Sorry … got stuck! I thought I'd be better by now.' I cry a puddle of self-disgust.

'You've nothing to apologise for,' Apple reassures.

'My ear is too loud,' I blub, pressing hot-achy skull.

We imagine taking Fourteen for ice-cream. Apple ensures I'm fully back before my hour is up.

July 27

I stand at my desk because my back muscles are clenched; too painful to sit.

Ms Lawyer emails. The Department have cancelled mediation and will not commit to another date until I undergo another medical, with a psychiatrist they nominate. *I agreed to that a year ago!* Their cruel delay sparks Good-Angry. Another exam and report could take months.

I call Steel: 'They're stalling.'

'It's progress, Cathy. Will you agree?' She holds her exasperation.

'By "agree", you mean …' I pace the room, holding fury, 'will I drag myself through *another* three hours with *another* psychiatrist to sum up Perp's impact on my life in *another* twenty-page document that I have to pay for?'

'You won't have to pay,' says Steel.

'This will be a *legal* cost,' I spitfire back. 'I'll have to regurgitate the awfuls … again!'

Steel waits. Her silence invites long, slow, deep, breaths.

Fill belly, not chest. Empty fully. And again.

I finally submit. 'OK, but not online.'

Steel says the Department will fly Vince and me to Sydney.

'Does that imply liability?'

She sighs: 'No.'

Vince distracts me with dream-van accessories. Big tyres. Off-road rescue ramps. A bull bar. 'Is there a *Mad Max* slicer-blade?' I ask.

He mimics Mel Gibson's deep drawl: 'You want outta here? Talk to me.'

~

I must have said appropriately suicidal things during the Flood Funding interview because Apple says they'll pay for more therapy. I'm supported because of a climate disaster, not because child sexual abuse survivors need priority help.

When I visit Apple, it's all in my ear: excruciating, high-pitched alarms.

'I have to look around to see if other people can hear it, or if it's inside my head,' I tell Apple, distressed. 'It screeches, stings my teeth and locks my jaw.'

'We'll try sound therapy,' Apple suggests. But today we're working on flashbacks.

'I don't know when I am or who I'm with,' I explain. *Could be him.* 'I get lost.' I cry and rub the itchy-back-head heat.

We use the pebbles as nausea erupts in fitful burps.

Apple helps me 'paint over' intrusive images of Perp's face with radiant sunflowers. We try to transform ear-splitting noises into gentle bee-hum. At home, I Panadol the stabs up my spine. I daydream into our escape van; a time beyond this wretched place.

Mid-August

In my blue cocoon office, I doomscroll. An investigation into the New South Wales Parliament finds 'unacceptable rates' of bullying and sexual harassment; half the incidents are perpetrated by Members of Parliament. Neither Premier nor education minister responded to my letter.

Noise overload. *Beep beep beep* of a reversing truck. *Scrawk scrawk* of Bitu-mill caterpillar treads, vibrating the whole house. Finger-in-ear, I go to investigate.

'It's only 7 am,' Vince whinges, quietly pleased that Council's stinky diesel trucks are scrape-fixing the flood channel across our driveway. I need to get out.

Magically, Gemma invites us to Cressie.

Sunshine swims are perfect therapy. On a rainforest walk, Gem asks, 'How's it going?' but I don't want to spoil the beautiful.

'Let's talk about something else.' Then a call from Amanda Steel interrupts our reverie.

'We need more details about incidents, on and off school grounds. Do you remember anything else?' *Dig deeper.*

Gemma gives me space, walks ahead.

I cat-furball at a spot where Perp took Fifteen once, for an oyster and Spumante picnic.

'Once, we were kissing in the music rooms ...' *Only kissing?* 'We had to jump apart because another student walked in ... I don't remember who.'

'Anything else?'

'On The Phone Call, Perp remembered Limeburners Beach.' *What happened at school musical camp?* I dig into murk-memory; the night I missed roll call. 'Perp came to meet me!' *Were other teachers looking for me?* '... Fingered me on the beach,' I tell Steel. 'He told me to "go in the side entry" while he snuck around the back.'

Ms Lawyer wants dates. I panic-mash memories. Forget others. On a public walkway, discussing intense details, without notes, I confuse years, stomp selves back into Body. When I catch up to Gemma, I'm hot-head buzzy. Mouth is cotton-dry, ick-sweet. She sees me spit into the 'Insta-perfect' Cressie view. He still pollutes my pristine places.

'It's going just great,' I grimace. We laugh.

Bullying administrivia

In news online, on TV, on radio: Grace Tame is still harassed by Nicolaas Bester, the teacher who groomed, raped and abused her as a schoolgirl. I should be grateful *my* perp is gone. But his lies still wander about, unchallenged.

September 1

Steel phones: 'The Department requests a list of witnesses, asks what each of them *allegedly* saw, where and when.'

They have a copy of a report from the 1980s. *They refuse to look for it.* They could call Donnelly. *But won't.*

'Regarding the principal, they want to know how and when

Mr Crepit *allegedly* reported to the Department. If in writing, please provide a copy.'

Phoophhh. 'They want *us* to provide copies of *their* records?'

Steel re-reads the request. 'They've asked for more details of each instance of *alleged* abuse; the day, month, year, location, time; whether during or after school; whether you were wearing summer or winter school uniform; what you were doing before and after the *alleged* abuse occurred; and the particulars of each instance of *alleged* abuse.'

More onerous *alleged*-victim work. A flood of administrivia.

I realise I've not taken a breath and suddenly suck in the world around me.

Steel throws a rescue ring. 'I've told them we won't be answering their questions ... your clothing is irrelevant.' *Steel fights for me!* 'By law, a school owes a non-delegable duty of care to a student when the perpetrator is in a position of power over the claimant.'

Brain clutches her legal words. 'He had special access to me; for musicals, band practice, saxophone tutoring—'

'Yes, but,' interrupts Steel, 'recent cases have been shredded because the abuse occurred *off* school grounds. We'll argue that duty of care extends beyond the school gate.' Then she adds: 'They have an obligation to investigate. They have the resources, but ...'

No-one can compel them.

Thirteen turns, like an unwanted pregnancy, sensing abandonment.

I try TRE but can't quiet the scream alarms. My eardrums bleed inside my head.

Therapy hurts

Sound therapy aims to strengthen the ear muscles. It doesn't help me. Besides, wearing headphones makes the hypervigilant more nervous. *We never know what's about to jump out.*

Other sounds emerge. Mantra-like bee-humms resonate in my chest. I make 'soap-a-pop' bubble noises, reminding myself I'm still here. Vocal *zhee*s relieve jaw tightness. It all feels desperate; the last gasp of a drowning. I'm dissociating more often, as if I might cleave apart.

Apple tells me I need to take extra care.

I squeeze my spiky ball, tell her I always have my scarf and jacket for the ice-freeze, and my forest-green water bottle, to hydrate. She means something bigger. I pool into worry.

'I can't seem to stitch my separates back together.'

Apple's gentle eyes watch me dive, into floodwater.

'I'm afraid I might leave them behind again.'

September

Every session yields something differently important. Sometimes I enter another age, inside body-memory. Sometimes we feel distant. Sometimes we're coiled tight, against breath. We children: abused, blamed, disbelieved, damaged. Trust is a frayed rope.

During one session, I drop into long-ago me, a chemical – not cognitive – exercise.

'It was all my fault,' Thirteen howls.

Apple jumps in: 'What if *I* told you something like your story, then said it was my fault?'

I know what she's doing.

'What would you tell me?' Apple prompts.

The adult-child shudder-gulps. 'I'd insist it's not your fault, you're not a bad person, he was a manipulative, evil man.'

'Now, hand to your heart,' says Apple, 'tell Thirteen.'

TiddlyBom flutters … 'I don't blame you.'

'As you deal with untapped emotions, deeper memories can surface,' Apple warns. 'A child's brain develops specific capacities in adolescence. Trauma at this time establishes neural pathways that determine how the brain responds to certain stimuli for the rest of your life.'

These journeys into younger selves involve neither magic, nor voodoo. They are not imaginary nor controlled by rational front-brain. The experience is intensely physical-metaphysical. Time-space bends, shoving my heart into recognition of deep sadness. In one session, I can only sit and cry. For an hour.

'Therapy hurts.' I let the tears roll as I restore trust in body signals, in my commitment to Thirteen, in my ability to speak. I am becoming more conscious of this subtle process; of how to navigate. I am beginning to understand how to grow myself back together.

Recently, I've felt more warmth in my chest, less threatened by eruption. Thirteen saved my family. *That* crying girl cannot change the past, but I can redirect focus, find sunshine between squalls, build myself into something unified.

Going back. Digging deep. *This is the only way forward.*

I flinch and *phoophh.*

'What just happened?' asks Apple, seeing my posture shift.

I let Apple in. 'Fifteen throws sawdust.'

'Where's Fifteen?'

'Still in the cage,' I say.

'Is anyone with her?'

'Eighteen comes and goes ...' I pause, sensing edges.

'Anybody else?' Apple waits as I prowl through her room.

'Twenty-Two.' Glimpsing Teacher-Beast I hack up a furball. Socks fill with shame.

Apple takes notes. 'And after that ...?'

'After that, I'm just me.'

Apple nods. 'What does Fifteen need?'

'She needs to know ...' Through Apple's window, I glimpse the RSL Club, then whisper: 'She didn't do anything wrong.'

Then I feel the blade and look at Apple in open-mouthed astonishment.

'What is it?' she asks.

Sliced open – I can't reply – from left shoulder, deep into breastbone.

'Cathy?'

'I've been … cut,' I gasp, shocked. The fissure burns ice and fire. So real I know my heart's been removed. Was that Lianne's 'felt-sorry-for-Dad' axe head?

You're crazy, some part snides.

Apple suggests we 'stay with the sensation.' Hold warmth to the wound, let the pain subside. I sit in silent tears, rubbing my chest.

Later, I'm stunned there's no scar.

A week later

'I'm so tired.' I flop into Apple's comfy chair, tugging boots off, earplug out. 'I'm dissociating even more. We all want this to be over.'

Apple waits for me to gear-shift down to her calm.

'How do you feel after last session?' she asks gently.

I rub my sliced chest. 'Well, it's …' Tears coat my cheeks.

Apple waits for the words.

'Weird that Fifty-Four feels the phantom injuries of a 15-year-old.'

'Weird?'

'It's profoundly confusing. I'm afraid I'm crazy and' – I jump up; shake legs and arms – 'I can't tell *anyone* about this time-travelling therapy!' Apple frown-smiles. 'How come?'

I sob-snort: 'No-one will believe me!'

Apple redirects. 'How do you feel about that wound?'

Mouth surprises me. 'I'm partly grateful.'

'What for?'

'It's a battle-scar trophy. A reminder: *I survived.*'

'You sure did,' she says in her kind-smiling way.

'Maybe I'll get it tattooed.' I laugh.

We discuss my fears about the upcoming second medical. 'It won't be "independent",' I blather. Apple reminds me it's normal for both sides to gather evidence.

We practise strategies: 'Ground yourself by foot-tapping; slow-breathing; fingers to thumbs; slide your tongue across your teeth; remember to eat, stay hydrated, and warm.'

Simple advice, given with love.

Keep going.

Preparations 14

Another medical

Late September

Kal is having surgery. 'You're brave,' I say.

'No, *you're* brave.' Kal smiles, knowing I'm the more afraid.

Despite cool weather, Body boils. Attempting TRE, I can't get under the frazzle. Maybe it's the traffic noise. Or the cigarette smoke from the guy downstairs.

Maybe it's because the Minister for Education pretends she didn't receive my letter to the Premier. Or that, when I finally got their dishonest reply, the Department's General Counsel claimed they 'communicated regularly with a view to early resolution'. Half-angry at their charade, I don't allow the distraction. I stock the rented apartment fridge, arrange for visitors to check on Kal. *I'm a good mother*, I speak against my horrors.

~

We start with a pre-dawn drive to Brisbane airport, two Sydney trains, and a greasy snack by a noisy road. Ears plugged, I'm shuffled by Vince through city-sound ambush to the Department's forensic psychiatrist,

Dr Ruby Willoughby. She reminds me of someone I like. But I don't trust her.

'You probably don't want to talk about this again.' She studies me with academic interest, asks about early family life; the grooming; first rape; missing memories. Thirteen flings from frosty to eruptible. Ears agony-slice as fire punches through skull. The beach incident ... *can't reach the silver string!* ... still the most difficult.

I conjure Apple's lovely face. *It's 2022. I'm 54. I'm safe.* We throw hand-holds to Thirteen. *Breathe! Tap your feet!*

Dr Willoughby sees neither freeze nor flight, nor practised rescue.

I skip the drunken sex of my college years, most of the Beast nightmare. I describe how my uber-confident 30-year-old 'triple-A+SuperBunnyDynamo' was always wired.

So tired now.

She asks if I can concentrate.

'I can read a book,' I say, forgetting I can't use spreadsheets or remember my bank login, and that simple tasks sizzle-melt my brain. I'm rambling, losing track.

After three forever-hours, Dr Willoughby asks if I have 'intrusive thoughts.'

A full-body shudder guillotines my throat and I shrink into the chair. I haven't even let Apple in there. 'I won't talk about that,' I snip, proud of my boundary-defender.

My evil is no-one's business.

'Can you give me some sense of those thoughts?' she persists.

Throat is slick with metallic goo. 'Horror,' I whisper.

'Can I have water?' I distract. Avoid. Crumble.

I'm done with being evidence.

'I suppose you think none of this was worth doing?' She tosses her trick question.

'It won't change anything,' I say, disheartened, 'but it had to come out.'

'What?'

'The awful' – she eye-scours me – 'my-selves.'

'Have you heard of the Sleeper Effect?' she asks.

'No?'

'Some adults who've been sexually abused as children appear to live symptom-free, but are actually in a state of shocked denial for years, even decades.'

Ear-siren wails. 'Oh.'

Vince's strong arms get me to the airport bar for a triple-hot-sauced Bloody Mary. The flight is delayed. By the time we arrive in Brisbane, we're so knackered we actually sleep.

September 28

I wake stiff-necked, needing to avoid noise and people. My fifty-fifth birthday gift is Kal time. Card games and cups of tea. From the safety of the couch, I become k.d. lang, floating 'Outside Myself', out over another flood-fouled river. At night, I struggle to keep my head above the slick. We spend a few days shutting out city sound and foul air. Then we settle Kal back into the student dorm and head for Tacking Point, through clots of traffic and reluctance.

Post office panic

Early October

I read that Brittany Higgins took the stand. Her perp-traitor chose not to be cross-examined. The system protects the defendant 'until proven guilty', thus assuming the claimant is a liar, undeserving of the 'presumption of innocence'.

I can't fight this.

Seeking ... camaraderie? solace? I return to Brisbane. The event flyer says Grace Tame will discuss her experiences. After her intense

Australian of the Year role, still copping it, still coping, Grace's bright voice appears distracted, deep-fried. She might phoenix-rise.

I will disintegrate.

October 11

I'm driving to humid-sticky Tacky 'Isle', memorising items: detergent, eggs, juice, Rocky's birthday chocolate. *Why won't they release Perp's employment file?*

On the wrong side of town, I rouse on Scatty-Brain: 'Re-route! Recite: *detergent, eggs … milk?*' But I've circled back, already heading home. *Sigh.*

I make a U-turn, notice thick clouds building, but navigate the too-bright, noisy supermarket maze and am back in my car, heading for the post office, without the chocolate. I'll get Rocky a gift voucher instead. Then I'm already driving past the post office!

Inefficiency irks me into anger. At myself.

I turn around, park, go in. Now I've left my phone (with Rocky's address) in the car. Already in line, I try to remember his street number, but concentrating ignites my head. I berate myself as the *boom-thump* of potential embarrassment amplifies. I step away from the counter, lift the envelope, and spot my phone. *Sigh.*

Now, I slow-instruct, *put voucher in the card, card in the envelope. Now, the address.*

Heading home, I realise I didn't activate the voucher, already mailed. It's useless. *I'm useless.* My skin is a bag of hot prickles. *C'mon stupid!* I force myself to go back and a nice lady helps me sort it. By the time I get home I'm a nest of frustrated, fuzz-headed itch.

'Did you get groceries?' asks Vince.

'My brain doesn't work anymore …' I storm past him and fume at the bathroom mirror. 'But that's not in any medical report!' Head throbs chase tremors down my arms.

'You *will* get better,' Vince reassures as thunder applauds the rain.

I lie in the bath, ensconced in steamy 'soap-pa-pop' noises. Vince brings me whiskey.

I'm on the rocks.

Amanda Steel emails: The Department says Perp was never investigated, but *the fact they ignore requests for* all *documents regarding* any *allegations against Cunning* … might mean, as Steel puts it, *there's something on his file they're not willing to release.*

No truth. Just games.

Mid-October

Steel phones. The Department wants my signed assurance I won't pass any documents to third parties. So they *do* have something?

'I suppose they'll want confidentiality too?'

'Of course.'

'Not happening.' I hang up. Angry sends her storm of chemicals through me.

'They want to gag me!' I yell at Vince, who encourages me to 'sign it and see'.

The Department then sends a 1981 'Duties of Teachers' memo, stating that 'a teacher is not on duty before 9 am or after 3 pm'. The memo says the Department is 'not responsible' if a teacher's actions were 'recklessly indifferent', 'intentionally harmful' or 'grossly negligent'.

This non-accountability memo *should* go to my secret posse of journalists.

If only.

Requiem

Sun mutes over slick-brown sea. I'm desperate for a wave. Driving to Cressie, hoping for clean water, I select Il Divo's debut album and hum with the Italian quartet.

I glimpse the blue-streak of a kookaburra, flying across the escarpment as the tenors croon 'Ti amerò'. I don't know what the lyrics mean, but the music soaks beauty into me and my heart fills the silver sky with memories of Fifteen. My jaw suddenly wolf-stretches. Grief howls for an endless minute as I clutch the steering wheel. The intensity stuns me.

Where was this pain smouldering?

Sob-waves dissolve Fifteen's hopes and dreams until I pull into the miracle of a Sunday parking bay. I sit for ages, unburdening.

We have a choice in grief, to yoke despair to hope and fix our eyes on joy; to rise towards light. Strangely sad-happy, Fifteen and I ride woo-hoo waves for two hours. I drive home in a peacefulness I've not felt for years. Healing, in its own time.

The next morning, Fifteen is no longer beside me. Disintegrated? Re-integrated? A soul I will miss. *Happy-sad. Goodbye Fifteen.*

Medicare memory work

Late October

Steel emails. I have to review my 38-year, 358-line Medicare history. Every doctor's consult, bulk-billed test and specialist visit. I must tick items that 'relate' to my 'injury', as if it's singular. Can I separate long-term cumulative from newly emerging damage? Breathe.

Cross out the easy ones: knee surgeries, baby Kaleido delivery! *But ... my lost second pregnancy? The hysterectomy? Do fibroids develop from too-early, too-often, painful sex?* The 1989 'cervix cauterisation' and 'uterus curettage' bring flashes of the Beast. *Do I tick those?* The pregnancy and HIV tests, when I feared the consequences of blacked-out inebriation outside Tacky RSL Club. Does that 'relate'? I shake out my arms, pop knuckles, make grumbly pow-wow sounds. It's soothing ... for a second.

I mind-spiral around years of phantom aches and gut-microbiome 'explorative tests'. None discovered my damaged child.

The ridiculous task takes all day. I do it twice because I stuff it up and have to print it out again. I run out of ink, then paper, then patience.

'How am I supposed to separate PTSD from other stuff?' I shout at Vince, trawling my damage. 'I've been tested for chronic illness, glucose intolerance, irritable bowel!'

'Keep it simple.' Vince shrugs. 'The lawyers won't debate the details of truth.'

'Truth *matters*,' I snarl.

Vince wisely exits.

Fog-Brain emails my ticked boxes.

A year from now, Medicare will, without notifying me, reject my claim and close my case. My lawyer will blame Medicare, who will blame my lawyer, for the one unticked box on the back of one form at the end of so many pages. I'll have to fight to get the claim reopened; redo the trigger dive.

~

Moody rain accompanies a post-nightmare morning walk. I'm nauseous again. Platoons of flood-smeared logs are beached, defeated dragons. *No swims today.*

I doomscroll, dismayed that Brittany Higgins' 'alleged' rapist will not face court because of 'juror error'. *A set-up?* In other news, an ex-football star, 'disgusted with himself' for sharing child sexual abuse material, blames his cocaine addiction, receives only community service. Society does not understand: the risk, the damage.

Ms Lawyer advises: costs are already $45,000. Mediation will take us over $100,000. Perp ensured his assets were held in trust for his children, to avoid paying for his crimes.

It will break us.

I drive to BrisVegas for a George Ezra concert.

'Mum, what are you doing?' Kal shouts when I flick my shoes off, dance past the crowd and shake it out to 'Green Green Grass'. I've moved on from 'Blame It on Me'.

November 4

The second medical report minimises my damage. Surprise! Dr Willoughby inserts the word 'alleged' before every mention of 'abuse'. I regret describing my 30-year-old 'triple-A+SuperBunnyDynamo'. She did not understand its 'too-tightly-wired' implication. She says therapy 'might get me back to some low-income earning capacity'. Well, great!

She acknowledges that the Teacher abuse enabled further abuse, but claims, bizarrely, it only accounts for 85 per cent of my 'psychopathology'. The Department's insurance lawyers will pounce on her assessment, to nickel-and-dime me down.

Steel emails: *Mediation is set for December 19.*

Nausea fills me like a sick bag.

Unveiling the intruders

November 12

The horrors have stitched my mouth shut for months, but I finally let Apple know they exist. 'I want them out of me,' I tell her. 'Fear of hurting a child makes me distrust myself.'

Apple helps me understand: such thoughts make me believe I'm a bad person.

Am I not?

'Your abhorrence makes it clear you would never act on these thoughts.'

I study Apple through suspicious eyes. Body sways.

'The thoughts intrude because something bad happened to you, not because *you* are bad.'

Intellectually, I get it; internalised blaming. The hurt baby represents *myself.*

Logical-Brain understands, but some parts missed the memo from the rational 'upstairs'.

Cottonmouth furballs sulphur into Apple's mint-fresh office. Throat spasms. Gut lurches into a wasteland of red terrror. Tongue slips across sharp teeth. I want to spit.

'There was another case at Tacky High.' I scramble to justify my panic. 'Same era, different perp … where the woman actually' – *Phoophhh!* – 'killed her baby.'

'How does that make you feel?'

'What do *you* think?' I snap. Apple doesn't deserve my angry. 'Awful,' I mutter. 'Sorry.'

'No problem,' – always kind.

'I know you care deeply about children.' She speaks calmly. 'You're loving to Kal and your grandchild.' *Yes.* 'You're not responsible for those thoughts … which emerged during immense confusion.'

After the volcano, the intruders came.

'Those thoughts are the reverse of everything you are. I understand you're afraid to speak about them.' Apple sees my agitated swaying. 'What does your body need?'

I bite down, taste metal. Sway. *I should shut up.*

'Your reality was distorted. Dissociation switched you between logical brain and survival responses.' *Some parts are listening.*

I feel heavy in my gut, tight in the thorax. Hand holds throat.

Don't tell her what we see!

I launch out of the chair, flick my arm, crack the knuckle. Feet stomp. Mouth *zhurr-zhee* gibbers.

'Is that a real language?' Apple asks.

'It … could be,' I laugh, breaking the ice-hold, but Apple sees the fear behind my eyes. 'What if, in mediation … I dissociate and … get stuck?'

'We can practise,' she reassures.

~

I wake in sunshine the next morning. 'Vince!' I shake him awake. 'I don't feel awful! I'm hungry!' I joyously bounce him out of bed. 'Will you make eggs?'

He sleep-walks into the kitchen, fries up a feast, watches me eat.

'My head feels like it's being operated on!' I beam at him across the table.

'That's great,' he yawns, heading back to bed.

It's 5 am. I take coffee to the beach and notice anaesthetic tingling in my head; the insertion of fine surgical instruments. Fizzy, like before, but different. Maybe the ants are moving on. I stretch and click neck muscles. Something is shifting.

I am not evil.

November 18

'Since the lobotomy …' I tell Apple jokingly, 'the nausea hasn't come back.'

Apple nods. 'And?'

'And I read that other people have intrusive thoughts,' I admit, swaying. Relieved.

'They're common with trauma,' she confirms. 'But we need to be careful … such thoughts can generate flashbacks and nausea.'

'Oh.' I sway.

'A particular thought, stuck in "replay", can overwhelm. But trying *not* to think it can trigger compulsive behaviours and other disorders.'

'Oh.' I stop. Swallow. Look at her.

'How are your younger selves?' she asks.

'Mistrustful.'

Apple nods. 'Unveiling intruders makes them less powerful. Would anyone like to share those thoughts?'

Phoophhh. Fourteen slams the screen door, propelling my chest forward.

'Did someone just exit?' Apple asks.

I freeze. 'Be. Very. Careful.'

'Why?' Apple prods gently.

'I can't tell anyone,' hisses Afraid.

'Why?'

'Because …' Chest tightens. 'Bad things are happening but … I can *never* tell.'

Fourteen listens at the door. I dry-swallow.

'It's OK,' says Apple. 'Take your time.'

I try to explain: 'Upstairs-Brain knows I'm OK, but downstairs, Fourteen doesn't know what we're talking about. She's frightened.'

Apple cocks her head but smiles. It all makes perfect sense to *me.*

Late November

It hasn't rained for ten days, but river sludge still swirls.

Nothing will ever be the same.

I distract from unwanted images into van-escape prep. We keep emptying the house. I give my guitar away. Vince browses camping equipment.

'Not yet,' I keep saying. 'We haven't got a razoo.'

~

Apple wants to chat with 'good, kind, caring Cathy.' Chin recoils at her words.

'Why do you think the intrusive thoughts must be kept secret?' she asks.

Naughty peers into her wise face. 'I was afraid.' *Am afraid.* I choke back words.

Apple is patient, but firm. 'Afraid of …?'

Chin pouts upwards. 'Of being found out.' *Phoophhh.*

Cold air rushes into my mouth, as if sucked through a pressure hose, flushing me with insight. *Afraid of being branded: the 'naughty slut'.* The masked intruders are just another blame-disguise! Not karma. Just swallowed guilt.

Now, Fifty-Five fills with clarity, and sorrow for my little selves. The back of my head, hot-itchy as mini-surgeons scrub the visions; neither memories nor flashes of a grotesque future. Logic-Brain was compromised; did not know how to process those intruders, who snuck in, fed off my distress and grew powerful. Now, I feel synapses rewiring.

I am a good person.

Apple and I attempt EMDR on a gruesome image. I reveal the details but, after only one revisit, it loses its charge. 'I can't get back inside it,' I tell Apple.

'You've learned how to recode those images as passing thoughts, not memories or intentions. Your logical brain knows you'd never hurt a child.' *It feels true.*

We hunt down other head-horrors, but their hiding places are empty. The shadow monsters hold less power. Where fear once reigned, peace blooms.

'It's strange,' I say. 'So much anxiety snowballed around stuff that's now ... defused.'

'Our brains do this,' Apple says, matter-of-fact.

'OK. What now?' I clap hands to knees. *Body wants to move on.*

'Well, you have the mediation ...' Apple watches me gag on sweet disgust.

'I want to be strong, but Ms Lawyer says I have to agree to *confidentiality.*' I push my tongue out, teeth-scrape the ick off. 'I don't know what I'll do if they try to silence me.'

'Try not to think about it,' Apple suggests.

Easy to say, I don't quip, because Apple closes her notebook, ending our session. I don't want to leave.

Becoming strong

'Confidentiality is a bullying tactic. Accept their best offer,' says Vince the negotiator. 'Then, do whatever you want,' says his footy brawler. *I need a legal expert.*

I re-read the Department's response to my letter to the Premier. Fury hammers out a reply, accuses them of 're-traumatising delays', challenges their archaic views that, as a child, I was not worth protecting; as an adult, not worth helping.

STOP. Check with Steel before you 'send'. Body flushes hot-cold. *Beach-walk it off.*

No! Last time I asked Ms Lawyer for a letter, she refused.

I am the grown-up now. Good-Angry tosses the bomb. Hit 'send'.

Within minutes, my phone rings. 'You've got my attention,' Steel says.

I stifle my apology.

Steel reminds me I don't have permission to use her firm's *gravitas.* She speaks 'client-lawyer privilege' words. I try to bite my truth-tongue.

'I won't privilege secrecy.' Strong voice escapes. 'Their letter was bullshit bureau-speak. You know it. They know it. I'm done being quiet.'

Ms Lawyer sighs. 'What do you want me to do?'

'I want someone to *fight* for me!' I shout, as my chest flares itchy heat. *It's not her fault.* But I don't apologise. I am strong. *I am Thirteen.*

I volume up Nick Cave's 'The Ship Song' and shout-sing, spinning through my living room, setting every Tacky Isle bridge on fire.

December 1

'I feel like a caged lion,' I tell Apple, puffing stab-breaths, tapping fingers to thumbs in a frantic digital circus.

'Move your body,' says Apple.

I prowl around her room, flicking my whip-knuckle. Gut-spasms gnaw my insides. I try vocalising *zees* and *pops* and *humms*, but end up walking in circles, tongue-clucking.

'How's your week been?' She already knows.

'I've been *Speaking Up*,' I boast, prancing behind the chair. 'I didn't let Perhaps-Mother drown me with saddy-news. I insisted on capital "B" Boundaries with the never-say-no grandchild about to jam-hand my curtains. I wrote to the Department highlighting their deceits, and I did *not* apologise to my lawyer.'

Apple watches my performance.

'I'mPractisingBeing*Strong*,' I declare, making fists.

'How much energy is that taking?' she asks as I zoom-cluck another lap, then chair-flop.

I admit: 'I'm exhausted; afraid of splitting off while driving; angry I can't even cross the road. Is this how I am now? … A PTSD mess!'

Apple tries to calm me, but the tremors crack all roads, from Richman Street to Lawyer Lane, to Barrister Alley.

'I'll take the spiky ball,' I say, as overwhelm slumps me into blue-balls flashback and shallow snort-breaths.

Apple sees. 'What's happening in your body?'

Fear. *Blue balls. That thing.* No air.

'What do you feel?' Apple repeats.

'I don't know!' little voice bawls.

'Cathy, take a breath,' says her calm authority. 'What year is it?'

I look through glazed eyes. 'Um …' *Concentrate!* 'Twenty … Twenty … Two?' I say, but don't believe. Slowly, air fills hot lungs. I straw-blow out. And again.

'Wriggle your left toes …' *I can do that.* '… your right toes.' *That too.* We breathe back.

'Twenty twenty-two. I am 55. *I am safe.*' I cry into a dozen tissues.

'No-one in that mediation room will know how to help me.'

'If you dissociate?' She offers Kevin Koala.

'Yes.'

'And you are …'

'Afraid.' Tiny voice sob-cuddles the toy. 'Afraid I won't be able to find my body.'

Apple lets me cry, then offers peppermint oil to rub into temples.

'Let's invite Vince to your next session,' Apple suggests.

'OK.' Vince is my solid. He's promised not to cook pork anymore.

~

It's raining again. Vince and I clean house, preparing to rent it out. If I can't have justice or truth, I'll try campervan freedom.

Steel emails, asking about my worsening dissociations: *Should we reschedule mediation?*

No! Please DO NOT reschedule. We've waited long enough.

In the media circus, Brittany Higgins is in hospital. The chief prosecutor says the case 'highlights the impact the justice system has on complainants … and how powerful institutions react when confronted'.

I will be silenced. The knowing snakes my throat.

I walk Pebbly Beach in my raincoat. Most of the pebbles are round. Centuries have beaten off their sharp edges. But one is broken, arrow-sharp, still fighting. I take it home.

December 6

I wake anxious. *Will Vince cope with details?*

'I've been keeping the yuck from you,' I say, breathing brave.

'I know,' he says, pouring chai.

'You should read my police statement and the psych reports.'

He goes to the deck. I sip tea. He reads for a long time. Lots of tiny sips.

'Oh darling.' Vince pulls me into a hug. 'I wish I'd known sooner, but I'll help you now.'

I show him my journal. 'I remember Dorrigo. You went cold.' He reads on. 'I'm glad you tossed that shirt.' He wipes my face. 'Keep going.'

Value

December 7

Vince and I take a three-way Zoom call. Ms Lawyer is concerned I 'might get angry'. Mr Barrister says mediation will be 'polite', which *does* make me angry.

'I'll have *my* Rottweiler ready,' I joke-hint, 'but I'll probably cry.'

'It will *not* be adversarial,' Mr Barrister reassures the adult, but Thirteen senses discipline: *Don't make a scene.*

'I'm afraid,' says little voice. *They're listening.* Take a breath, step towards strength. 'My habit is to silence myself.' Hand stills a throat spasm. 'I'm afraid I'll dissociate and won't be able to speak.'

Can they understand the horror of detaching ...?

Vince leans back, pyramids the fingers of his hands, takes long, slow breaths. *Solid.*

Mr Barrister explains his role: 'We'll try to get as much compensation as possible.' He talks numbers. *I'm not interested in numbers.* Body shrinks as hands patter-tap chest.

'I want truth.' I'm surprised the words get out. 'I want to see Perp's employment record, and the maths master's report. When did Dad meet the principal? Did they know about the schoolgirl at Loggerville High?'

I wait inside their long pause, tapping fingers.

'We might not get to that,' warns Mr Barrister. 'Document discovery is only available via court proceedings.'

Mediation will not reveal truth.

'*We* have to decide' – he indicates his Barrister self and Ms Lawyer – 'what's of judicial value and in the court's interest.'

Is he being ethical or just bollocks? My fingers slow.

'It can't be just for your curiosity,' he explains. *Bollocks.*

'So ... truth is not in the interests of the court?' I choke. 'Don't you represent my interests? ... based on what *I* value?' Fifty-Five shakes her head in disbelief. Thirteen is more than curious, wants more than mere survival.

I want Truth. 'Was it reported? When?'

I want Justice. 'What's a fair settlement?'

I want Freedom. 'Stuff confidentiality! … There's more to this than money.'

Their Zoom faces bore into me. I pyramid *my* hands.

'When I reported to police in 2021, schoolboys were being sexually threatening. This is about the kind of society we accept.' No-one says anything. *Silence is ugly.*

Mr Barrister redirects, listing over-confident compensation targets.

Numbers bore me. *Money is not justice.* I find my big voice: 'When a public institution won't reveal truth, and doesn't encourage others to speak truth, it perpetuates abuse.' *Don't tell.* 'The Department is keeping the abusers' secrets. Retired teachers are afraid to put on record what they know to be true.' Then, someone shouts: 'Stop cowering! If mediation won't get truth, let's go to court!'

Wait, did I just …? Throat seizes. I start clucking. Embarrassed, I cover my mouth.

Mr Barrister warns: 'Court will be expensive and take another two years.'

Drop the crusade.

The Zoom ends, I sit on the blue daybed with my laptop and type: *Mediation Goals: Truth, Justice, Freedom.* In a burst of imagined power, I add *Social Outcomes. The Department should: support expert counselling; encourage witnesses to assist; release data on abuse cases, to inform the public of costs and damaging effects.*

I send it to Steel, who replies: 'The Department has offered to write an apology'.

'No more empty bureau-speak,' big-me demands.

December 9

Awake before dawn, I scrape oyster-cotton off my tongue, drown it in black coffee. Vince and I encourage each other to accept 'whatever comes'.

In Apple's office, Vince fills the other blue chair. He sees me twitch and *phoophh*. He learns about dissociation; my different child-selves; how my posture and voice changes. Apple gives tips on getting me back through breathing, tapping, mints and water. We practise.

'Where are you now? How old are you? What year is it?'

Vince understands that Thirteen is still frightened. He listens with his lama-palms pressed together, breathing slow. *Solid.*

Mid-December

'Mediation is just blame-sharing,' Lianne dismisses on the phone. 'Is this the last dance?'

'That depends,' hedges strong voice, 'on whether truth gets a whirl.'

'Cathy, you don't want this to go on any longer.'

She doesn't know what I want.

On-team Maggie meets me in Tacky-town, buys me an earthy bracelet 'to remind you of your power to speak', and hugs me. 'You've got this.'

The bracelet has forty-two stone beads, one for each year of silencing.

Perhaps-Mother texts:

How aare you?

Me? I'm asking the powerful to do the right thing. I'm trying for brave. It's frightening.

She replies with emojis: a duck, a frog, an owl.

Well, I'm proud of me, I reply.

Pre-mediation Friday

December 16

In Barrister Alley, I realise Fog-Brain wrongly accounted for the Queensland time difference. *We're late!* Vince steers me through traffic. Ear-plugged and sweaty, I flounder into the striped wallpaper and linen shirts of Mr Barrister's chambers.

Parts are scrambling; it feels like I'm meeting Jason Harbour for the first time. *Did he always wear glasses?* I'm seeing with different eyes. He hasn't changed; I have. I'm stronger. Rejoined. Clearer. But now, the fight seems bigger.

Ms Lawyer is seated, pen ready. Mr Barrister closes the door.

He assures me I'll 'be heard'. Steel says I'll have access to a separate space during mediation. I imagine fresh air, potted plants, herbal teas. Coping things.

'Cathy?'

Hand hovers at throat. An involuntary *cluck* escapes. Mortified, I close my eyes and breathe into the not-me.

Barrister-man itemises settlement: *three hundred thousand* for this; *two hundred thousand* for that, 'plus interest, superannuation, medical expenses'. The numbers drip off his cedarwood desk, into puke-yellow carpet. I'm trying to be polite, to not interrupt.

'Their first offer will feel insulting,' he warns. 'Their apology will not admit liability.'

Ms Lawyer does not look up.

Vince wants to wrap me in a blanket, but he's my lama sidekick today. We're in training for Monday's long-awaited, twice denied, rescheduled, mediation.

I raise my hand and Mr Barrister stops, like a dentist.

'You've lost me in the numbers.' I shake my head. 'I need you to understand why I did this.' Throat spasms.

Mr Ironed Stripes sits up straight. Ms Lawyer puts her pen down.

Release hand from throat. Allow breath to balloon. Focus on Vince's hands.

They're waiting. I twitch, cat-furball, cluck, and then ... *speak.*

'If the Department aims to dissuade me from speaking, then the predator is still in the room.' Perp flashes behind my eyelids. 'I will *not* be quiet.' I Apple-paint over his face.

Barrister-man tries reassuring: 'The Royal Commission made it clear that silencing a survivor is not acceptable.'

'My freedom to speak is non-negotiable,' says newly integrating self.

Vince asks to see the confidentiality clause, but Mr Barrister points to my fantasy list of 'Social Outcomes', shaking his head. 'Mediation can't make policy. This is not a justice system, but a *legal* system. We are bound by it.'

Mediation has no interest in social good. It aims to buy silence.

'Why can't you make Donnelly speak truth?' I demand, wanting to skip mediation and dump dirty laundry in the New South Wales Supreme Court.

Ms Lawyer boils over. 'We can't compel a witness. If we subpoena him, we can't even cross-examine.'

'*What?*' Nausea surges. Some parts levitate towards the window. I cluck-choke a swallow. 'So, even justice will silence truth?'

Barrister and Lawyer look down, say nothing.

Dry-retching, I push up from the big wooden desk, can't see a bin-liner, so I launch towards the closed door.

'Do you need me?' Vince panics.

'No!' I vomit-shout, desperately turning the slippery gold door handle. *Trapped?*

It finally opens. I dash to the bathroom, retch, teeth-scrape and spit. I square up to Big Brave in the mirror. 'Stay strong,' I say, unsure whose eyes look back.

As I re-enter, I shake my legs, cluck and flick-click my arm.

'Shall we?' Jason Barrister nods to the chair, but I prowl about as he outlines court options if mediation doesn't work: 'Two years is a huge cost risk. Resolution … uncertain.'

'What about the maths master's report?' I ask, forgetting that 'access to documents' requires a court case.

No-one speaks.

'They're hiding it!' I scrape oyster-tongue. 'Donnelly knows. Schiller knows—'

Vince jumps in: 'We're willing to sell the house to take this public.'

There's my crusader!

'You won't have to do that,' insists Mr Barrister.

I plonk heavy head to cedar desk, search the carpet for dead ants. Pretend I don't notice his ruling out of the court option. *I'm not worth the risk.*

Barrister-man focuses again on dollars and nonsense.

Voice interrupts him: 'Last time, you said you'd take half of any settlement.'

'Oh, we don't talk about fees here,' he flippants.

I lean in. 'I know why everyone else will be at that mediation, but money is not *my* motivation.'

Mr Barrister sits back. We all take small, separate breaths. He reassures me *he will listen*, that I *have a voice*. The snake flexes, squeezing my jugular.

'I have one more question …' I jump onto the elephant. 'Won't they just pass on blame; say my parents didn't do their job?'

'Ah, I've been avoiding that,' he admits. 'Your parents had a professional duty of care. You didn't deserve less than other students. You deserved *more*, because they were parents *and* teachers. The fact that so many others suspected, that your sisters felt unease … it will be clear in court, that your parents' *professional* duties were breached.'

And there it is: my family poop, on Mr Barrister's polished cedar.

Steel asks if she should contact Perhaps-Mother.

'Go for your life.' I toss my hands up. 'You won't draw a drip from that stone.'

The elephant pirouettes out into clouds, and I follow-float above the winding river.

Vince stands to leave. I scurry back to Body, to Voice: 'So, their apology will be bureaucratic blah, the settlement won't be just, the document of truth is inaccessible, and system improvements are outside your remit.' *Pause.* 'All I can fight for is my freedom to speak. So, *any* confidentiality gag is a deal-breaker.'

I surprise us all with my clarity.

Ms Lawyer slips a large white envelope across the desk.

'For you to be informed of ... costs to-date.' *Classy.* 'But don't open it until after Monday. Don't worry over the weekend,' she says, ensuring we will.

Already pushing for settlement. They don't want this to go to court. *I never did.*

Back in our cheap Airbnb, we fall for the ruse, open the envelope.

I've racked up $70,000, not counting mediation. They estimate $100,000 in total. If I don't agree to their offer, court will risk another $250,000 to $400,000.

'It's up to you,' says Vince.

'No Vin, I can't sacrifice *our* life savings, *our* future ... for *my* truth crusade.'

We cuddle on the musty sofa. *Solid. Together.*

'It's funky though,' I ponder aloud, 'how we take advice on the chance of a win from the people *we* have to pay if *they* lose.' We laugh at the absurdity.

Later, we meet Kaleido for Turkish kebabs and garlic dip. I embarrass Kal by joining in the belly dance. I shake and shimmy with the sparkly, buxom lady, imagining cape and boots as the entire restaurant claps me on.

Don't be greedy

In slick humidity, Vince and I agree to 'not talk about my stuff'. We visit Aunty Marion and Uncle John. It's nearing Christmas, so of course we tear the flimsy wrapping off 'my stuff'.

'Don't drag yourself through another two years,' advises John.

'Retired teachers are still hiding truth,' I argue through mince tart.

'Fair enough, they don't want to get involved,' John absolves, as if he were a priest.

'Nothing fair about it,' says Voice. 'Truth would cost Donnelly nothing.'

'He let you know there *was* a report,' John's volume rises. '*That* was the right thing.'

'No, John,' I raise my voice to match, 'the *right* thing would be to sign an affidavit, so I don't have to go to court to see that report.' I suck in hot air and sugar-ick. 'Being a gutless arse is *not* the right thing.' I walk skin-ants to the balcony and spit cherry pips.

Reliably charming, Aunty Marion swims over. 'Those teachers probably rallied community spirit during the floods. I don't get why they won't help you.'

I hold onto her lifeline, listen to her garden windchimes.

When Marion and I go back inside, Vince tells them: 'Cathy doesn't want to talk about it,' and diverts to campervans. But my stuff is all-consuming. We slide back into the muddy topic of confidentiality.

'I won't be gagged.'

'You're brave, Cathy,' bolsters Marion. Supportive. Motherly.

'You said you don't want to talk about it,' John snags my contradiction. 'So why care about confidentiality?'

'Cathy might want to tell *her* story,' rescues Vince.

'I'm not afraid of the truth anymore, but …' I falter.

Marion wraps it: '… but other people are.'

'I only took up a civil case because a National Redress lawyer advised me to.' *Sigh.*

'You'll have to compromise,' John decrees. 'Don't be greedy.'

An awful taste flushes through me and Vince extracts us for a walk.

I'm so tired of other people's words.

~

The bridges flash Christmas lights all night. We don't sleep.

At 4 am, I watch Argentina beat France in the Soccer World Cup, pretending it represents the possibility of perseverance over power. At 6 am the cool breeze reminds me that things *can* change. La Niña *can* move on.

15 Mediation

Openers

December 19

I have my comfy power-clothes on: crisp white shirt, dark pants, black leather hi-tops and Maggie's 'strength' bracelet. I've got my water, scarf, Vicks sniffer and ginger bears. I grip the arrow-shaped rock and push my earplug in as Vince guides us through city noise. Wearing rain-forest-green, he's my lama-calm today.

Already it's not working. My breath scrapes and I nostril-snort, skimming air, stimming through spasms and finger-knuckle clicks.

In Mr Barrister's reception, I inspect the Raj-esque elephant lamps, olde-world globe maps and sketches of Elizabethan ladies without waists. It all reminds me: the legal-not-justice system reflects centuries-old power imbalances.

I'm scrutinising the marble bust as Barrister-man enters. Navy suit over striped linen.

'Your marble man's not labelled,' I point out.

'Yes,' he admits.

'Who is it?'

Jason shrugs.

'So, you honour some random white guy?' I spot the wrapped boxes beneath a faux snow-dusted Christmas tree. 'And the presents aren't real either?'

His cheeks ripen with the fakery.

Amanda Steel enters in serious black, and we step into his office. I ask for the door to be left open. They talk words as I dissolve into dusty books.

Jason Barrister doubts the Department will argue for a 'stay of proceedings' which would kill my legal action, but he admits: 'Recent cases have been shut down using this loophole.'

I'm not really here – or hearing. I hope Vince is taking it in.

'You *could* speak,' ventures Barrister-man, 'but I can't control what you'd say.' His words flash-stun my eyes open.

Control what I say? I shake my head and cluck.

'I do know how to *behave*,' I manage. 'Let's go.'

~

Vince shuffles me in and out of lifts, across a road, around a corner, up an alley, to the mediator's office. Ms Mediator's fine-wool black dress glides us towards a black-walled room, where she indicates for us to squeeze to the far side of a seriously-too-large-for-the-space, ebony table, gleaming under one tiny downlight. Even the chairs feel trapped.

I stall on the threshold. Body limbo-leans back, scans for an exit. No windows. No vomit pot-plant. I flush with dehydrating panic and twist towards the door handle.

Jason Barrister, behind me, sees my alarm, sees that he traps me in the doorway.

'I need to know I can get out!' I shout at him, wincing at echoes.

Ms Mediator dashes off to find an escape room, so I don't have to stay with the Department's minions. She parks Vince and me in a vacant office. The window won't open.

'Wait here,' she instructs, closing the door. *Can't breathe!*

I nudge the door ajar and overhear hushed rearrangements. Trying to not-panic, I prowl about, opening drawers. Gut grizzles as I arm-flick, knuckle-click, *phooff* out sour.

'Do you want to sit?' Vince unhelpfuls.

'Nope,' I cluck and fidget.

My three legal eagles swoop into the un-safety nest. I barely take in their word-squawks as I Vicks-sniffer menthol-calm, hum away the twitches.

'Today is a pre-court meeting,' Ms Mediator begins, 'to negotiate an outcome that will involve less time, less risk, and less difficulty than court proceedings.' She 'cannot give legal advice', only 'a pathway likely taken by a judge'.

Barrister-man asks me to trust him, mentions the Department has sent a Position Paper.

Wait! *When? Does it mention Perp's employment record, or the maths master's report?*

But there's no time for questions because the Department's representatives arrive.

They're waiting.

We file back into the soulless midnight room: Ms Lawyer, Ms Mediator, Mr Barrister, Vince, and Us-Me. This time, I'm seated near the open door.

Across the shiny slab sit three black-clad, overly made-up representatives: a barrister, a mid-level bureaucrat, and a talon-sharp insurance company lawyer. All women. *Strategic.* I can't look at them. They symbolise the perp and the institution that stifles truth.

I ask to be called 'Cathy'. They call me 'Dr Byrne'.

They'll have a pre-approved financial limit to reach settlement. I wish they'd just tell me. But, like any dance, the legal tango has rituals. First, we must bow to each other. Then step forwards, backwards, sideways. Someone will hold a foot up in the air and wait, still as a hot-rock lizard. I watch as my Barrister-man spins shiny words, seems nervous. I puff-breathe as he glances at my typed 'Goals', begins again, conveys my reasons for coming forward: my need for truth, my desire for systemic change. He concedes 'some changes *may* have already begun'.

He's being polite. Coaxing them towards humanity.

Barrister-man highlights the Department's awareness of child sexual abuse throughout the 1950s, 60s, 70s. 'There were rules for reporting' but 'lack of teacher training and departmental investigation created a context for criminal harm.' He suggests that my sisters' early sense of 'wrongness' and my parents' moral responsibility *should* have triggered their professional duty of care.

He says a proper 'justice system' would have imprisoned the Cunning Perp-traitor for up to fourteen years, and that his suicide continues to cause me damage.

I am quiet. *Behaving. Being polite.* Occasionally clucking. The sharp beach arrow digs into my palm. I could drive a scratch down this magnificent table. *Would that be 'horrific'?*

Mr Barrister says the Department's 'constructive knowledge' means they 'should have known'; they hold 'vicarious liability'. He talks of the 'open-secret relationship', described by multiple students and some teachers, my father's 'direct knowledge', having been told of its sexual nature, and of his, and the principal's, breach of their duty of care.

Thirteen is grateful for truth.

Then, with certainty, Mr Barrister spotlights the contradictions in the Department's medical report, which describes 'severe dissociative amnesia' when I was Thirteen, but claims 'no long-term psychological damage'. He challenges the Department's trio of tough chicks to consider how 'a little girl, subjected to serial rape her entire high school life, suffered in many areas of life, all her life, and is consequently, irrefutably psychologically damaged'. *True.* 'Just because Cathy achieved academically, doesn't mean she didn't suffer: financially, emotionally, and physically, for a very, very long time.'

Jason the Argonaut fights for me!

'If this situation had been properly reported when the perp was *still* teaching, it would have been investigated. There *would* have been disciplinary action and Cathy *would* have received the help she needed and deserved – *still* deserves,' he emphasises.

We feel his torchlight on our faces.

'If the abuse had been reported earlier, Cathy might not have been re-victimised. There is no doubt, in the mind of any court, Cathy's life would have been significantly better if not for this gross negligence.'

I breathe deep into belly as Jason-my-safe-Harbour proclaims: 'In court, the case is likely to succeed, and the damages *will* be significant.'

Hooray! yells my inner squad. I'd like to leave now, to have tea and scones served, to start court proceedings, to request the 1980s report. *I want to see it.*

But now it's their turn.

Attention shifts to the vampire ladies, half-hidden in shadow. *Faceless.*

Cluck goes my chicken. A hand smacks over mouth, trapping me in putrid bog-water.

I watch Vince's lama-palms and straw-breathe.

'We are very sorry this happened to you,' begins the Department's barrister. 'We all empathise and thank you for stepping forward. You've shown great courage …'

She's pretending nicey-nice. To disarm.

I stifle another cluck, but nod, to show her I'm in-the-room.

'We acknowledge the importance of reviewing how these matters are handled.' She seems sincere. I try to see into her hooded eyes. She surprises me by speaking of grown-up Cathy as 'a person of high calibre'.

I smell the lie of false empathy but can't tell if they want to tango or tussle. *How do they treat those of 'low' calibre?*

Body is swaying. Brain feels two-lobed, swings back and forth like a double-armed theme-park ride. Friction melts my back-scalp as I pendulum-scissor; shunt towards collision.

'Having said that …'

My jaw clenches. I flinch at the steel-on-steel scrape. Brace … slice off a piece of ear and suddenly I understand, their job today is '… to defend the public purse'.

I am a commodity, begging at the counter of 'Ca$h for Coping'.

Her mouth keeps moving, despite my laser stare. She shuttles through arguments from the Position Paper I've not yet seen and will never be allowed to disclose.

Truth is not allowed out.

[*Some words in the following exchange have been redacted on legal advice.*]

Then, the cloak of cunning slides across that shiny table. She says: '██████████.' My throat seizes. *He's in the room.*

Jason shifts in his chair as my escapedoor-side attendees come to understand: '██████████.'

Death rots the bones of truth.

Confidential legal-not-justice words snake through my mind. Six chicken clucks escape.

Everyone that could have helped … gone. Now only Donnelly and Schiller, and the maths master, and Perhaps-Mother, all corpse-like in their cowardice. No-one will ever hear of Cunning's *alleged* inappropriate dealings.

My Argonaut snides a polite 'Good luck with that!' and whips out his notes. 'In 2020, the New South Wales Court of Appeal argued that … "██████████." Furthermore,' states Jason, '██████████,' and, '██████████.'

But their cold stares dim his eyes a little.

The Department will never contact Gutless Donnelly.

Fog-Brain wonders if the maths master's report, or my sanity, would make it to court? I watch the Department Barrister's mouth; opening, closing. Hear my loud *CLUCK!*

Does it mean 'Don't be a chicken' or 'Beware of foxes'?

Soothing my ruffled feathers, I sink into the dark wall, wondering what my father's face did in the school playground that day.

Settlement is not justice

In the mediator's floor-to-ceiling bathroom mirror, I can't see who I am. I think of how horrible court would be, dragging Perhaps-Mother through fear of her own guilt and the trashing of her otherwise honourable husband.

Vince guides me back to our airless huddle room. I *tap-tap-tap* my arrow-rock along the windowsill. TiddlyBom flaps in desperation. All seated at a small desk. I keep tapping, tap out. Jason, across from me, speaks legalese, while Steel reviews her notes, *tap-tap-tapping* her pen.

'Cathy, do you understand what Jason is saying?' Vince is tapping my arm, trying to find me, under water. I'm surprised there's no sound from the three faces, peering.

'Oh! Hello,' I greet Jason. He 'hellos' back as I resurface. I'm fighting the impulse to cluck. I ask for the Position Paper, but its words glaze my eyes. I stomp my feet and flick arms, wishing for fresh air, hot tea, and an Apple.

Steel number-crunches my pain on a notepad: *Suffering and loss of amenity; Travel, treatment, medication; Past economic impairment plus interest and superannuation; Future economic loss, medical and therapy; plus legal costs = $x.*

'I know this is hard for you,' Jason says, 'but, Cathy, you *can* trust me.'

I shrug as they venture back to the dark side, carrying my single sum.

'Patience, grasshopper,' Vince whispers.

Tap-tap-tap, I spasm and cluck. Trying to read, I get lost in the Department's blame-sliding assumptions and continuing negligence. They wipe their hands on my teacher-parents.

I'm still clucking as Jason re-enters, advises us to wait.

'Need … air,' I urge Vince, grabbing my earplug. *Chicken gotta run.*

'Don't go far,' warns Jason.

Vince and I seek freshness in a flood-stenched city. On my phone, I search 'vocal tics'.

Google says that suppressing my inner-chicken might lead to more severe episodes, even rage attacks. *Chicken gotta gun.*

I twitch-wait. Jason phones, disappointed, relays their starting offer.

Air puffs out of me and I retch into the muddy river.

'No,' says all of me, barely holding bird-bones together. We haul back into stuffiness.

I shrug as Mr Argonaut presents his 'reasonable' step-down counter-offer, then toddles back into darkness, to play-battle the mercenaries.

Cluck. Twitch. Flick. Crack. Retch. Wait.

Ms Mediator brings a draft Release Agreement so we can review the confidentiality clause. Vince nods as he reads the already-Jason-revised version: *Nothing in this Agreement prevents the Releasor* – 'that's you,' explains Vince – *from disclosing the facts, matters, and circumstances contained within the Agreement, the circumstances of the Claim, or the Releasor's experience of the Claim's process.*

Outside, a patch of blue peeks through bleak grey. I picture Vince and me on the road in our sea-green campervan and finally, the realisation … *I can tell my story.*

Freedom surprises me. But we're not finished. The draft agreement is taken away. Offers resurface. We step down several times. Jason Argoes, back and forth; 'unacceptable' figures fly as the vampires tap-dance for the taxpayers. *Lizard-dancing is not justice.*

'I feel floaty.' I melt into Vince, nauseous-hungry. 'When will they bring the egg sandwiches?' *I'm paying good money.*

Everyone smiles, as if I didn't speak.

Vince leans over. 'Jason seems nervous,' he whispers, loud enough for lawyers' ears.

Jason cuts a stern laser-gaze through us, highlights the reality of the Department's threat.

A head drops heavy on the table.

'I need food,' I tell the skin-ants, then shake my empty packet of ginger bears.

Vince and I find stale sandwiches in Barrister Alley. People walk too close to our table as I try to read. Brain can't decipher their 'Position Paper'. I feel odd, eating chicken.

Vince's phone pings. Jason wants us back.

What now?

We wait. Jason asks Vince about his job. I feel irrelevant. My clucker is irked. Steel asks if we have dinner plans, mentions her young son. *She's a mother!* I flush with guilt at my impatience, shrink into my shoes.

Ms Mediator steps into our stuffy pod, closes the door. She has their 'final offer'.

I am 55. It is 2022, and I am ... done with 'blameless' bureaucracy. Done with bargaining for my pain. I flick-crack-twitch again. Puff and squirm.

I picture the faceless ones zipping their briefcases, expecting acceptance.

Here in Team Cathy's huddle, Steel and Argo watch to see how I react.

I look, sigh, close my eyes.

Vince asks if filing court proceedings would incur immediate costs.

'Yes,' Jason says, 'and there are other risks now.' He nods towards me, as if I'm not 'there'. *Maybe I've gone again.* Jason whispers, he's 'not sure Cathy would make it through the ordeal of the New South Wales Supreme Court'.

I snatch up my Goals.

'Whatever happened to their written apology?' I scowl.

The lawyers look around as if someone just farted.

No! I scream inside. *A bureaucratic brown smear is not good enough!*

The Department kept their documents hidden, their investigation un-started, their witnesses un-subpoenaed. They will never publicly admit to protecting a pedophile. I will never know why the principal chose the school's reputation over my wellbeing. Never understand how my parents turned a blind eye. Never comprehend the cowardice of the teachers, even now, willing to *speak* truth, but not write it.

I am tired of chasing shimmers. Ms Mediator sees I'm struggling.

Thirteen flutters in her heart-shaped cage. *Will I be locking her back in?*

My insides respond with a glottal *cluck* as someone says to 'take my time'.

It's been two years already since Perp came back to town.

Vince and I leave with the unsigned agreement.

I numb-shove my jitters under too many vodkas.

'Let's take 'em to the Supreme Court,' I slur as Vince pats me to sleep.

Survival counts

December 20

I dream I'm trying to sign the agreement, but I'm underwater. The pen oozes ink and the paper dissolves at the edges. I scribble in different places, then the page disintegrates.

'*Take your time*', urges me from semi-sleep. I'm done taking *my* time. My whole lifetime. I scrape the waking oyster-scum off my tongue, the bridge-light dryness from my eyes. I look across my snoring lama, at the unsigned agreement and the pale dawn.

Could I endure another two years?

I feel utterly drained. Doing 'the right thing' has burned through all my brave. I'm nothing but the powder-ash of a dying volcano, panic-flutters, and chicken squarks.

Acceptance feels like defeat, betrayal, cowardice … but also: relief. Two years of adrenaline fires and cortisol floods have singed my fibres. Another two will obliterate me.

Do I want truth out of the cage, or myself?

The Department has worn me down, but if I keep fighting, I'll be the one doing damage. My bravest move now is to prioritise the innocent: get child-self to safety. Complete the rescue. It makes no sense at all, except it finally does. I am not responsible for the cowardice of others. Their fear of truth is not my burden. It cannot set me free – only I can do that.

Breathe sky. Deeply in. Slowly out. Survival counts.

I watch Brisbane's joggers, puffing about in mango-coloured light. Sunlight strikes something reflective on Mt Coot-Tha. Something shimmery.

I realise now, at least their offer is more than I'd receive through National Redress. Our efforts weren't futile. By accepting, I *can* finally move on. With the strength and power of all my selves, I *can* claim the freedom to leave it all behind, take time to heal.

I sign the document. One day it might feel like some justice.

16 Freedom

A clear voice

For days, I cry relief and regret: for truth's lost opportunity; for questions unasked. I wonder if I'll ever let go of disappointment-in-myself, for not fighting harder, longer, stronger. I manage polite responses to texts that urge me to 'celebrate'. *This is no victory.*

In Tacky, we collect our gypsy-sea-green campervan. It feels safe, inside turtle armour. Vince stashes kitchen gadgets, finds space for the pastry brush, tosses the oyster-shucker.

During the months that follow, my nausea, clucking, insomnia, flashbacks, panics, and floaty-forgetfulness continue. Apple was right; legal resolution does *not* cure PTSD.

I recall the Department's psych supposing that 'none of this was worth doing'.

Actually, it was.

After forty-two years, I finally wrestled shame to where it belonged. I got back together with who I am, released my trapped selves from the fear cage.

There's healing to do. Plenty. But I choose freedom.

January 2023

It's a blustery blue day as Lianne and Perhaps-Mother walk into our driveway. Vince steps into the van, avoiding. Perhaps-Mother sticks her beak in, spouting advice on what he 'won't need'.

I encourage them away, to the beach. Perhaps-Mother walks ahead; doesn't want to hear about mediation.

'I know you're angry with me,' Lianne ventures into my quiet.

I close my eyes. *Not angry, waiting for a miracle.*

'Dad should have complained. Something should have been done.'

'That's all I ever needed from you.'

Lianne reddens, then admits: 'I've been working with someone who knew Perp … they asked whether you ever considered *his* family!'

I breathe away the belated blame.

Sensing tension, Perhaps-Mother circles back.

'Your father didn't know any …'

'One day—'

My clear voice interrupts her, takes a big-ocean breath and exhales deep into warm sand. I expand through time, connecting myriad ant trails, calling all my selves through the Pebbly Beach car park, along the 255 steps up the street to the floorboards of my childhood, releasing long-buried hurts from that grey dust. 'One day … you might fully acknowledge *my* truth.'

'Perhaps.' Mum gives a wry grin as they walk away.

But I am content. I've started my wild, freedom countdown.

~

I rock on bare feet, listening to kookaburras. The cool south-easterly invites me to the wide, blue-again expanse. I dive under waves and swim past the breakers. There, floating alone, I swallow a belly-full of sky, tasting rainbowed salt-spray. I feel a gentle tug across my chest as a glowing ribbon of sunlight unfurls inside of me, slowly refracting, warming me with Thirteen's wilful copper marmalade; Fourteen's lime-green stripes; Fifteen's searching emerald eyes and the pathos of Eighteen and Twenty-Two's blue-hued journeys; then the insight, settling indigo, discovering something more to this strong self. So much light and colour now, the stuff of me. The ocean holds me, enfolds me in the hum. Thirteen's gift: I see how my own silence left too much space for misunderstanding; how I've held Thirteen down, below black ice. It's time to rejoin all my wild, confident, curious and clever selves. *Time to resurface, into voices of joy and gratitude, into sparkling colour, and a future.*

I bodysurf to shore, massage skin in sandy tingles. At home, I feel strong.

Vince steps onto the deck. 'The van's packed.'

'Let's drive into the big empty.'

'Which way?' he asks.

'Let's decide at the end of the street.'

Beginning, by ending

We carry history in skin.

April 2023

I'm at the intersection for Cape Hauy, the last along Tasmania's Three Capes Walk. It's starting to drizzle when I get a text from Vince, at the other end. *Already?*

I've had four blissful days, in pointless beauty. Walking snake-brave, under enormous sky; releasing pain into cool, green undergrowth, transforming fear into intricate flowers. Four days being present, breathing crystalline, southern air.

Now, I'm nearing the last trail head. *I can't keep him waiting.*

Dozens of perfumed, chatty daywalkers swarm in from the other end, bringing the shrill of civilisation. Should I skip the final leg? *He can wait.* I should go. *No.* I don't deserve such beauty. *You're being ridiculous.* Overwhelmed, I make the mistake of keeping my pack on.

Now I'm stupidly carrying it down steep, rocky steps. There's not enough room for me, my pack, and all these lurid interlopers. *Embarrassment feels like shame.* In the gully, before the last spectacular view, I'm crying, not wanting people to see me. Angry at myself for becoming small. Undeserving. Frustrated because now, down here, I've lost reception, lost my balance. I'm not at the end, but …

He's waiting.

Just thinking it, shrinks me into a confused, self-sabotaging fraidy little thing in someone else's skin. *What if he's angry?*

The mere thought floods hot prickle-panic from guts into chest. Breath fights through a straw, then the back of my skull starts to rip. *Where'm I gonna run to?*

Back up those steps. Heart thumping. Ears screaming. Sweat inside clothes. Tears and rain. My hiking boots, hitting the ground, running …

And then, out from the drizzling grey, Vince scoops me into strong arms and spins me around like when we got married. He whisper-sings Sinead O'Connor's 'Thank You For Loving Me' and wipes my crying face. I suck in air and remember: *He's not the one that gets angry.* Breathe. *Deep in, slow out. Touch fingers to thumbs.*

Say it with me: 'I am 55. It's 2023. I am safe.'

Epilogue

November 2023

In the news:

... Australia's High Court rules against the use of 'stays' to shut down historic child sexual abuse cases.

... Brave Grace Tame campaigns against mandatory minimum sentences for child sex offenders which may cause abusers to plead 'not guilty', forcing victim-survivors into distressing trials.

... Brave Brittany Higgins is accused by her perp-traitor's lawyers of 'making up' her rape allegation. Her old boss, a senator, pursues her for defamation.

... A Tasmanian man sexually assaults three girls, aged 6 to 10, in front of a 5-year-old boy but avoids prison by pleading 'guilty'. The magistrate is 'hopeful' that, given the age of the children, there'll be 'no lasting impact'.

Gratitude

Thank you, Julia Gillard, for establishing the Royal Commission into Institutional Responses to Child Sexual Abuse.

I am grateful to (but legally advised to not name) many people who listened, believed, and supported my efforts.

I thank my siblings (especially Tony), and my children and grandchildren.

Thanks to the braves: Grace Tame, Brittany Higgins, Saxon Mullins, Chanel Contos, Tiffany Skeggs. Also Pariss Baker and Michael Bradley of the Grace Tame Foundation, Miriam-Rose Ungunmerr-Baumann, and Jess Hill.

The Australian Society of Authors and Arts Tasmania 2025 Writers and Illustrators Mentorship Program and mentor Alexandra Payne. Sydney Writers Studio, Jen Stonier, Elise Greig and Melissa Butcher. This book owes much to my talented, patient editor, Bianca Millroy, who helped me find my voice/s. Thanks also to Susan Young of Ashwood Publishing, who helped me get this story told.

Special heartfelt thanks to Anja Draper.

And you, Mr Lovely, Alex (Vince), *Thank you for loving me.*

Deepest gratitude for Thirteen, and all my little voices. Thank you for being so brave.

References

Chapter 1: The Upending

Chanel Contos: quotes are from her article, '"Do they even know they did this to us?": why I launched the school sexual assault petition', in *The Guardian* online, 15/03/2021 at 03:30 AEDT.

Chapter 2: Little Brave, Asking

'Children are to be protected': Report (uncorrected proof) of proceedings of the Standing Committee on Law and Justice Inquiry into Spent Convictions for Juvenile Offenders session of 29 March 2010, p 14; https://www.parliament.nsw.gov.au/lcdocs/transcripts/521/100329%20Uncorrected%20transcript%20-%20Hearing%201.pdf.

'One in four': These figures were challenged at the time as an underestimation. According to the 2023 Australian Child Maltreatment Study, 'more than one in three girls and almost one in five boys experienced child sexual abuse'. See Mathews, B., Pacella, R.E., Scott, J.G., Finkelhor, D., Meinck, F., Higgins, D.J., Erskine, H.E., Thomas, H.J., Lawrence, D., Haslam, D.M., Malacova, E., Dunne, M.P. (2023). The prevalence of child maltreatment in Australia: Findings from a national survey. *Medical Journal of Australia*, 218 (6 Suppl.), S13-S18. doi: 10.5694.mja2.51873.

Chapter 4: Criminal Justice

Saxon Mullins: the quote is from the ABC TV show *Q&A*, broadcast 18 March, 2021. https://www.youtube.com/watch?v=i3C41QYy-Hk

'justice in NSW': See NSW Bureau of Crime Statistics and Research, Attrition of sexual assaults from the New South Wales criminal justice system. https://bocsar.nsw.gov.au/documents/publications/bb/bb151-200/BB170-Report-Attrition-sexual-assaults.pdf.

Chapter 5: Family Justice

'more than a third': The 1998 United States National Institute of Justice and Centers for Disease Control and Prevention research report 'Prevalence, Incidence, and Consequences of Violence Against Women: Findings From the National Violence Against Women Survey' found that '33.4% of women who were raped before age 18 went on to experience physical assault, rape, or stalking by an intimate partner as an adult.' Australian data reinforces this trend but broadens the understanding of abuse to include a child being subject to or viewing domestic violence. The Australian Bureau of Statistics Childhood Abuse statistical report estimates that '43% of adults who suffered abuse before the age of 15 went on to experience cohabiting partner violence or abuse later in life.' https://www.abs.gov.au/statistics/people/crime-and-justice/childhood-abuse/latest-release

Ursula Le Guin: from the Afterword to 'The Farthest Shore', in Ursula K. Le Guin and Charles Vess, *The Books of Earthsea: The Complete Illustrated Edition*. Saga Press 2018.

Chapter 6: Some Justice

'After the first time': from Part One of the three-part SBS documentary *See What You Made Me Do*, broadcast on May 5, 12 and 19, 2021. https://www.sbs.com.au/ondemand/tv-series/see-what-you-made-me-do.

Chapter 7: Facebook Justice

Professor Ian Coyle: quote is from an ABC News report by Susan Chenery and Jennifer Feller: 'How career criminal and notorious bank robber Russell Manser turned his life around'. https://www.abc.net.au/news/2022-05-30/how-russell-manser-went-from-robbing-banks-to-turning-his-life-/100631408.

'child sex-offender suicide risk': this passage draws from Key, R., Underwood, A., Farnham, F., Marzano, L. and Hawton, K. (2021), Suicidal behavior in individuals accused or convicted of child sex abuse or indecent image offenses: Systematic review of prevalence and risk factors. *Suicide Life Threat Behavior*, 51: 715-728. https://doi.org/10.1111/sltb.12749.

Chapter 8: Community Justice

'Opera chief': This refers to Judge Geraldine Davison's 2021 ruling and 14-year sentencing of Opera South Australia's artistic director and chief executive, Timothy Sexton, found guilty of maintaining unlawful sexual relationships with two teenage girls. Additional information can be found at https://www.abc.net.au/news/2021-07-02/sa-opera-timothy-sexton-sentenced/100262056.

Chapter 10: Somatic Justice

Tasmanian Department of Education: Some information from the radio report mentioned in the text was also published online as 'Tasmanian Education Department shielded paedophiles, disbelieved students, Inquiry finds.' https://www.abc.net.au/news/2021-11-09/tas-tasmanian-education-department-shielded-paedophiles-inquiry/100606012.

bell hooks: quote is from her article, 'Beyoncé's Lemonade is capitalist money-making at its best', in *The Guardian* online, 12/05/2016 00:00 AEST.

Chapter 12: Commitment

National Student Safety Survey: The quoted statistics are from Heywood, W., Myers, P., Powell, A., Meikle, G., & Nguyen, D. (2022). National Student Safety Survey: Report on the prevalence of sexual harassment and sexual assault among university students in 2021. Melbourne: The Social Research Centre.

Chapter 13: Civil Justice

icare cost blowouts: reported in ABC and *Sydney Morning Herald* news articles. https://www.abc.net.au/news/2022-08-22/government-spent-1-9-billion-on-icare-bailout/101357898 and https://www.smh.com.au/politics/nsw/icare-chief-s-pay-tops-1-million-as-embattled-insurer-boosts-salaries-20221114-p5by3z.html.

investigation into the NSW Parliament: this investigation into bullying and sexual harassment found that attempted sexual assaults, sexual harassment and everyday sexism occur at unacceptable rates, with low trust in reporting arrangements. More at: https://www.parliament.nsw.gov.au/about/Documents/Independent%20Broderick%20Report.pdf

Chapter 14: Preparations

Brittany Higgins: The prosecutor comments were reported in *The Guardian*, 3 Dec 2022. https://www.theguardian.com/australia-news/2022/dec/03/right-to-be-scared-brittany-higgins-and-the-harsh-realities-about-justice-and-power.

Epilogue

'No lasting impact': https://www.abc.net.au/news/2023-11-16/tas-wildlife-rescue-volunteer-child-sexual-assault-sentence/103104616

www.ingramcontent.com/pod-product-compliance
Lightning Source LLC
LaVergne TN
LVHW090308210926
848480LV00001B/171

* 9 7 8 1 7 6 4 7 8 4 2 0 7 *